*Praise for*

# DECISION SPRINT

One of the greatest challenges of leadership is choosing between speed and accuracy. Based on decades of experience at some of the world's most successful organizations, Atif Rafiq has learned that this is a false choice. In this book, he presents a remarkably practical model for accelerating decisions without sacrificing quality.

—**Adam Grant,** #1 *New York Times* bestselling author of
*Think Again* and host of the TED podcast *WorkLife*

Atif Rafiq's *Decision Sprint* takes what successful leaders already know—that to grow and innovate takes collective intelligence—and puts that playbook into your hands to capitalize on your most meaningful ideas and opportunities.

—**Jeffrey J. Jones II,** President and CEO of H&R Block

At both Google and Peacock, I've seen first hand how team-based problem solving is essential for success. *Decision Sprint* distills best practices into a guide that is both accessible and indispensable.

—**Kelly Campbell,** President of Peacock and
Direct to Consumer at NBC Universal

Atif is a well-known Silicon Valley innovator who helped modernize several Fortune 500 companies at pivotal junctions. I'm glad he's taken the time to pen his methods so that more companies can build their great futures.

—**Dr. Vishal Sikka,** former CTO of SAP, former CEO of Infosys,
and Board Director of BMW and Glaxosmithkline

The bar for promising ideas has been raised in today's business environment. Every company needs a way to move faster and smarter on their most important ideas. *Decision Sprint* is the guide to make the leap from ideas to action—it's perfect for this era of uncertainty and heightened expectations.

—**Adam Bain,** former COO of Twitter

I have seen many great ideas not be executed. *Decision Sprint* captures the need for both upstream and downstream thinking, and provides an elegant solution to moving promising ideas to action.

—**John Bryant,** former President, CEO, and
Chairman of Kellogg Company

# DECISION
## SPRINT

THE NEW WAY TO INNOVATE
INTO THE UNKNOWN AND MOVE
FROM STRATEGY TO ACTION

## ATIF RAFIQ

**Mc Graw Hill**

New York   Chicago   San Francisco   Athens   London   Madrid
Mexico City   Milan   New Delhi   Singapore   Sydney   Toronto

1  2  3  4  5 6 7 8 9   LCR   28  27  26  25  24  23

ISBN        978-1-264-60959-8
MHID        1-264-60959-0

e-ISBN    978-1-264-60986-4
e-MHID    1-264-60986-8

McGraw Hill books are available at special quantity discounts to use as premiums and sales promotions or for use in corporate training programs. To contact a representative, please visit the Contact Us pages at www.mhprofessional.com.

McGraw Hill is committed to making our products accessible to all learners. To learn more about the available support and accommodations we offer, please contact us at accessibility@mheducation.com. We also participate in the Access Text Network (www.accesstext.org), and ATN members may submit requests through ATN.

*This book is dedicated to my father, Ahmad Choudhry Rafiq. His one-man business in New York City's Garment District planted seeds for everything I've learned in business.*

# CONTENTS

PART FOUR

## A BOUNDLESS PLAYBOOK FOR GROWTH

# INTRODUCTION

hen it comes to an important initiative, idea, or problem space, companies need a new way forward.

Collaboration is no longer centered around the office, most problem-solving takes place at the team level, and the velocity of business challenges is only increasing (supply chain, energy, and financial market crisis are disruptive issues as I'm writing this book).

Yet decision-making in companies is built for a different age that is long gone. Gone are the known commodities and the long, safe way of deciding what to do.

Existing know-how, stable workforces, and the fail-safe of command-and-control leaders who've been there and done that have given way. These past strengths have vanished, replaced by constant exploration of new territory—of the unknown—by teams. Business needs a guide for these teams to navigate the unknown. *Problem-solving needs to be reinvented for the modern era, and solving for unknowns is the key. Let me explain why the future of your company depends on it.*

The short answer is the devil. In business, the devil doesn't wear Prada. He always appears in the form of unknowns and ambiguity. As leaders, we face new and unknown territory constantly yet struggle to make strategy actionable. One of the biggest challenges in business is to convert ambition, strategy, or intent into the right course of action. It's not enough to have a corporate purpose, strategic pillars, and a list of underlying initiatives or projects. A useful development in the business lexicon over the last decade has been the OKR, which stands for "objective" and "key results." But somehow we forgot about the part in the middle. How do we—leaders and teams—traverse the

1

space between objective and results? That's the hard part. A world of unknowns will always characterize anything big or meaningful. And a large, unsorted pile of unknowns is exactly what makes it hard to lift off. Without a method to address unknowns, our work can feel like operating in kryptonite.

What do I mean by unknowns? They vary, of course, depending on the nature of the project, problem, or initiative. When it comes to a strategic opportunity, a company might struggle to explore key matters involving customer needs, business model, economics, or market considerations. On an operational challenge, participants may fail to surface all the contributing factors to a failure or breakdown. When these unknowns remain lurking, it's impossible to solve the complex puzzles that we hand to teams in our organizations, and equally unlikely these teams can place the right recommendations, conclusions, and decisions on the table.

So if you're wondering why there's lack of momentum on key initiatives in your company, reflect on how unknowns are being addressed. The answer to this reflection will likely illuminate.

So how do we get these initiatives moving in the right direction? If unknowns are the norm, what methods help build clarity? Can we systematically turn unknowns into knowns? How can this show up at the project level? And in day-to-day work? What is the role of teams? What is the role of leadership when teams are enabled? What is the role of the CEO to usher in new ways of decision-making by embracing methods to navigate unknowns? How do we make it an ongoing feature of how the company works?

Companies react to unknowns with one of two reflexes. They can shy away and rush ahead to planning based on what they already understand. In this mental model, it's viewed as weakness to acknowledge unknowns, so it's best to move on from them rapidly. In such a workplace, the desire to explore and try new things can be limited. It can be bureaucratic to navigate the workplace for permission. Curiosity is absent.

The other reflex is to allow autonomous exploration, but often in isolation, with multiple teams doing similar work without communicating and benefiting from each other. It's a breakdown in the collective intelligence of an organization. This leads to missing important inputs and problem-solving that fall short of the mark. As a result, initiatives experience fits and starts, with pockets of support and enthusiasm, but not of the sustained variety. To employees, this can feel chaotic. The organization runs hot and cold on promising ideas.

Does this sound familiar?

In my experience, the response to unknowns is most visible when it comes time for decisions. Did we play small ball and kick the can down the road, or did we go forward with more questions than answers? Neither path is optimal. Decision points can feel rife with these pitfalls, but the tables are set *upstream.*

That is my key, perhaps counterintuitive, message. To experience speed and quality in decision-making, organizations must start further upstream. Too often, companies are cavalier or circular about how they handle unknowns. Then when it's time to make a decision, they're paralyzed or they blunder into a poor decision.

Decisions are often not as hard as you believe when the workflows preceding them are obsessed over. I dedicate an entire chapter to these workflows and spell them out in great detail, after having put them into practice within the C-suite of well-known companies.

Without a method for handling upstream work, companies often must choose between bureaucracy and chaos. CEOs of large incumbents fear the former but struggle to identify the root cause and solutions beyond slogans. CEOs of high-growth companies can't afford to soften the pedal as survival depends on continued innovation.

So what exactly is "upstream work"? It's the part of an initiative or problem space with more questions than answers. Questions always stream in much faster than answers at the start of a promising idea or important problem space. We only get to quality execution if the answers begin to outweigh the questions, no matter how promising the opportunity or urgent it is to take action on a problem. Upstream work is how we connect *exploration* to *alignment* to *decision-making.* Only after connecting these three phases can an initiative move downstream, where execution lives.

Use this simple definition of upstream work to reflect on your current initiatives. Is your organization spending more time downstream on a priority that needs more upstream effort? Has a priority been unable to move downstream even though enough is understood to make the transition? That's why the first thing we'll cover is the difference between upstream and downstream.

Where does upstream work matter? Consider a project or strategic initiative in your organization. There could be a dedicated working team formed with a set of sponsors. There may be a cadence of touchpoints to steer the work. Everyone wants to see the plan and move on to execution. But to produce a plan, we need to sort through the puzzle pieces. Brainstorms and deep dives fill our days, but how effectively do they help discovery of these puzzle pieces and their implications? It can be like a rabbit hole of detective work. It's essential to get the right inputs on the table. Only with the right inputs can we get to a point of drawing conclusions or recommendations. It's painful to reach a decision point for an initiative only to realize the quality of the inputs leaves more to be desired. An obsession for the right inputs is one of the quickest ways I've found to create momentum around a promising idea. Otherwise the enthusiasm can outweigh the substance. And that opens a wide ravine for skeptics to nip innovation in the bud. You'll read about how some of today's most successful CEOs are input obsessed.

Operational problems can be just as vexing. A site or service is not working. Management wants it "fixed," but it can be like a game of whack-a-mole. Ever wonder why? It could be a rush to execute a superficial fix. Meanwhile, the fact-finding mission to surface underlying factors is shortchanged. Upstream doesn't just relate to new spaces and products; it's important whenever there's a new kind of problem to confront.

It's impossible to develop a sensible plan without flowing through this upstream journey. But how well does this type of journey progress in your organization? Does it take weeks, months, even quarters? Probably. And is there a method to get this done? Can anyone describe how it's supposed to work? In most organizations it's likely art more than science—and it varies considerably from project to project.

## WHAT YOU'LL LEARN IN THIS BOOK

Let's turn back to organizational reflexes when encountering uncertainty. There is a sweet spot between the two extremes. This way is better than either blank-check autonomy or corporate microman-agement. It's a system built ground up for the world of unknowns. The system is a collection of methods that will systematically turn unknowns into knowns, producing the clarity needed for faster and better decision-making. I call this system "Decision Sprint."

In 25 years of business, I have never encountered a systematic way to deal with unknowns. Yet they are the common characteristic of any big bet, innovation, strategic initiative, or new growth opportunity in any organization. And you'll read about, they are just as relevant to operational problem-solving and established parts of organizations.

In the chapters to come, I will introduce Decision Sprint as a system to handle every aspect of upstream work while feeding into today's project and planning activities. I will guide you through con-crete methods that empower all levels of an organization to meet unknowns head-on. Once you see the massive unstructured nature of upstream work centered on dealing with unknowns, you will suddenly discover new and better solutions.

You'll learn how Decision Sprint is situated within the familiar set-ting of how work happens today. Your organization can drop it in and begin to see immediate "error correction" when flowing through com-mon project and planning milestones. Decision Sprint starts to enable bright ideas even before they are formalized as a "projects."

It's not hard to convince others that Decision Sprint is the painkiller for many types of headaches. Most people can understand the difference between upstream work that makes things clear before downstream work where execution takes place (Decision Sprint connects the two). Most colleagues understand that alignment is desirable (especially in cross-functional work) and that establishing a way to make sense of unknowns is the key to achieving it. Most are open to steps that can make everyone more confident to enter decision meetings or decision points.

To implement Decision Sprint, you won't need to "clean sheet" today's approach. You simply need to make some powerful modifica-tions to begin to rewire existing ways of working. Learn about that in the Chapter 9, "Hack Today's System."

What's more, Decision Sprint can be embraced by a variety of contributors in an organization—from innovators to skeptics, from strategic thinkers to pragmatists, from those focused on today's horizon to those charged with a horizon in the future. Each persona has a role to play in tackling unknowns. You'll learn how Decision Sprint activates the players in your organization in the right way instead of tolerating legacy behaviors or blank-check experimentation. Both extremes are costly, if not deadly. We hear a lot about failing fast, but personally, I'd rather see you start winning.

Decision Sprint can apply to almost any initiative, project, or team in an organization. It is a horizontal solution that is accessible to all functions and participants—supply chain, customer experience, product development, marketing, innovation, digital, and more. Today's most meaningful business challengessustainability, business model change, evolution of customer experience, and digitizationcan benefit from a problem-solving system that embraces the unknown.

Given its capacity to transform organizations, Decision Sprint can become a major cultural accelerator. It will reach down into virtually every interaction between people to help navigate unknowns in their day-to-day work. Day-to-day collaboration is the best signal of a healthy culture, not slogans. I dedicate an entire chapter to culture change through workflow, over slogans.

It is a game-changer because ultimately, it shapes the day-to-day experience of employees by enabling them to bring out their best. That's the promise of Decision Sprint.

## A BRIEF DESCRIPTION OF THE CONTENT

This book is organized into four parts. I encourage you to read *Decision Sprint* sequentially, as each part builds on one another. You might approach each of these four parts in a particular mode. Part One provides insider stories to illustrate a big need. You'll be a fly on the wall in a room of high-stakes corporate environments. Part Two provides a high level recipe or methodology on how to solve for this big need. After reading it you might be thinking, it makes so much sense, why has no one taken the time to break it down into components before this book came along? Part Three explains how to apply the solution. It will have you rethinking many of your current meetings and their effectiveness. Part Four will stretch your thinking on the future of management and the role of artificial intelligence (AI), once companies and teams are working effectively upstream. The work of management will be transformed in a way that would make Peter Drucker roll in the grave. The partnership between knowledge workers and AI will make today's management techniques look absolutely primitive. AI will help teams jump-start their problem-solving efforts and provide managers with radar into whether initiatives will realize their objectives. It will raise the bar on all of us. Having set your expectations on the various altitudes this book traverses, let me overview each part in a bit more detail.

Part One explains why the failure to uncover and address unknowns is so troubling, and why doing something about it contains so much upside. The key is to focus on upstream work. That's where unknowns are sourced, synthesized, and reasoned through to arrive at conclusions that drive decisions. Effective upstream work enables us to turn unknowns into knowns, create greater clarity, move with better velocity, bring conviction to decision-making, and achieve successful project outcomes. The problem today is that very few companies and teams have a method.

Part Two, "From Strategy to Action: Driving Growth Through Decision Sprint," provides the solution to all aspects of upstream work at the high level. It breaks down and explains the three components of Decision Sprint: *exploration, alignment, and decision-making.* These steps come before planning and execution. Handle them well, and the downstream activities of planning and execution are simplified.

You will read about the three components of upstream work often, so let me briefly define them. *Exploration* is a concerted effort to surface the relevant considerations, especially unknowns, and get to the bottom of them. *Alignment* is about bringing together what's been explored to draw conclusions. *Decision-making* is committing to the necessary actions.

Part Three, "Installing Decision Sprint," describes how to put Decision Sprint into practice through 13 workflows:

**Workflow #1**    Initiating an Exploration

**Workflow #2**    Sourcing Matters

**Workflow #3**    Sourcing Questions

**Workflow #4**    Calibrating the Exploration

**Workflow #5**   Sharing the Canvas

**Workflow #6**   Answering Questions

**Workflow #7**   Calibrating Answers

**Workflow #8**   Drawing Conclusions

**Workflow #9**   Preparing for Alignment

**Workflow #10**  Conducting Alignment

**Workflow #11**  Identifying Decisions

**Workflow #12**  Preparing Content

**Workflow #13**  Conducting Decision Meetings

The workflows I provide are at a practitioner's level. Your team or organization can start to implement them rapidly. They are the ingredients to faster and more effective problem-solving and decision-making. The cultural side effects are extremely positive as well. They help create a more engaged workforce and healthier culture. Finally, they allow individuals to thrive and grow in their careers. There is no greater source for job satisfaction than feeling acknowledged, valued, and rewarded for contribution. Helping an organization solve problems faster and better is a major contribution, and will become more visible and measurable at the individual level.

Part Four, "A Boundless Playbook for Growth," discusses how digital tools can help everyone involved in Decision Sprint and how AI can create a management system that unlocks the growth possibilities in organizations. Yes, AI and professional managers will come together in profound ways to drive the future of business decisions. You'll learn about the vast data lakes that can emerge from establishing upstream workflows and bringing them to life with digital tools, setting the tables for AI. I will share detailed use cases where AI will help companies problem-solve faster and better.

The final chapter, "The Upstream CEO," looks to the future and how AI and upstream work may radically shift how CEOs perform their jobs, including how CEOs drive valuation, develop strategic plans, and calibrate the most critical business initiatives through an AI-based radar. Data-driven signals will provide CEOs and executives a much better sense of where time and energy are required.

Rest assured, the ideas in this book resonate with today's most progressive business leaders. That's why you'll find interviews and perspectives of CEOs of major companies, including Volvo, H&R Block, Peacock, Restaurant Brands International (which owns Burger King and Tim Hortons), and OrangeTheory Fitness, featured within. You'll also hear from executives who've been pushing boundaries at McDonald's, Hyatt, and MGM Resorts. On the personal front, you'll read how the world's preeminent venture capital firm—Andreessen Horowitz—put in motion one of my career moves and injected Silicon Valley DNA into a 90-year-old business.

To make Decision Sprint concrete, you'll be taken through detailed case studies involving a range of business challenges, including Amazon's disruption in self-publishing, McDonald's massive transformation of customer experience through digitization, the highly secretive launch of Apple Pay, Volvo's push for sustainability, and more.

## HOW THIS BOOK PUSHES BOUNDARIES

Decision Sprint starts from a big-picture theory standpoint yet lands in the day-to-day work of new ideas, projects, and opportunities. The big picture is consistent with the most advanced know-how that exists on topics of innovation, mindset, neuroscience, business agility, and decision-making. I did not originate any of that theory, but as an operator, I have the real-world experience of placing these ideas into motion to help companies grow. The big ideas within this book coupled with the practical guide level haven't been offered in any prior work.

One of the most influential works on innovation is the *The Innovator's Dilemma,* a series of four books by Clayton Christensen, which I see as highly influential in real-world innovation for a place in time, say up to 2010 or 2015. In his work, Christensen explains why internal innovation gets stymied and why setting up autonomous projects outside the company's core is the best way to avoid the premature death of good ideas.

I have done this at companies like McDonald's, Volvo, and MGM Resorts. As Christensen elaborates, providing these teams with the space to develop their ideas can kickstart wider interest. Design thinking practices including prototypes and lean UX are so common in today's innovation work. But even promising concepts need significant calibration on the road to becoming market-worthy. They must be vetted to surface and understand a wider set of unknowns. And that's where design thinking hits a limit.

Critical unknowns only come to light when concepts are socialized and brought into contact with the company's operating core. Operating staff possess a ton of institutional knowledge to shed light on the critical steps between promise and reality. The paradox is the company "mother ship" can easily overwhelm a promising seedling. Therein lies the challenge.

It's a huge conundrum. Autonomy in a vacuum will produce a limited idea. Subjecting an idea to overwhelming skepticism (masked as input) at the start will kill it. I will show you a way out of this trap.

In this trade-off, Christensen proposed a model of autonomy as the better alternative. As I said, this model has been effective in helping companies create a pipeline of innovation. Still, it doesn't solve for increasing the ability of the company's core to contribute to innovation. The time has come for such a solution.

With the current growth objectives of a large business, ideas need to move much quicker from the edge to the core. Growth objectives need to go from zero to billions in a few years. This requires input, problem-solving, and contribution centered on these promising ideas from across a company.

It's time to solve for getting the mother ship comfortable with unknowns. It's a mistake to separate into worlds of those who deal with "business as usual" and those that work with the new.

It's my hypothesis that this separation eventually hits a wall, and we need a better way. This book will show how to create a system that harmonizes these worlds. Decision Sprint neutralizes the tendency within the organization to veer too much in the directions of skepticism or wishful thinking. More than self-correcting for too much of the glass half full or empty, it doesn't force a choice between speed and quality. Until now—when it comes to unknowns—teams and companies have had to settle for one or the other.

There are some amazing books on how our brains use different systems for various types of decisions. These books hold exciting parallels to how companies think. What's the connection? Since companies are made up of people, we can find some of the same pitfalls and traps in decision-making within companies as people face in their personal lives.

One book from which I draw inspiration is *Thinking Fast and Slow* by Daniel Kahneman, who received the Nobel Prize in Economics for his research and theories. He lays out how our brains consist of two systems. System 1 is optimized for quick decisions based on known patterns. In business, we call this execution mode. System 2 is designed for new situations where we need to "slow down" and reason through matters, including unknowns. If we don't "slow down" enough to question, we can easily miss important considerations and apply the wrong weights to them. Our opinions or recommendations can be standing on poor assumptions. While companies and teams need both modes, they tend to be more capable at execution. Yet companies regularly face new type of problems that they have not encountered. I have introduced the notion of upstream work to bring attention to the need for this kind of problem-solving. Upstream work is where system 2 thinking needs to be king, and Decision Sprint is how companies activate it. (See Figure I.1.)

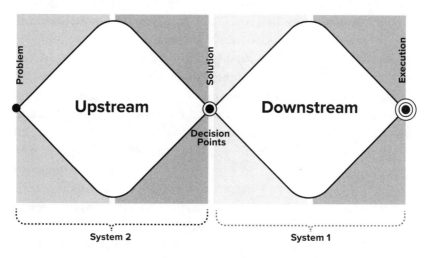

**FIGURE I.1** Systems 1 and 2 for companies

I hypothesize that companies tend to be better at system 1 and that there's not a practical way to establish routines for system 2 in today's workplace. It's a big gap, and this book will provide concrete methods to fill it. But before coming to that, let's clarify the terminology.

It's not that system 2 decisions need to be slow, as measured by time. It's that failing to activate system 2 can lead to mistakes. You must be aware to activate system 2 thinking for the purpose of avoiding blind spots and mistakes.

I've built my career on honing system 2 thinking in a variety of business situations. I was able to rise through the ranks quickly with system 2 thinking, and I'm only decent at it. I've seen many people who excel at system 2 thinking far more than I, yet my career has gone further or produced a bigger impact.

The difference is I could craft an environment for system 2 thinking at a team level. When you can enable a team to perform system 2 thinking effectively, watch out! It's very powerful. The proof is in the pudding. Many of my direct reports have risen to the C-suite in well-known companies, benefiting from our work together. Getting the upstream right is a win-win.

This book treats an organization like a collective brain, which faces constant unknowns that require system 2 thinking to solve. When unknowns are the norm and central to your growth or innovation project, you must enable the team to use system 2 thinking to make sense of matters. This is the "thinking slow" part of Kahneman's model. What the methods in *Decision Sprint* teach you to do is to speed up the "thinking slow" part. In other words, your team will be able to think slow and do it fast. That's the promise of *Decision Sprint*.

When it comes to books about mindsets, they are relevant because they help us see possibilities instead of closing them off. Observing more of the environment opens the door to creativity. It helps us see more information that could lead to novel ways to approach something.

Carol Dweck's book *Mindset: The New Psychology of Success* is very popular in today's business vernacular. Dweck coined the terms "fixed mindset" and "growth mindset" to describe people's underlying beliefs about learning and intelligence. In business, people tap her ideas to create a degree of openness to new ideas.

Microsoft's CEO Satya Nadella, who's tenure has seen massive growth in the company, is well-known for bringing Dweck's ideas into Microsoft's culture. "I'd rather be a learn-it-all, than a know-it-all," is a famous Nadella quote. In sharing these words, Nadella is encouraging staff to shift their attention from opinions to collecting knowledge— prior to drawing conclusions. But how do you make that real in the day-to-day? *Decision Sprint* will make it real.

Many books about how companies and the teams should work spend a lot of time on theory and not enough on making it real in practice. *Decision Sprint* is more of a how-to because I'm first and foremost a practitioner. I've always run teams, or divisions, or companies. And that's the perspective I come from.

My objective for this book will be achieved if you can apply the thinking *immediately*.

A team can use the methods described in this book on any project, problem space, or initiative. So how do you apply these methods? Part Three, which provides detailed workflows, will be the place to start. *Decision Sprint* helps you make easy yet powerful adjustments to your existing day-to-day interactions, which will then lead to an immediate boost in speed, quality, and outcomes.

## FIRST CHIEF DIGITAL OFFICER

To understand why I care so much about upstream work and have developed Decision Sprint to "solve for it," let me introduce my career journey. Spoiler alert. It's more metamorphosis than a straight line. (See Figure I.2.)

The challenges of managing and leading in the post-Covid global economy call upon us to adapt to a constant flurry of unknowns. Ambitious companies always considered this state of affairs the norm. I've lived in this deep end for 25 years, initially in Silicon Valley companies led by billionaire founders, and later in places I'd never imagined working, where it's a new muscle.

My experience with major adaption in the C-suite started in 2013 when McDonald's pulled me out of Amazon. I was, by some accounts, the first chief digital officer in the history of the Fortune 500. And the

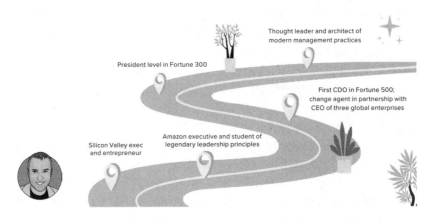

**FIGURE I.2** Mission to spread what I've learned

youngest person in McDonald's 60-year history on the company's senior leadership team (the set of 12 individuals from across the globe in the most senior positions). Because of career moves like this, people in Silicon Valley jokingly referred to me as its "ambassador" to the Fortune 500. My network is a Venn diagram of elite venture capital firms, startup executives, and C-levels of global behemoths. Over the last 10 years, I bridged these worlds in a unique way that I don't believe anyone can match.

The charter at McDonald's was transformation. Transformation is often defined as making a generational leap from here to there, whether related to customer experience, business model, or new offering of some kind. We often measure the results of a transformation by "what is shipped" to the customer. I learned it was just as much about "how we work" as "what is shipped." The two are intertwined in a rate-limiting fashion. The more "how we work" evolves, the bolder and bigger "what is shipped" for the customer or business outcome. (See Figure I.3.)

This was not an easy lesson to acquire. Coming from a culture like Amazon, I was a little spoiled. The company is storied for its continued march of innovation on a mammoth scale. The "how" is very well encoded into the day-to-day. It's Amazon's secret sauce and the reason behind its mind-blowing growth into context.

To grow by 20 percent in 2016, Amazon needed to add $21.5 billion of new revenue. For it to grow by 20 percent in 2019, it needed to add

**FIGURE I.3** Two halves of innovation

$46 billion of new revenue. And to grow by that same percentage in 2021, it needed to add $76 billion of new revenue. These figures are new revenue on top of what was produced earlier. In each case, it exceeded the mark. Amazingly, Amazon's annual growth alone is greater than the total revenue of many Fortune 500s.

I was fortunate to get a strong grasp of how Amazon works—particularly its excellence at upstream work—during my time as general manager of Kindle Direct Publishing, one of the company's fastest-growing businesses. However, I could not simply export what I learned at Amazon (or the things I picked up in 15 years of Silicon Valley companies) into my new position at McDonald's. It's not possible to franchise a novel management system built up around a founder—whether that be Amazon or other notable examples like Bridgewater (the world's largest hedge fund). The iconic management systems built by Jeff Bezos and Ray Dalio have been written about and publicized. Yet it's not easy to replicate these problem-solving and decision-making approaches within "mere mortal" organizations.

Transforming McDonald's into a digital business was a tall and tough order, but the goods were delivered to the tune of billions in incremental revenue. The pioneering nature of the role and the scale of the impact put me on the map as someone who could activate and manage transformation. And that led to C-level responsibilities at more influential brands. I helped revitalize Volvo as their chief digital officer (CDO) and chief information officer (CIO), and rose to the president level of MGM Resorts, another Fortune 500 company. So what is the red thread?

My secret sauce is a deep comfort with unknowns of big ideas or problems and the ability to put them into action (I refer to this as "workflow"). In that 10-year ascent across the C-suite, little did I realize I was building a "system" that many companies simply lack through a collection of these workflows. I put great energy into living these workflows. I helped companies and teams see how doing a good job with the upstream work produces downstream impact that is meaningful and lasting. Now, I am looking to scale what I've learned by authoring a system that any team in any company can utilize.

If you're looking for a better way to put strategy into action or solve important problems, tap Decision Sprint. It took me 10 years to put together and a daily iteration to refine and develop real-world fit. It's not elusive theory. It's borne of practitioner's work. The grind is why I know it works.

PART ONE

# THE METHOD

# The Hidden World of Upstream Work

When I was appointed chief digital officer at McDonald's, culture change was just as much a deliverable as delivering new experiences, business models, or services. My mindset was to lead teams in the way that had produced results for Amazon and other Silicon Valley companies where I grew up. Start with big thinking and then problem-solve to bring ideas to life.

But these ideas don't have a shot when culture is a headwind. Culture is less about slogans and words than about how work and collaboration occur in an organization. That's why I dedicate an entire chapter to workflows and another chapter on how to reinforce the substance of these workflows with language.

I demonstrate how workflows express culture and, more important, how to develop workflows to move culture. The power of this can't be understated, because it enables a team to change the culture from the bottom up.

In this chapter, I discuss my experiences with transformation at McDonald's and Volvo. Transformation is the generational leap companies attempt in an important area, whether it be the customer experience, product, or business model. Some companies—especially

consumer brands that are now direct-to-consumer businesses—
are making the leap across multiple facets at once. While much was
accomplished at both organizations, I've learned a lot about the promise and pitfalls of solving for big ideas in an organization. I've had
experiences with top-down and bottom-up change and explain how
they come together. Teams don't need to wait for top-down change.
In fact, it's best when they kick-start it. What motivated me to develop
Decision Sprint is to unlock why and how this makes sense for everyone in the organization.

## ME AND MICKEY D'S

My first major project briefing at McDonald's involved the mobile app,
something we wanted to roll out globally. That's a big deal when you
serve 100 million customers daily. The project itself had been struggling to get off the ground. And the tension was building.

The CEO had charged a corporate squad with building it, but when
your company operates in over 100 countries in a decentralized model,
there were also competing efforts in countries that were trying to build
something similar faster. You may think McDonald's is a single corporate behemoth, but in some respects, it can be more like a federation of
many companies. There's a power in that for marketing and sales, but
it's muted when it comes to consumer technology.

Before I arrived on the scene, these competing forces had been
in play for almost two years, and no one was happy with the progress
on digital. Corporate was viewed as proceeding too slowly, while the
countries were taking shortcuts in building apps that ultimately hit a
wall. Consumers were baffled.

When I arrived, we counted no fewer than 25 apps for McDonald's
in the US app store. These included apps that worked only in Brazil and
Poland, and even apps for specific regions within the United States.
Digital was a hugely fragmented effort, which was not set up for success. Now add the big picture: McDonald's needed new ways to bring
in customers and business. The company was in a real pickle, with
several consecutive quarters of same-store sales decline and no major
growth drivers on the horizon. The heat was on.

Most people were skeptical about digital being a growth driver—but not our CEO, Don Thompson. He was out in front of the trend. Through his Silicon Valley relationships and his passion for what's next, Don created the first chief digital officer role in the history of the Fortune 500 and hired me to take it on.

At the time, very few could see how technology would reshape the experience of doing things in the physical world, such as getting a meal from McDonald's. Remember, there was no Uber Eats, Airbnb, or Instacart. There was much at stake for Thompson to prove digitization was a good bet and accelerate the company's business turnaround. He was confronted with a compound challenge: the company badly needed a customer breakthrough and internal forces were tugging in several directions, making collaboration very difficult.

James Floyd, who was general manager and VP of operations for McDonald's company-owned restaurants, put it this way:

> ❝ The mood with respect to technology when Atif joined was skepticism. We are the #1 QSR (quick service restaurant) in the world. It's easy to take the position "if it's not broke, don't fix it." Especially because the company has tried innovations that didn't work, like McSalad Shakers and McLean. Maybe digital will just die on the vine. And the complexity for McDonald's is very high to begin with. Globally we have 34,000 restaurants. Germany, France, United Kingdom, Australia, Latin America, Brazil—everybody kind of had their own technology. The idea of company-wide product development and strategy seemed a reach. There were a lot of moving parts to pull together into a combined effort on behalf of the juggernaut. ❞

## INPUT OR OUTPUT?

I remember my first executive project briefing. To be at the head of the table in such a meeting is both a luxury and a mountain of responsibility. First, you occupy the power seat and need to be ready. If you're not careful, your tone of voice and small nuances in words can be interpreted differently than you intend.

Many people attended the meeting, probably around 30. It was a signal of how seriously people in the organization perceived our mission.

Being so new to the company, I wanted to respect the flow of the meeting and how the team had crafted the agenda. The presentation was not very interactive; it was led by different people across facets of the project. Curiosities and clarifying questions piled up in my mind. I realized that with so many people involved in the project, I was unclear where to direct questions. We were heavily resourced, yet everyone was operating in silos.

Reflecting on that first meeting, I had one regret. A single question I could have asked would have changed the entire tenor. A question that would challenge people to think differently and begin to shift the norms of the company: *"Is this an input meeting or an output meeting?"*

An output meeting is like the end point of sausage making. You taste the product and like it or not. Then you try to guess why. An input meeting shares how the sausage is planned to be made. And you can help steer what it becomes before sending it down the assembly line. (See Figure 1.1.)

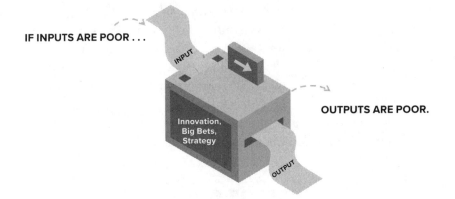

**IF INPUTS ARE POOR . . .**

**OUTPUTS ARE POOR.**

Innovation, Big Bets, Strategy

**FIGURE 1.1**   Upstream work is focused on the inputs.

Consider a typical strategic initiative in a company. Typically, these initiatives are characterized by many unknowns. But many large organizations approach an innovation challenge with an execution mindset. That's how their culture develops during periods of scale, as they move from being led by founders to professional managers. So when faced with an important initiative, companies resort quickly to detailed project planning, taking comfort in tasks and dates. When such plans are built on weak or insufficient understanding of the problem, they create a false sense of confidence. (See Figure 1.2.)

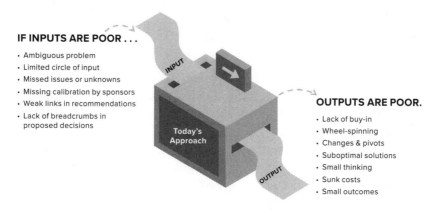

**IF INPUTS ARE POOR . . .**

- Ambiguous problem
- Limited circle of input
- Missed issues or unknowns
- Missing calibration by sponsors
- Weak links in recommendations
- Lack of breadcrumbs in proposed decisions

Today's Approach

INPUT

OUTPUT

**OUTPUTS ARE POOR.**

- Lack of buy-in
- Wheel-spinning
- Changes & pivots
- Suboptimal solutions
- Small thinking
- Sunk costs
- Small outcomes

**FIGURE 1.2**   Upstream work is reflected downstream.

In essence, with a stable business formula, organizations lose muscle memory when tackling the new and fall back on execution culture. Execution culture emphasizes the known commodities, whereas competitive advantage is at the edge of what is already understood. The new territory comes with more unknowns than knowns, which tends to be where the execution culture cannot cope. It lacks agility. By that, I mean the ability to dance with the unknowns.

As the leader of a big bet at McDonald's, I did not want to create a false sense of confidence along these lines. We needed to dance with the unknowns rather than taking comfort in our excellence with execution. Knowing execution culture wouldn't serve the company's interests gave me discomfort in the meeting. To help McDonald's succeed, I quickly realized I needed to shift the focus to the upstream work.

# WHERE IT STARTS: INPUT OBSESSION

Let's turn back to the question from my early days at McDonald's, "Is this an input meeting or an output meeting?" Input meetings allow you to spend time with the unknowns. Output meetings require that key unknowns are explored to the right level and sufficiently understood. You want to get the sequence right.

It's fair to seek to understand how conclusions and recommendations are drawn. Nothing is more relevant for leaders of growth and innovation efforts than understanding if the right unknowns surfaced, what was learned about them, and how the exploration of these issues impacts the plans on the table. With input meetings, we provide a space for that. In their absence, leaders are left to make decisions from the other side of the glass without feeling the texture. It's more like window-shopping than actually touching the fabric.

In those early days at the fast-food icon, I could not put my finger on the disconnect between the management culture I was trying to establish and what the organization was accustomed to. All the dynamics that make meetings easy, encouraging the path of least resistance, also make them a dangerous pitfall. I did not want us to step into them in my early days at McDonald's.

It's easy to sit back, make remarks about accountability for results, and take comfort in forecasts and plans. The hard part is surfacing the reasoning, thought process, and considerations behind the issues—to know whether you're on solid or shaky ground. Many leaders simply do not do it or lack the methods. Input meetings provide a way to perform this calibration. But an output meeting that needs to be pivoted to an input meeting is a delicate maneuver.

At that first McDonald's meeting, I remember saying to myself—I am sitting here, responsible for the digital future of a $100 billion company and about to make a multibillion bet to turn strategy into results. All eyes in the room eventually turned to me—and I'm feeling uneasy about things. I am being spoon-fed the output, yet I want to understand and shape the input.

Should I start asking questions and get my head around the inputs? Or maybe I should trust that everything has been vetted the right way? The team isn't accustomed to a senior leader being drawn into the fabric making and testing. It's not a norm for leaders at the top at McDonald's like it is at Amazon. It's unfamiliar territory because it is not the model.

The problem was just as rooted in me as it was in the process. Let me be clear about that. I couldn't even explain how the meeting should flow or how to reverse the course of it to address my concerns. We were coming from two different planets at this point in the journey. There was no language to connect the two planets. I could not explain my expectations. Over the next 10 years, I developed the language, words, and methods to connect the planets. (See Figure 1.3.)

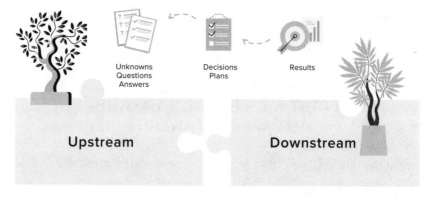

Unknowns
Questions
Answers

Decisions
Plans

Results

Upstream

Downstream

**FIGURE 1.3**   Upstream provides space to address unknowns.

The story has a happy ending, as far as the bottom line is concerned.

McDonald's experienced a sustained business turnaround and sales growth through new digital experiences like in-store kiosks, curbside pick-up, delivery, mobile order ahead, and new ways to drive promotions. Billions were served since the company's founding in 1960—and billions more were served through digital since those efforts started in 2013.

We modernized stores, we were a founding partner for Apple Pay, we introduced new service models and digital experiences, and we developed new roles, skills, and capabilities. And we did it on a *global scale* most companies could not imagine. Most of the customer experience behind McDonald's runs on common platforms, whether you order food in Sweden or Morocco.

Most important, it became "real in the restaurants" and made the leap from corporate PowerPoint slides.

James Floyd, reflecting on the impact in the United States, remarks:

> 66 At one point, we were getting so many sales from digital channels like delivery, we couldn't keep up with those sales. The iPads in the restaurant would just ping, ping, ping, another order, another order, and another one. We needed somebody just to manage those orders. Sometimes people disconnected the devices because they couldn't keep up with the orders that were coming in via mobile. That was early on, so we developed remedies. It was a learning curve to service the incremental customers and business in a different way. 99

## FIRST MOVER, ADVANTAGE AND DISADVANTAGE

As McDonald's gained notoriety for success with digital, the role of CDO spread like wildfire, with almost every large company establishing the position—a development that created visibility for me. I subsequently helped three global household brands boost their agility and drive business growth as a result.

But could it have been more? Could McDonald's have become Uber Eats before there was one? Or at least driven customer orders through the McDonalds' app, and limit Uber and DoorDash to fulfillment (using their dashers), so it could keep the customer relationship? What about cloud and ghost kitchens? A loyalty program that might have been rolled out five years earlier? Coffee subscriptions? How about going big on Tesla Superchargers in parking lots (our team tested this with progressive franchisees)? New menu items that change the perception of the food while bringing in new customers? And what about bringing new, agile ways of working throughout the entire company, not just on the customer experience or digital side of things?

Can a company that lost one million existing customers a year for the last 10 years afford to slow the pace of new ideas? The unknowns behind these questions were too challenging to fathom or even muster the willingness to explore. If we embraced more change on "how we work," could we put in motion more of "what is shipped" to the customer?

While McDonald's introduced new customer experiences and service models, the inner workings of how those experiences and models were developed were anything but smooth. It was choppy for everyone involved. We rode the fault line between two cultures.

We failed to develop the right interface between an execution culture that drove the company for decades and a newer learning culture necessary to grow and innovate. At times, I felt like a surfer riding a 100-foot wave. The company was hungry for a vision and definition of what good looks like, but less open to changing its way of working to get there.

And that's where the rubber meets the road. Unless the day-to-day work of teams changes to embrace learning and exploration of unknowns, vision is watered down, even cast aside. How teams work through unknowns will determine what portion of an ambition or vision is realized. The "what" and "how" are interlinked.

To affect this cultural change, I was driving a massive global transformation involving talent, structure, and operating models that McDonald's had never experienced before. It was one of the largest transformations of any kind across the Fortune 500.

When companies speak of transformation, they typically point to tangible changes in roles, talent, responsibilities, and processes. Along those lines, we rolled out a formal program with lots of PowerPoints and support from McKinsey & Co.

What were we trying to achieve with the transformation? To me, it seemed obvious: the new must be the "tip of the spear" to point the established ways in the right direction. My view is there are no half measures when undertaking top-down internal disruption. The overwhelming strength of established ways in the organization can neutralize "new norms" in a heartbeat.

That's why a formal transformation effort needs to remain steadfast as well as years of unwavering commitment to get fully rooted, to rewire things around it, and for people to feel the benefits. Signs of progress will be there early on, but you have to know what to look for, and skeptics will only provide support when positive change is obvious.

Few companies and leaders have the stomach for that kind of horizon. After three to four years of a push, it seemed McDonald's had enough. It turns out I was a hired gun meant to catalyze the system—a creative injection of ideas around customer experience, the digital road map to bring it to life, and the development of the technology stack to enable it. All of that was supposed to unfold within the norms of execution culture. Operating as an upstream leader without an upstream system can only continue for a period of time. So I moved on from this iconic company. I took with me a valuable lesson. Top-down change is only one way to go about it.

## SWIPE RIGHT: VOLVO AND THE UPSTREAM CEO

Marc Andreessen, the famous venture capitalist and creator of the Mosaic browser, coined the phrase "software is eating the world" in 2013. It was the year I joined McDonald's. It succinctly explained why most companies in every industry began to place digitization as one of their main growth drivers.

By 2017, across every industry, you could hear CEOs echo a common refrain: "We see ourselves as a technology company sitting inside the [XYZ] industry"—where the industry could be everything from groceries to hotels to cars.

Speaking of cars, it was Marc who introduced me to the next stop on my journey—Hakan Samuelsson, CEO of Volvo. Marc was impressed with his curiosity and intellect and graciously shared with me his impressions of Hakan and Volvo.

Hakan was an engineer by background who never lost his itch for understanding the details of how things work. Except when I met him, he was tinkering with how to build, or rebuild, the culture of Volvo Cars into a progressive, innovative, customer-centric organization.

If you've seen a Volvo lately, you've seen the fruits of Hakan's 10-year run as CEO. He and his team transformed the company from a dying business to a producer of compelling alternatives to any German car or Tesla vehicle. Indeed, Hakan did more than turn around a failing business. Some say Volvo today is the most innovative company in automotive other than Tesla.

When I met Hakan, a dinner scheduled for two hours turned into a four-hour mind meld. We reimagined many aspects of the industry, from car subscriptions sold directly to consumers to in-car systems that work as well as your phone.

I took a leap of faith and joined Volvo as CDO and global CIO. Interestingly, I had never run an IT department before, yet Hakan gave me 1,500 IT people to manage. We'll touch on why that turned out to be a smart move.

Hakan was very curious to learn from me. How do things work in Silicon Valley? How does Amazon work? What did I learn at McDonald's?

The learning was certainly two-way. When your leader, in this case, the CEO of a $20 billion company, is fully engaged in meetings, comes from a place of curiosity, and seeks to understand your thought process, it can be a little jarring. But once you overcome the sense of pressure or judgment, it's very powerful.

Hakan is gifted with the ability to start with questions even when he has a good instinct of his own on a subject. He is a questioner-in-chief. He lives in the upstream. And he is not shy about it. Repeatedly in meetings, he has demonstrated a hunger for inputs and reasoning that helped the topics reach the next level of clarity. So it's no surprise that when I suggested "clarity of thought" be the job title he listed for himself on the company's website, he instantly took to it.

The job title change arose because in some egalitarian fashion, Volvo decided to do away with titles and replace them with what each executive believed was their main contribution to the company. The company went so far as to remove the official titles of the executive management team on the corporate website and replace them with a variety of pithy descriptions.

When Hakan asked to hear my thoughts on the role of chief executive, I shared with him the idea that at Amazon, Jeff Bezos viewed his job as promoting clarity of thought. While I never heard that directly from Jeff, it's what one of his direct reports shared. It stuck with me. I connected with the idea that a CEO's highest contribution is to calibrate thoughts of the organization, to straighten out any clumsiness from them, and to make sure that understanding is driven into the teams. Hakan liked this notion as well. It's what I saw him do every day.

The company badly needed it. In 2010, Volvo was nearly extinct. Sales had receded to $10 billion, and Ford, which bought Volvo for $6.5 billion in 1999, sold it for a mere $1.5 billion 11 years later.

Things got so bad, Volvo nearly pulled out of selling cars in the US market entirely. By 2013 when Hakan arrived, there was some fixing up to do. He was up to the job. By 2017, revenue had soared to an all-time high of $20 billion (it's approaching $25 billion at time of writing this book). With the turnaround accomplished, it was time to look ahead to the future.

Hakan and his team decided to go for it on all fronts. For starters, they committed to electric vehicles, modernized the designs of the boxy Volvos, connected cars to the cloud, and built autonomous vehicles.

New frontiers were explored, including (1) making it easy for consumers to subscribe to a car through an app, (2) working with Google or Apple to make the infotainment in a Volvo a native version of these mobile operating systems, and (3) making Volvo cars that could power Uber or Waymo's burgeoning fleet of self-driving cars.

Volvo was jumping straight into the unknown. And yet it was still a 90-year-old car manufacturer that, like others in the industry, was accustomed to setting plans for cars five to seven years before they hit the market.

Talk about a culture shift.

Hakan and his team knew well they had to change the culture as much, if not more, than change the strategy for new products and services. While much was involved in changing the culture, I was struck with one simple thing they did. To remind staff of what was expected in the new environment, the executive team printed slogans and taped them to the doors and hallways. Slogans like "Bring Out the Best" and "Group People Around Challenges."

## *Excerpts from an Interview with Hakan Samuelsson, Former President and CEO of Volvo Cars*

**Atif:** In looking how far Volvo has come, would you point to any initiatives that you are particularly proud of in terms of your tenure?

**Hakan:** I have always been interested in design and how the cars look. At Volvo, every second week, the executive team gathers for a design review where we go through the exact colors, trim, and styling of the cars. Of course, we also look at the technical specifications. Should we have hybrids only, should we have plug-in hybrids, or should we go all electric, and so on. All of that to develop attractive products for future consumers. I think that's number one in the success of Volvo. We upgraded the cars and met consumer expectations. That would not necessarily happen if we just gave the order: "We need a new car, here are the cost targets, ask some customers what they want, and the car must be ready in three years."

We started a big initiative by going "direct to consumer." Consumers today are frustrated because carmakers cannot answer: What is included in the price? What are the specs of the various models? And when can I get it? These are basic questions all customers have, which the industry today can't answer. Pricing is confusing because you need to shop around, and every dealer has a different price. People today want transparency around pricing. We also need to be better at answering what's included in the various models and when will the customer get it? That's why we need new systems for transparent, direct digital interaction with consumers. We now have attractive, good products, and we are making them available directly to consumers. That is what we have been working with in the last years, and I believe that's one reason why we have been successful.

We are today globally present, growing and more profitable.

**Atif:** Your ambition was for Volvo to lead the industry and invent new ways to build cars and to sell to consumers. How did you go about that as a 90-year-old company?

**Hakan:** We wanted to modernize the car business by introducing a more direct-to-consumer approach using new digital tools. We started from the consumer expectations and worked backward to define what we should do. I think that was the right approach.

If you introduce a new idea in the organization, you normally get a lot of resistance. If you take Volvo, for example, it is a carmaker, and like other carmakers it is basically a factory and a wholesale organization. There are many people called sales managers, but they are not really selling cars. They are more into logistics, providing production allocations to distributors, and negotiating transfer prices.

Our two systems—direct and wholesale—were colliding.

To be successful with direct-to-consumer, you have to see digital capability as a business capability. We started discussing consumer expectations and the purpose. Then we wrote clarifying narratives of what we wanted to achieve and formed teams around that.

Creating clarity was something we always emphasized. Also important is forming small teams with ownership working together instead of big cross-functional meetings where things tend to get more complicated. We built teams that had a common understanding about the problems to solve in meeting consumer expectations, and we empowered them to take responsibility and act. That is something that many companies lack. There are too many processes and time spent on monitoring and follow-up instead of having people with the right competence focusing on how things should be done.

I remember something that you said very early in your tenure that impressed me. It went something like this: "We work too much with targets, KPIs, and project management and we talk too little about how to understand the problem. We really need teams who are empowered to explore, create clarity about the problem, and understand the big picture." To me that's crucial. To really empower and trust a team requires that you have this clarity. I want to know that the team really has understood the purpose to drive what should be achieved before I can empower it.

**Atif:** How does the CEO activate the transformation of the company in a day-to-day sense?

**Hakan:** I like questioning because you cannot run an organization just with positive feedback. You need to question why and how.

I like dialogues where you ask inquisitive questions. Why can that not be done? Why are we doing this? What's really the idea with this initiative? What are the trade-offs? Can we stop doing this?

Because normally when we want to improve, we add more and more complexity. Management should also be about stopping things that no longer serve a purpose. Asking why with a smile five times is very efficient. That is part of my management style, not just going out and saying "great, that's perfect," without really understanding what they are doing.

Sure, you want to provide encouragement and motivation, and one way to provide that is to be curious—show interest in the progress. Don't ask people what they have done; ask them what they want to achieve. How are you thinking about it? Why are you doing that? Will that work? That type of dialogue requires that the CEO have a certain understanding of what the team is doing. This creates energy, motivation, and ownership for high-potential employees.

**Atif:** What do you see as the long-term impact of your leadership as CEO?

**Hakan:** Volvo changed. We don't sit in meetings and ask people to report numbers and results. There's a risk everybody paints a positive picture and says they have been delivering their numbers. You need to go deeper, focusing on how they are thinking about critical matters that will shape the outcomes once things are in execution. How should those things be done? It's a more input-focused approach.

I don't like management by objectives. People say, if you can't measure it, it's not worth doing. To me, that can be nonsense because often the most important things to do are difficult to measure. You must be more involved: have discussion to reach a commitment on the strategic direction—that people can relate to. The results will be the consequence of clarity that comes from helping shape the inputs.

**Atif:** Would it be fair to say one of the things you mentioned was that you focused more on inputs over outputs?

**Hakan:** Yes, "input" and "output" are good words. We should focus on inputs because normally we focus too much on outputs. You cannot influence much by talking about outputs or results. Defining the right inputs is key.

**Atif:** What about the people side? How did you approach that?

**Hakan:** I value the spontaneous interaction between people because the best ideas don't typically come up in scheduled ordinary meetings. They often come up at the coffee machine or waiting in a lounge in an airport. It's very difficult to be creative at an 8:00 in the morning meeting. You are most creative when you're not expected to be. People are much more creative in open, exploratory interactions rather than in scheduled meetings with PowerPoint presentations.

Questions are critical. How are you thinking? Do you really mean that? How will that work? I think questioning is something you must build into your way of thinking. Questions are a very good way of creating clarity because they are much faster. Don't waste time on what everybody already agrees to. I often say when I lack time, let me ask questions. Why are you doing this? What's the purpose? How will it work in the United States? Can we have the same solution?

It's a very effective way to ensure the right things will be done.

Because doing the right thing is even more important than doing things right.

## THE VOLVO CHALLENGE

Entering the fray of this massive endeavor at Volvo, I saw parallels with McDonald's. Perhaps that's surprising to hear. Sure, burgers aren't cars, but there's much in common when reimagining a business around customers and transforming the structure, talent, and teams around that vision. Both companies were well-known brands, but neither was organized to interface directly with customers. Customers were largely anonymous.

So I went to work on the transformation. It started with giving the board a presentation on "What does good look like?" in terms of engaging customers. I recommended making structural and talent changes, such as putting a few key lieutenants already wired for innovation, speed, and tackling complex unknowns in important positions.

Along the way, I realized this "change initiative" shouldn't wait for the perfect organizational design. Yes, we needed to add new talent and skills. But we had a ton of great internal talent ready to be activated. They just needed to be shown the way and given the methods to bring change into their pocket of the company. If we didn't change the legacy culture at Volvo, it wouldn't matter whom we hired.

I began to add to my toolkit for modernizing culture. I started with this principle: meet the company where it is. Rather than starting with redesigning what the company or team should look like, we worked up from the current setup at Volvo.

We worked one interaction at a time with the existing players and configurations of teams to ground them in the new methods. It wasn't about training anyone. Training is not in-line with the day-to-day work of teams. Training is a separate, outside activity. Instead, it was about experiencing it within our interactions. I'm convinced it's a better way to learn.

With a wider remit at Volvo, I was able to run experiments in my sizable organization. I set up methods like input meetings, usually in two distinct steps, on the path to reaching a decision. Enough people got the hang of these new ways or at least appreciated them to make them work.

We shifted how teams worked without needing as much top-down restructuring as I had imagined. When people experienced a different workflow designed to bring out their collective intelligence, there was an appreciation and hunger for the new methods. Enough company veterans stepped up, embraced the mantle, and teamed with newcomers. Several pockets of a new cultural way were established in the organization.

## WELCOME TO SWEDEN
## (AKA THE FACTORY INCIDENT)

My first day on the job at Volvo was not exactly what I imagined. We had many consumer-facing innovations on the horizon from autonomous vehicles to car subscriptions that I would be leading. But the circumstance I walked into on day one was a bit of a shock. The main factory producing the company's flagship XC90 car had come to a halt—not for hours but days.

Millions of dollars were being lost each day, and the bleeding was intensifying. As global CIO, it was my job to fix (and understand) the software glitch that was responsible for it all.

Lemons into lemonade, as the saying goes. Once you look past the challenge, it's possible to see the upside. A chance to bring the team together, understand our capabilities and gaps, and showcase my management approach. Cut through the layers and show up with the team on a common challenge.

My first action was to gather the involved people in a standup. A standup is a no-prep interaction to problem-solve as a team. For an operational incident, we trace the issues and surface everything we know. Then we identify what still needs investigation. It's like organizing detective work. We used methods like "Toyota's 5 Whys" or the "root cause" approach that Amazon uses when there are defects in its service.

I'd like to say the standup was a smashing success, but the truth is that it was a cold start. It took three or four sessions to gather enough clues and even begin to understand what was broken. Part of the cold start was activating the team to be less passive about fact-finding and to continue digging beyond the surface. The prior regimes didn't have this expectation, and people were not accustomed to it. But things changed once the team began to see that standups were not a call to the principal's office but instead a way to solve a puzzle together.

In the coming chapters, you'll learn about this kind of team-based exploration. Suffice it to say at this point, people at Volvo began to feel safe when they understood that the questions I posed weren't a threat, but were rather a purposeful exploration of the problem. Safety unlocked their higher-level problem-solving abilities. We continued standups until production was flowing and there was assurance it wouldn't stop.

In a situation of such urgency, you typically find a fix for the problem and take more time to get to the real underlying factors. Those root causes can take weeks or more to fix while the bandage solutions are in place. You might have to explore what a more resilient system would look like now versus when it was designed 20 or 30 years ago.

Reflecting on this crisis, which eliminated any honeymoon period in the new job, I saw a silver lining. I joined Volvo to help introduce new offerings and navigate new spaces. But what about everything else? What about all the groups and teams behind or outside the exciting innovations? They typically don't get sexy projects or much love from the company. This was an opportunity to bring all parts of my organization into a common drive for cultural change and to learn together as explored unknowns. Rethinking software for an assembly line may not be as enticing as a consumer-facing offering, but they are both meaningful and come with unknowns. Both require upstream work.

I didn't know it then, but some of the leaders involved in the factory incident became some of the best advocates for new ways of working, new mindsets, and new workflows. Two years later, they would blow me away with a successful agile coaching center, spreading these approaches throughout the company. And it all started with the factory incident.

That's one reason I rebranded "IT" to "enterprise digital." I was not only the first CDO of a global company to expand into CIO responsibilities, I was the first one to kill the notion of IT. The reason made a ton of sense: we leave no woman or man behind on our journey. We need to activate the entire organization in our ambition to grow and innovate. In this case, it meant that every aspect of IT would evolve to a digital products mindset with new roles, skills, and operating models. It's great to run an IT transformation and a digital one at the same time, but dealing with unknowns or teaching people how to do it goes well beyond ambition.

While at Volvo, I helped people to think through unknowns when they were involved in an initiative, but I was too close to the action to describe or canvas out my methods in a general way. In other words, I did not have a documented or written approach. I was doing it in real time. Like you, I was time constrained, so this meant I had limited ability to affect more than a handful of initiatives in any period.

Hakan refers to this as the artisan way. An artist can produce something meaningful but may not be able to describe the method. That's a huge limitation because I could only affect things by being involved in them.

Since my time at Volvo, I have reflected on and canvassed the methods. I've documented upstream work—what it is and why it matters—and Decision Sprint as the solution. I've started with a way to enable companies at the team level. It's a more bottom-up approach to boost any given initiative, with a bigger role for leaders.

## BE A SYSTEMS BUILDER

Artisanship can seem an odd concept in large companies and their systems. If you're a leader, I will demonstrate how to move from artisanship to develop a systematic way to address constant unknowns that hold strategy back from action. It will turn the art of *upstream excellence* into methods. And that will allow you as a leader to bring systematic change.

Systems are prevalent in every company, even if they are not formalized. There's a system operating in your organization as we speak. It shows up in nearly every interaction, like a convincing whisperer, rarely leaving a breadcrumb for its influence. It sits above any person, project, function, or strategy in your organization and impacts performance for years and decades. Yet it's rarely discussed or managed.

So what kind of system does your organization need? Decision Sprint can make innovation and fearless problem-solving a cornerstone of your company's DNA, and can begin to show benefits one project or team at a time.

Leaders of new, emerging, and established companies can use Decision Sprint to achieve their strategic ambitions without compromising speed or quality. It provides a way forward for leaders of incumbent companies who are urgently seeking to reverse the tide of legacy culture.

Leaders of innovative businesses that are already fast-growing can learn how to keep their edge as they scale up and lay the right bricks to establish an enduring culture like Amazon. They want to keep "day one" pace and thinking while steering a more expansive and complex ship. It addresses the issues that keep CEOs of the most innovative companies up at night—the slow creep of bureaucracy, institutional thinking, and the quest to move with speed that doesn't feel like chaos. They don't want to be the next Peloton.

Tap this groundbreaking system to continuously make the leap from identification of white spaces, innovation, and growth opportunities to taking decisive action on them. Let's dive into how teams and companies can innovate in the unknown.

# Why We Need
# Decision Sprint

**D**ecision-making is the ultimate superpower of companies. To grow, innovate, capture new markets, and stay relevant, a company must decide quickly and more effectively than ever. Complex problem-solving is also the name of the game when it comes to operating existing services and products. Operations is not immune from forks in the road. Operational decisions can feature ambiguous and uncertain issues, challenges, and root causes. Whether it's white space or a mature part of business, action can only unfold on the heels of decisions, but they are harder to make than ever. As a leader, you may instinctively agree. In this chapter, I will elaborate on why.

To develop this superpower, a company needs a method of dealing with the unknowns that come along with new territory and problem spaces. Let me emphasize this again because it is so often missed. Any new idea, opportunity, or innovation has a critical mass of unknowns at its center. Make the unknowns leading characters in the script, not last-minute substitutes.

In simple terms, when an organization can work through unknowns, it will make faster and better decisions. Unknowns often trip up companies into inaction, lack of commitment, and reduced ambition. And when companies trip up, teams feel it. They feel stuck, powerless, and frustrated. How does poor handling of unknowns lead to this?

Let's start at the beginning. Let's say a team is asked to develop a plan for a new idea or solve a new problem space. Typically, a leader may share the objective and wait for well-baked plans to be presented. That leaves a ton of problem-solving activity in the middle. As executive reviews near, teams feel they need to have the "answers." Tolerance for ambiguity shrinks. Expectations for answers are high as time elapses.

Questions are always greater in number than answers at the start of problem-solving. Without the mechanism for leaders and teams to spend time with the ambiguity, there's a lot of guesswork and blind spots we can introduce. If a leader senses these gaps deep into a project, it could trigger an urge to control, and that's not good for anyone. Many teams have experienced a level of command and control where the autonomy is stripped away. At the team level, there's also a number of pitfalls. No single person can own or be accountable for a meaningful project. The unknowns are too numerous and multifaceted. Progress within a team halts when people don't see unknowns with some common understanding. Teams can spend a lot of time trying to align each other to polar positions when they are weighing a different set of considerations. Before drawing conclusions on what to do, they need to see the same canvas of the problem—the knowns, an investigation of the unknowns, and the weight they hold on the scale. Yes, complexity and ambiguity are like kryptonite. The opposite is also true. That's the good news. We can turn kryptonite into superpower.

We must rethink decision-making practices to incorporate unknowns. Designing the work leading up to decisions with unknowns in mind changes *everything*. New initiatives take flight and build momentum. Growth materializes. The internal lift to get there is lighter and less taxing. This is the promise of the methods I will share with you. Only with these new methods and practices can companies experience a sustained way to move from strategy to action or solve the problems that matter. (See Figure 2.1.)

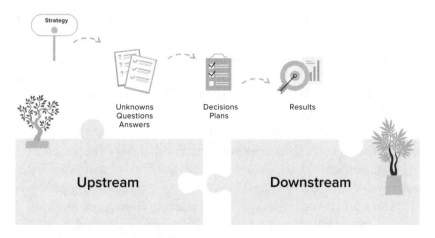

**FIGURE 2.1**   Upstream focus moves projects from strategy to action.

It's not easy to deal with unknowns on the path to confident decision-making. Any strategic problem or major innovation will face a pile of unknowns. Yet most planning approaches treat unknowns like a nuisance—an unwelcome guest at the dinner party.

That's why the first thing to know about dealing with unknowns is they deserve space. Welcome them in at the start, before any decisions are even considered. This simple change will pay consistent dividends as a project or initiative is developed. I've built a career in the C-suite of well-known companies through this practice of hungering for unknowns as we drive a big idea. The faster we identify them and seek to understand as much as we reasonably can, the more likely we will create enough clarity. Clarity is what gives the confidence to green-light, hold, or fold.

## UPSTREAM AND DOWNSTREAM

We provide this space through upstream workflows. You're already familiar with downstream workflows because they are all about execution. Companies are capable of crafting project plans, KPIs, and desirable goals. These characterize the downstream.

The downstream is not kind to unknowns. The downstream runs on answers, not open questions. It often rejects unknowns because it feeds on the well-defined bit that push execution along. The upstream is where we can do something intelligent and purposeful about unknowns to create clarity. Upstream work exists in our companies but typically lacks a method. It can be clumsy and depend on the players involved. Often the method is a flurry of circular brainstorms and deep dives. We don't experience the pain of this until too late in the game.

Decision Sprint enables movement from upstream to downstream, with speed and effectiveness. Decision Sprint not only provides a structure for the upstream, which is missing in most companies, it knows what the downstream wants. And it serves it up like a warm buttery biscuit. Put the upstream and downstream together with Decision Sprint, and you have a problem-solving, action-oriented, thinking machine that is constantly shipping.

As you get deeper into the book, you'll learn about upstream and downstream workflows, how they're handled, and what could go wrong. I'll explain the typical pitfalls and traps of dealing with unknowns. You'll be able to relate to these pitfalls and learn how behavioral science allows us to avoid them. As part of establishing upstream workflow, you will learn about exploration and alignment practices. These are often where the pitfalls live. If the upstream had three major phases, exploration would come first. Alignment would follow. And decision-making would be the third phase.

Exploration is where a better way of working starts. Exploration is a concerted effort to surface the proper considerations and get to the bottom of them. Alignment is about drawing conclusions based on an exploration a team has performed containing these puzzle pieces. One pitfall you will be hearing more about is aligning before exploring. This happens when execution hunger shortchanges the effort to examine unknowns that affect the direction of a project or initiative. It's the rush to form an opinion based on what's already known.

Often this comes from a place of fear. Channeling this fear into something constructive is one behavioral method I will demonstrate. A lack of commitment to exploration is always going to backfire. It locks in a lower ambition because it forces decisions on incomplete understanding. Often it means settling before knowing what is possible.

Here you will learn how to use questions (and questioning) to channel this fear and redirect it into a constructive exploration effort. Questioning is never something to shy away from, but it must be neutral. Otherwise, it clouds judgment and overwhelms creativity and problem-solving. A questioner personality can help if it's coming from the right place. I'm known for coming from a place of questions (see "The Questioner Personality").

Exploration holds many potential pitfalls as well. Weak links in exploration happen when we miss a key consideration or a consideration is surfaced but only understood in shallow ways. You'll learn how to source input for an exploration and practices to address these pitfalls effectively. Sourcing input is essential at the start of exploration. It's progress in and of itself—like getting to first base before scoring a run.

## THE QUESTIONER PERSONALITY

Do you know what a questioner personality type is? Or what it's like to work with a questioner?

Let me share a story. Ten years ago, a friend who's an executive at Google and previously worked for McKinsey described what it's like to meet me for the first time. "At first, you begin to think he's quiet and reserved. Then he starts asking questions, and you wonder why it's so hard for him to understand. You think he's quite slow and the hype about him is all wrong. He may even come across as downright stupid. Half an hour later, when you understand his questions, it flips. He's expanded your mind and you think it's pure genius. Everything is clear and better."

Close friends can be a mirror unto ourselves.

I took this story to heart as a reflection on where my strengths lie (and where they do not). Many of us admire the charismatic leader who speaks fast and evangelizes followers with each word. That's not me. In the last 10 years, I've discovered charismatic leaders are less of what we need to build companies and teams in the future. I'll elaborate why "thinking together" is a superpower for organizations, how questions are the starting point for it, and what methods can systematically bring the superpower to life.

I am constantly working on big ideas and initiatives. Big new territory in business is not for the faint of heart. It's like solving a gigantic puzzle. Uncertainty. Ambiguity. High stakes. Big decisions. Upside. Risk. Many puzzle pieces.

In business, our puzzles are mental; we don't have physical game pieces. So where does the puzzle reside? In whose mind? Yours? Your colleagues'? Your boss's? Ideally, it's like in the board game world, in the center with people gathered around making contributions to solve it. But if many people are solving the puzzle in their own minds with no consistency or common understanding, you can only imagine the result. So where does the puzzle reside, and how is it being solved? The answer will inform how constructive or dysfunctional an organization happens to be. More important, it's the best indicator of success. It will determine how likely any strategic ambition, objective, or initiative is likely to materialize.

Back to the story related by my friend at Google. The people involved didn't realize that we were solving a puzzle together. I happen to be very good at drawing the puzzle out, placing it in the middle of participants, and guiding as we sort the pieces.

My brain formulates a construct but suspends judgment and is hungry for inputs. Questions are the best way to get those inputs and feed them in. With enough of the right inputs from the right questions, puzzle pieces can start to fit. A whole puzzle is hard to connect because smaller sections need to come together first. This is what makes thinking together a challenge. Some puzzle pieces may be in your head or that of your colleague. I never assume all the puzzle pieces are in mine. That's my assumption even when I'm the expert on the matter. I assume the opposite. I work consciously to bring out puzzle pieces around me. It can make me look unsure, but in the end, it makes everyone more sure. This is hard work, and I'll elaborate on how to do it.

My questioner personality has served me well in business. I've built a fast-track career without realizing that my superpower is "questioning." Over time, it became the basis of a management style ideally suited for dealing with big ambiguous initiatives, innovations, and transformations. Having this superpower explains why big roles in the C-suite came calling and why I was able to tackle them with success.

Being a questioner is hard. You must conquer ego. It's easier to be a "know-it-all," but one has to decide. Do we want to be right or come across as the smartest in the room?

In this era of leadership, we need more people and teams comfortable with tackling unknown territory rather than doing more of the past a little better. We need to appreciate, explore, and master a new approach to link unknowns, questioning, and the work of leadership.

As mentioned, alignment links what's been explored to a recommendation or conclusion people must agree upon. Imagine a scenario where everyone works from a shared understanding to draw conclusions. This scenario can radically streamline approvals, support, and buy-in. I've used high-quality exploration to make high-stakes meetings drama-free and straightforward. You'll learn about this approach to alignment. Exploration and alignment are part of the upstream. But to make them stick, you will need to understand them in concrete detail.

In fact, the entire upstream work in companies needs elaboration and clear methodology. That's why I developed a system, or solution, to tackle the entire upstream flow of work. It centers on Decision Sprint.

## DECISION SPRINT: 13 WORKFLOWS

When it comes to making decisions, they are not isolated but instead directly influenced by the workflows leading up to them. That is the key reason to think in terms of sprints. *Long before reaching a decision point, the tables are being set. I will help you set the tables in 13 steps or workflows.*

A company cannot hope for better decisions by narrowly thinking about the decision points themselves. So much takes place under the hood. Relevant considerations have been surfaced or not. Depth of understanding for these considerations has been reached or not. Recommendations can be connected back or not. And the right actions to put recommendations in motion have been developed or not. This is a lot of activity. And it takes place in the weeks or months leading up to decision points. It's critical to weave them into common fabric. The notion of a "sprint" provides a continuous backbone to the workflow. Keep it moving. Don't stay stuck.

In this book, you will find a set of 13 workflows that set the tables in the correct sequence. Taken together, I refer to them as Decision Sprint. (See Figure 2.2.)

**Workflow #1**   Initiating an Exploration

**Workflow #2**   Sourcing Matters

**Workflow #3**   Sourcing Questions

**Workflow #4**   Calibrating the Exploration

**Workflow #5**   Sharing the Canvas

**Workflow #6**   Answering Questions

**Workflow #7**   Calibrating Answers

**Workflow #8**   Drawing Conclusions

**Workflow #9**   Preparing for Alignment

**Workflow #10**  Conducting Alignment

**Workflow #11**  Identifying Decisions

**Workflow #12**  Preparing Content

**Workflow #13**  Conducting Decision Meetings

With Decision Sprint, we organize a flow of work that makes decision points a natural output of the work leading up to it. Each workflow is a well-defined step with clear inputs and outputs. You'll learn who to involve, where to start, and what comes out of each workflow.

Decision Sprint combines three components: exploration, alignment, and decision-making. Its purpose is to embrace unknowns and help teams pull them forward into action. It informs what unknowns are being worked on, where the work is headed, and for what purpose. Decision Sprint is how everyone involved in a project makes the proper contribution at the right time and in the right way. It sits above personalities and agendas.

You'll learn how Decision Sprint unlocks benefits before, during, and following decision points.

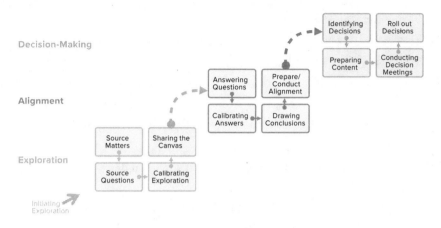

**FIGURE 2.2** Workflows you'll learn about

Following this process leads to more confident decisions because you and your team now have higher-quality information to make vital decisions. It creates a connected trail or breadcrumb of findings that sit behind a recommended decision. When colleagues and bosses want to know what sits behind your conclusions, the line of thinking is easier for everyone to draw.

This documentation simplifies the path to decision-making, reducing churn and bureaucracy for teams. It makes it easier to roll out and explain decisions across the organization. It creates transparency. Cascading decisions and the why behind them is simplified. These are just some of the benefits for executives, sponsors, and working team members. But the main benefit is something everyone is seeking.

Making the leap from strategy to execution.

## THE WHY BEHIND DECISION SPRINT

In the end, this book is about a sprint to decisions. Business is always a sprint to decisions—whether we hold, fold, or double down on them. It's what executives get paid to deliver. And it's what teams need to move their work forward. I've coined the term *Decision Sprint* to combine these workflows into a singular purpose. (See Figure 2.3.)

**Decision Sprint**

**FIGURE 2.3** Teams use Decision Sprint to build and run explorations, drive alignment and speed up decisions.

You'll learn about Decision Sprint and its elements shortly. You'll learn how to tap into Decision Sprint to ensure you and your team make the right decisions at the right velocity. I'll explain how to effectively work backward from strategic objectives to run explorations to identify key points of alignment and surface decisions that will drive a project forward.

You'll learn to use Decision Sprint to power important meetings where leaders gather to calibrate and set direction. The lift of getting the organization onboard is much lighter and easier to achieve. High-stakes meetings won't be a mad dash of preparations.

Oh, while we're talking about making goals easier to achieve, upstream workflows won't mean adding more work to the plate. Decision Sprint will streamline ongoing activities while making them more effective. I've learned an important principle over the last 10 years: "meeting a company where it is." Decision Sprint does precisely this because it meets you in a state where there are many questions and not many answers. Every project or hairy problem begins like this, so it's easy to place Decision Sprint into any initiative. Decision Sprint looks at questions as the best starting point for project work.

Everyone talks about culture. Do you want a learning culture? Or maybe an agile culture? Decision Sprint is an effective way to drive culture change. It's much better than slogans or campaigns. You might ask, what does upstream work have to do with culture?

I've designed the workflows to be enablers for teams. As you've read in Chapter 1, there are two ways to bring change. Top-down and bottom-up. Top-down change happens to teams, and bottom-up change is what teams make happen. Teams should not make excuses. There's a learned helplessness in teams, and I will provide a way out of that mindset.

Ultimately, it's powerful to work from both ends, but the team level is much easier and faster to initiate. Here's why. When you form a project team, what follows are endless meetings, emails, messages, and other interactions to reach milestones (such as check-ins or updates with senior leadership).

I'm not proposing any changes to how milestones with senior leadership are conducted. Instead, I lay out a different workflow to get there. Milestones can continue operating in standard practice while the work to get there is within the team's liberty to design. If you're presenting to senior leaders, they want to see the output of team-level collaboration. They typically don't get into the guts of the workflow driving that output (unless there is a major problem or best practice to spread).

If senior executives are curious about workflow behind the scenes, they will be impressed by Decision Sprint. Decision Sprint provides a transparent, effective path to decisions and simplifies how executives "calibrate" the work of teams leading up to decisions. When they see higher-quality information, everyone benefits. Senior leadership may notice the difference when you hold up a project powered by Decision Sprint against one that is not. More clarity, better velocity, more conviction, and momentum: these are some of the upsides. With differentiated outcomes, senior executives will likely look for best practices to spread in the organization.

What about the roles of senior executives, and how they complement the role of teams? As you do upstream work, many people will ask what the roles executives should play in interacting with these enabled, empowered superteams. You'll learn how in this new upstream environment the roles of executives shift to higher-leverage activities; they're calibrating work, not micromanaging it.

In this new world, leaders need to think about team enablement. Enabling teams is not a passive exercise for leaders. It doesn't devalue leadership work. Back to a hypothetical situation where a team is asked to develop a plan for a new idea or solve a new problem space.

Leaders play a role in actively shaping inputs the team is sourcing and the conclusions being drawn from these inputs. I refer to this as calibration. In a calibration model, a leader doesn't wait for finalized thinking to provide feedback. By then it's too late to "calibrate" whether the right inputs have been collected to canvass the problem. When calibration goes well, it provides leaders with evidence to provide teams with space. With this space, teams can run ahead with deeper work.

Executives can come into the front end of exploration work to see how stuff is being built and validate the build. They can review the running of an exploration as the team investigates the key unknowns. Once it's time to make recommendations and review them, executives will more clearly follow how the team got there. As a leader, you'll learn there's great upside to shift your efforts to calibration.

Beyond this, executives can play at a more systematic level. They have a significant role and can place these workflows on steroids. They can establish these workflows to become systematic at the level of teams. New norms for the content, cadence, and agenda of meetings will require help to spread the power of Decision Sprint throughout the company.

Coaching project teams to use Decision Sprint will also help spread the method. You can establish indicators for evaluating how people perform in terms of upstream contributions and incentivize success. Taking advantage of the data when Decision Sprint comes to life through software will change where and when your company invests time and energy. It's a massive reveal of data that is missing today, and it will usher in new AI-based applications.

Ultimately, there is an AI component to how we'll understand the development of intellectual capital generated by Decision Sprint. It comes down to this: the rate at which unknowns are being understood gives us the best indicator for the success of projects, strategies, and company goals. You'll learn about the role of AI in providing new radar for leaders on key initiatives and their progress. I am a huge believer in the human + AI partnership that will fuel the next generation of how companies are managed. A system to handle unknowns, a backbone for upstream work, and faster movement from ideas to action—Decision Sprint provides the foundation for it all.

# The Power of
# Moving Upstream

In your organization, how does a typical meeting unfold? Does someone "present" for most of the time, ask if there are questions, receive sparse input, and then receive a passive green light? This may feel like a win until somewhere down the line, out of the blue, the project is stalled because support evaporates.

Perhaps the meeting unfolds differently. The audience doesn't connect with the recommendations. People don't follow the conclusions and want to back up to understand how the team got there. The team struggles to explain and lacks enough buy-in to move on. The team did not "pass go" and has to return to the drawing board. A wasted opportunity and it slows things down. Uncertainty. Letdown.

Was the team subjecting people to endless meetings in preparation and for alignment beforehand, only to fall short of confident decision-making? Why do decision points and meetings feel so risky to navigate, onerous to prepare for, and difficult to get right?

The answer lies in the idea of upstream work and how *underserved* it is.

As I've shared in previous chapters, anything new and meaningful a team is trying to create or solve will start with unknowns. Unknowns deserve space and a way to be transformed into answers or perspectives. If this work is shortchanged, the results are painful because they show up as blockers later.

Enter the idea of upstream work. In Chapter 1, I described "upstream" as the state when there are more questions than answers. *Upstream work is how unknowns are sourced, synthesized, and reasoned through to arrive at conclusions that drive decisions.* That may be a mouthful, but it will become super clear how Decision Sprint brings all that together for faster and smoother decisions. There is an entire body of work to flip the script on the unknowns.

Remember, the start or any new phase of a project is characterized by unknowns. Unknowns describe the upstream world. They are like puzzle pieces when you first open the box. Plentiful and unclear how they all relate. When enough is understood about these unknowns, we can draw conclusions, set direction, and decide on actions. Your organization needs a way to address this. Only then can we get on with downstream activities like detailed planning and execution. It's time we stop shortchanging the upstream.

## WHAT GOOD LOOKS LIKE

Upstream work is not a new thing to add to the plate of a team. Upstream work happens continuously in teams, but it's often hidden and approached without a transparent method. The quality can vary. The impact of those quality gaps may only show up further down the line, for example, when the decision meetings are taking place and it's "showtime" for the project team. Trust me. You don't want to realize the quality gaps in a high-stakes decision meeting. By then, it's too late and embarrassing. And the project can take two steps back. I can often trace the *root cause of underwhelming outcomes in decision meetings to the quality of upstream efforts.* There is a better way to drive your initiatives and projects, and it starts by recognizing that upstream work is critical.

Let's take a glimpse at "what good looks like" for upstream work. Imagine a fork in the road within your project. You need to make a strategic choice, and there are seemingly "good" reasons for each alternative. The choice will impact the execution, so it's more of a one-way door rather than something that can be undone easily. The working team convenes to discuss and reach some common understanding.

Now imagine in this meeting, for some time, no one is allowed to provide answers or opinions, only questions. A good question feels like digging and striking gold. The questions are on the right track. They help us see more. The team sorts, organizes, and explores the questions in an open-ended manner. No one knows what the dialogue will conclude or lead to. Everyone is in the moment. The questions feel like they are surfacing the correct issues and provide a guide to how the team should explore problems. The rush to answers is gone, and the flow of the room is geared to surfacing important considerations. What matters? Can we see why they matter?

When the questions feel right, the team moves on. Someone takes a crack at answering a question or really exploring it out in the open. In doing so, this team member shares insight, explains why it matters, and reasons through how it weighs on a potential answer. It's a solid contribution. Others around the table nod their head with understanding. Or perhaps someone views it differently. This team member shares perspective and reasons through a different or improved answer to the same question. Several issues, underlying questions, and explorations of those matters take place in an organic way. The team has done some "thinking together." There is a point where everyone, by and large, feels confident to move on to draw some conclusions. Why? Because the group feels it's standing on high-quality information. The team has canvassed the topic with good questions, exploration of potential answers, and reasoning through their exploration. The team stands on solid ground to draw conclusions or recommendations.

No one held the spotlight, and virtually everyone had a common understanding. It feels like a collective IQ lift. *These types of meetings are possible and are anything but chaotic. There's a method to them.* It's an input meeting more than an output meeting. Recall in Chapter 1, where I experienced unease at McDonald's when I headed a meeting that was very output-focused when I was looking to engage on the inputs. Since that time, I've had plenty of constructive input meetings. But that's because I saw the need and tinkered with small changes to meetings and leaned into my calibration skills over a period of 10 years.

Input meetings occur routinely when learning is an active part of an organization's management culture. So why don't they exist in your world?

The answer is that many organizations miss entirely the notion of upstream work in projects, initiatives, and problem-solving. The input meeting I described needs to be supported by a methodology built on the workflows you'll acquire through this book. Yes, it's a lot to ask for a meeting dynamic to promote "thinking together." The workflows that you will learn about are designed to promote these behaviors. They start with the unknowns and provide concrete guidance to handhold the organization until these behaviors become the norm. The meeting I described can quickly become natural to your organization and teamwork. Decision Sprint will kick-start the change and make it stick.

## THREE COMPONENTS OF UPSTREAM

High-performance organizations have a method for upstream. Their teams can connect the unknowns that we must tackle at the start all the way to decision points. That's an expansive journey to traverse. Most initiatives, projects, or problem-solving activities struggle to connect the dots. Before racing ahead to KPIs, outcomes, and execution, high-performance organizations intensely explore the inputs that influence outcomes. You can't do upstream work if a system is built entirely for downstream execution. In Chapter 1, you learned why I was so focused on inputs in my efforts to revitalize growth at McDonald's and why the CEO of Volvo spent much more time on inputs than on hearing reports about results. So the first step in the Decision Spring is to recognize that we need to build a new planet—call it the upstream world.

This world has three components we've mentioned: exploration, alignment, and decision-making. These steps come before planning execution. (See Figure 3.1.)

*Exploration* is a concerted effort to surface the relevant considerations and get to the bottom of them. *Alignment* is about bringing together what's been explored to draw conclusions. *Decision-making* is committing to the necessary actions.

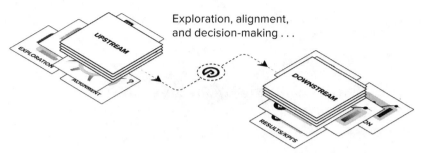

Exploration, alignment, and decision-making . . .

impacts the quality of *downstream* work.

**FIGURE 3.1** Exploration, alignment, and decision-making are key upstream workflows.

Three simple yet powerful descriptions. When these components work together, the results can be compelling. Teams can craft plans and move on to execution with confidence and the right backing in the organization. The three components are meant to feed the other and to make the next component an easier lift for everyone involved. They are part of one continuous thread of work—Decision Sprint.

## UPSTREAM PITFALLS

Many companies claim to have a way of fact-finding, learning, or investigating before planning a strategic initiative or a solution to a problem. When push comes to shove, they will claim to use brainstorming, working sessions, workshops, stakeholder interviews, and other means to prove how they've done the necessary work. But there's a real intensity and method required to the upstream work.

Here are some pitfalls I've observed at companies, whether they are Fortune 500 companies, fast-moving tech companies, or a 30-person startup. (See Figures 3.1 and 3.2.) Note: I've been part of all types of organizations over my 25-year career.

One of the most common scenarios, especially in so-called legacy cultures, is "alignment before exploration." This occurs when a limited set of matters and limited understanding of these matters cement a conclusion that is hard to undo. It is all too common for teams to

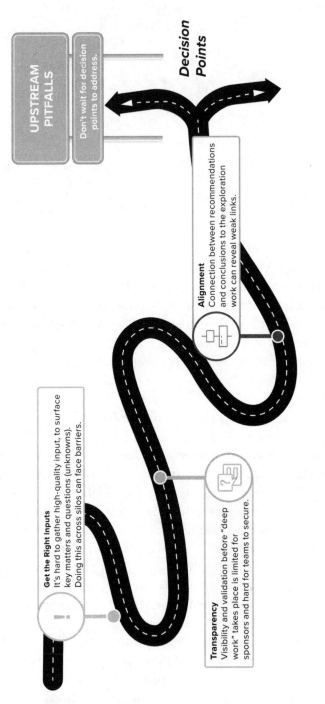

**UPSTREAM PITFALLS**

Don't wait for decision points to address.

**Decision Points**

**Alignment**
Connection between recommendations and conclusions to the exploration work can reveal weak links.

**Get the Right Inputs**
It's hard to gather high-quality input, to surface key matters and questions (unknowns). Doing this across silos can face barriers.

**Transparency**
Visibility and validation before "deep work" takes place is limited for sponsors and hard for teams to secure.

**FIGURE 3.2** What makes upstream hard

experience executives who cement a decision based on limited understanding. The limitation could be a single overweighted matter or consideration. The consequence of this is to limit the amount of stretch or big thinking in the project. It locks in small decisions and, therefore, small actions.

Alignment before exploration can water down a strategy or opportunity without surfacing what's possible. It could be that something bigger was entirely doable without major risk, yet those possibilities were never given wings. If you wonder why projects in companies are big and get a lot of attention internally but don't move the needle for the external world, lack of exploration is often the culprit. Everything has been watered down, so what is being shipped to the customer is a "so what." Big companies are replete with this. Teams are in a tizzy for months, even quarters, but what gets out the door is just catching up to the world. They're perpetually behind the curve. But the LinkedIn posts celebrating launch continue to show up in our feeds.

For a company to endure, it needs to deliver "wow" and "OMG," not "so what." So we need a way to overcome or outsmart this potential pitfall in our organizations. I'm going to show you how to do that. But first, let me share a story.

Back to the early days of digitization of McDonald's in 2013 when no one viewed mobile as a way for the company to grow (yet that was exactly my charter). The mobile app needed to be much more than a way to deliver promotions and coupons—what a yawner. I was instead motivated to use mobile to introduce new ways to use McDonald's. To tap mobile to make McDonald's convenient for the next decade and beyond. That's why I was super intrigued by the idea of curbside pickup or fulfillment. A customer would be able to arrive at a parking spot and have food brought out. Some bright people on the team were bullish about the idea, and I wanted to give it a chance.

In my conversations with everyone from the board members to employees, I framed digital as a way to provide customers "new ways to use McDonald's." And that to enable this we would "introduce new service models" like skip-the-line ordering. It was all about taking the McDonald's customer experience to the next level. It's not a big stretch to say I was the first technology executive in the Fortune 500 to frame my work as the customer experience of the future.

The company had grown to $100 billion in system sales on the back of three ways to get McDonald's: (1) drive through, (2) stand in line + order + get a bag for takeaway, and (3) stand in line + order + get a tray for dine-in. What if we could invent two to three new ways to use McDonald's? It could lead to billions.

Turning back to curbside fulfillment, we didn't know whether the idea could fly. After all, there were some real issues to solve. Would customers be allowed to order before arriving so we could save them time? When should we check in the order to the kitchen? Would the location services technology be accurate? What if customers didn't show up and food was wasted? Would it translate to customers coming more frequently in order to justify the investment? What kind of training would the crew require? What if the parking lot was full of people loitering after finishing their meals in the car?

These were some of the unknowns. The unknowns did not scare me. As we've said, unknowns always characterize the start of anything big and meaningful. That's why I didn't want to kill the concept either. There was promise in thinking about what comes after the drive-through. Could this be a way to self-disrupt?

It was natural for me to push to innovate in the unknown. I'd felt my way through the dark before; it had been deeply wired over years and years. But some executives, understandably protective of what they saw as the McDonald's way, had a fear of introducing a service model that would confuse and slow down operations. "Align." It's a word that can mean almost anything. That's why it was uncomfortable when my peer desperately wanted to align the mobile app's scope to limit it to the safest possible option. "Safe" usually means underwhelming to the customer.

And when he mentioned it, I was like "sure, of course."

Who wouldn't want to align? But as you hear people out, you realize that what they want to cement or align is closing the door on new thinking or even collecting enough of the inputs to take a position.

It's uncomfortable when parts of a company need to work together to ship something yet come from opposite mindsets. One part feels "this could be a game-changer" and another feels "we should come back to this later." I knew that coming back to this later meant it could be years before we get to it.

In many companies, you'll hear about a "crawl, walk, run" approach whereby all the exciting possibilities are laid out in some sequential priority. *Crawl* describes some of the easy wins, *walk* characterizes more advanced ideas, and *run* is when the team runs with the bigger and harder ideas. In many projects, items pegged for walk or run are never prioritized. They simply never materialize. The exception is when your upstream machine is working, and the velocity is high enough where we move through the crawl-walk-run stages quickly.

If we didn't prioritize "looking at it" now, I knew it would be years before the idea could have a chance at getting commitment as a core part of the customer experience.

Here's where alignment before exploration can be a real pitfall— when a conclusion is reached that an idea is too complicated to act on before it's been explored. There's a big danger when people at the top do this because they have the power to close doors for a long time. In fact, I was not "aligned" that we were ready to "align" on delaying this type of customer experience. I would be more comfortable to first surface enough key factors to inform a conclusion. To draw a conclusion (go/no-go, now or later, important or nice to have, promising or not), we needed better inputs.

My peer was accustomed to two people agreeing on a direction and informing the teams about the decision. At the very top of the organization, we could do this. Yet we were not close enough to the action to make the call unless there was an exploration of the issues we could review.

There was some good reason for my peer to hesitate to consider curbside as part of the mobile strategy and customer experience. Exploring in a big company like McDonald's could take a long time. And as a corporate group building technology, his team already suffered from a reputation for moving too slow. Markets like Australia, France, Sweden, and China were already building competing apps, and corporate needed to ship something that would satisfy enough of the market need to be a good alternative.

One could look at curbside or another feature as pushing availability of the app further out. More scope could mean more time. That could be risky. At the same time, we needed to deliver something meaningful that would be noticeable to customers worldwide. And you can work upstream on an idea to explore its merits before committing to execution.

As I've mentioned in the Introduction, people have two reflexes regarding unknowns. They can shy away from them and rush ahead to planning based on what they already understand. In this mindset, unknowns make for a distraction. During the early days of transformation at McDonald's, this is how I was asked to align—to push away the tough questions.

The other approach is to stay in research mode on an idea, which sounds promising, but can lack urgency and pragmatic focus. This is the risk my peer was reacting to. If we simply stepped back to give a team autonomy to study the curbside opportunity, a lot of time could elapse, and we wouldn't know if it were worth it till the end. It felt like too much of a "trust and wait" model. Keeping initiatives in the lab for a long time without the prospect of seeing daylight would be wasteful.

## DON'T BAN ALIGNMENT, REDEFINE IT

There is a better way—I just didn't know it at the time. Exploration that is purposeful and fast is the better way. And I will show you how it's done in the next chapter. Exploration speeds up, not slows down, the outcomes you're seeking. It's not about giving people endless rope and being distant from their "research." It's about being quick and deliberate about what needs to be understood and building understanding together, pronto.

So how did things unfold at McDonald's? It was somewhat tug-of-war. I leaned toward exploration, not only on curbside but so much more. New and more convenient service models to order food, our own payment card, contactless payments, loyalty, and even our own fleet for delivery. I offered that my group focus on problem-solving these concepts to see what's possible. Another part of the company thought curbside delivery was a distraction and wanted to nip it in the bud.

We tried to convince each other. But we had no interface, common language, or way to communicate our instincts. We needed a better way to team up. And that's why I'm writing this book. Unknowns should not drive a wedge; we should find better ways to team up around them to create a shared understanding. In business, we can't afford distractions, nor can we afford to water down ideas and their potential.

It got to a point at McDonald's where I banned the word *alignment*. I would not allow anyone in the team to use it because it would spread the wrong way to think about our work. That was a blunt move, and I regret moving to such extremes. I did not have the language to explain why it would lead to pitfalls. I would invent the language over the next 10 years and am sharing this story so you're equipped with the language to meet this maneuver with a more elegant tactic.

Banning alignment was a defensive move. It would have been better to push for exploration. Purposeful exploration to feed alignment. Aligning without exploring is limiting our ambition without necessity.

If a team had the methods to show how exploration could be structured, I believe my peer would support this effort. I'm referring to exploration that feeds into alignment and a concrete decision point. Crafting a workflow that would be transparent and connect to a decision point, one way or the other. But the workflow was missing.

I will show you the steps in that workflow, how to get the sequence right and much more. You'll learn how to avoid the pitfalls and traps, while being streamlined about upstream work.

What do I wish had been done differently? For starters, I would offer a solution to our disconnect. Yes, I would like to align after we've run an exploration. The exploration would be purposeful and would not require months. We could have some content to review in as little as a month. We would be able to shape the considerations going into the initiative to avoid blind spots. This strategy would be better for everyone involved. The most senior people would have high-quality inputs upon which to draw a conclusion. The working team would have breadcrumbs to connect what they explored to their recommendations. Keep in mind the refrain: exploration, then alignment.

## UPSTREAM AND STRATEGIC PLANNING

Most companies have documented their overall strategic direction. Often this starts with some visual, like a pyramid, where at the top is purpose. Purpose is why the company exists and its relevance to the world. Below the purpose is a set of strategic pillars. These represent the main foundations allowing the firm to achieve its purpose. The pillars are the biggest focus areas for the company in years to come. It's OK for these pillars to be not yet realized. We often have pillars that are early in their definition.

Pillars allow us to place a stake in the ground with our focus, resources, and investments. To bring a strategic pillar to life, companies may launch new initiatives that are separate projects but all part of a common overall objective.

For example, a consumer products company may want to connect to customers and diversify from the retail channel. Its pillar may be D2C (direct to the consumer). Many companies aspire to this because it can be more profitable and allow for stronger customer relationships. This pillar may require a host of initiatives from e-commerce to managing customer data to direct marketing. Each initiative is a massive effort for a company to "stand up" or get going.

An industrial products company may want to get into the twenty-first century and move from selling widgets to selling a recurring service. Its pillar may be "business model transformation" and that may require several projects, from subscription revenue models to redefining their offerings (charging for data instead of the products) to new billing capabilities to developing new versions of products that are cloud-connected ("IoT" and telemetry capabilities).

As you can see, each pillar in our two examples consists of several initiatives. Leadership will form project teams for each pillar, and the teams will be cross-functional, meaning no one part of the company has all the answers. The executives will charge the teams to pursue over months and quarters high-level objectives at first and then build the road map to real functioning capabilities and market success. In the middle is upstream work.

I know a lot about strategic frameworks because I authored them for well-known companies and startups. (See Figure 3.3 for an example.) Frameworks such as strategic pillars are a great starting point. But they are words on paper unless we mobilize teams to act on them. Teams hold the accountability and ownership for the day-to-day work of mobilizing these projects. I have spent the last 15 years working closely with teams in ways that not every executive is comfortable doing. Rather than being on the receiving end of the team's plans to

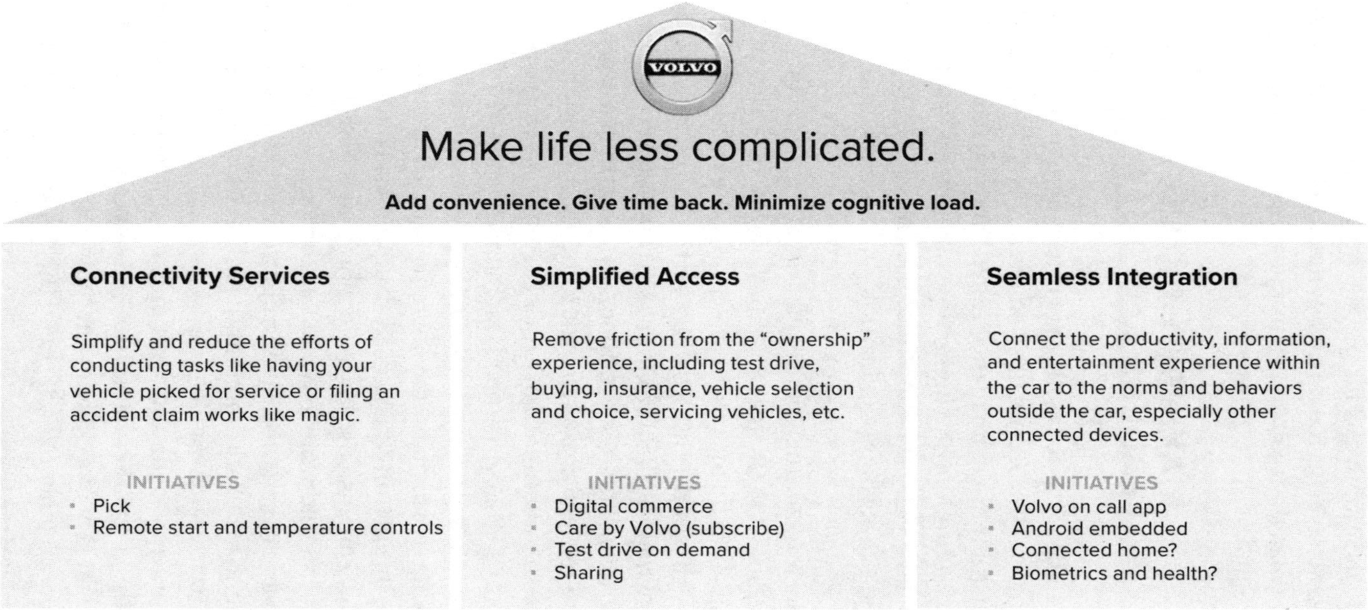

# Make life less complicated.

**Add convenience. Give time back. Minimize cognitive load.**

## Connectivity Services

Simplify and reduce the efforts of conducting tasks like having your vehicle picked for service or filing an accident claim works like magic.

INITIATIVES

- Pick
- Remote start and temperature controls

## Simplified Access

Remove friction from the "ownership" experience, including test drive, buying, insurance, vehicle selection and choice, servicing vehicles, etc.

INITIATIVES

- Digital commerce
- Care by Volvo (subscribe)
- Test drive on demand
- Sharing

## Seamless Integration

Connect the productivity, information, and entertainment experience within the car to the norms and behaviors outside the car, especially other connected devices.

INITIATIVES

- Volvo on call app
- Android embedded
- Connected home?
- Biometrics and health?

Example of Volvo's digital transformation strategy, shared publicly

**FIGURE 3.3** Common strategic-planning framework

tackle strategic initiatives, I have made myself available for upstream work. Being involved in the upstream means being a thought partner at the stage when there are just many questions and few clear answers.

## MAKING THE CASE—
## LEADERS AND TEAMS

It can be challenging to be the executive sponsor of a major initiative. For starters, you are not likely in the day-to-day. The challenge is often about guiding a team in the limited time you have. I call this the process of calibration. The higher up you go in an organization, the better you need to be at calibration. I define calibration in management as fine-tuning how people think about matters and doing it very efficiently. People who work for me know one of my catchphrases is "calibration over control." You've read about this in Chapter 2 and will read more about it in Chapter 8, "Tap Workflows to Express Culture."

You can't suck up too much time from the team and micromanage every step—those are control behaviors. Instead, you must quickly put the finger on how they're thinking about things, identify what needs to be tuned, and help them see it. Then empower them to move on that.

If you're the leader of a strategic initiative, upstream work should occupy more of your time than it does currently. As you've read, Hakan Samuelsson, CEO of Volvo, spends far more time upstream than downstream. If the CEO is doing this, what about your allocation of time? By the time things get to plans for your review (downstream), it's tough to unpack the line of thinking, quality of inputs, and information people used to draw conclusions. So your calibration is going to be challenging to perform. And while it could be correct, it will be disruptive to the initiative. Back to the drawing board. The fits and starts coming from this tend to deflate momentum and set us back weeks or longer. Get ahead of any letdown.

Do yourself a favor and shift engagement with the team from downstream to upstream. I'll show you how that engagement works and how to make it one of your superpowers.

Let's turn to other roles. If you're the day-to-day lead of the initiative, life can be like herding cats. Herding cats is one thing. Aligning them with a point of view can be like herding them up a snowy mountain. It's hard work to channel the collective input, but without it, project recommendations and decisions could miss the mark.

A project leader may spend an unbearable amount of time surveying people across the company for inputs, finding the patterns, identifying the main considerations, reporting their findings, confirming a working group agrees, conducting deep dives on various topics, pushing people with "day jobs" to think about new problems, synthesizing thinking, and driving some common understanding or recommendations.

It's challenging to manage personalities and to track everything and everyone involved. There's more. Email, Slack, Teams, digital whiteboards, PowerPoint, and spreadsheets are the tools where the inputs, ideas, and feedback sit. Often that content is incomplete, vague, or requires discussion.

Let's say you're not an initiative's main sponsor but are an important stakeholder. Your challenge could be finding the space to provide input and landing it. Often, work in companies is siloed. Whoever is point may not plan or know how to tap the inputs and intelligence from other parts of the organization. It's a baffling situation in companies when one part of the organization is running point to drive an initiative but doesn't make an effort to tap collective intelligence.

High-performance organizations know that collective intelligence is better than siloed intelligence. And with upstream workflows we provide ways for this collective intelligence to take place. If you're in the role of having input but not leading, ask the responsible team how collective intelligence will be achieved. How will it show up in the interactions and day-to-day work? What makes for a high-functioning working team in terms of day-to-day workflow? Ask these questions and challenge the organization.

Upstream is just as much about unleashing collective intelligence as anything else.

## COLLECTIVE INTELLIGENCE AT H&R BLOCK

Let's turn to an example of how a leader brings out the best of an organization by promoting collective intelligence. Jeff Jones, president and

CEO of H&R Block, articulated in a detailed discussion that upstream work takes patience and care: "When I first arrived at H&R Block," Jeff said, "I asked a ton of questions. People were freaked out a bit because I was never giving them the answer. They didn't know what to do about it. They thought I was holding my cards too close to my chest." Jeff is referring to the early days of his tenure as CEO, when he began to set the tone for his brand of leadership and principles.

> 66 So, I said, I am going to ask you a ton of questions because I want to deeply understand how you think about what you do. When I stop asking you questions, it's because I have gained total confidence in what you are doing. As time progressed, we established operating norms. But you never have a perfect team. We constantly evaluate how we are doing. I say "let's figure it out together" all the time. This creates conditions for emotional safety. People can be vulnerable so they can contribute 100 percent and not be afraid to express themselves if they think there's a better way. I think that's what it is all about. 99

Jeff is clearly a natural at the art of leadership when it comes to innovating into the unknown. And he has established—and really cascaded—within H&R Block the art of leading with questions and getting people to think together for stronger solutions to problems. While it was wise for Jeff to role-model these behaviors when he started as CEO in 2017, there's no reason any leader should hesitate adapting knowing the upside on culture and performance. As you'll read about in Chapter 14, Jeff and his team reversed over a decade of flat growth by creating what they refer to as Connected Culture, which places a premium on speed, trust, relationships, and teamwork.

You'll also learn how AI will play an increasing role in helping CEOs. In Chapters 13 and 14, we'll look to a world where upstream work is digital, and AI comes into the picture to provide CEOs with a powerful and almost unimaginable radar. It will inform on the velocity of new intellectual capital being produced, whether it's enough to signal project success, and provide clues for necessary improvements.

# PART TWO

# FROM STRATEGY TO ACTION: DRIVING GROWTH THROUGH DECISION SPRINT

# Exploration

Have you ever been involved with a game-changing or valuable idea and hit a mental roadblock? Have you ever witnessed a huge opportunity where your company is naturally positioned but not yet mobilized? Or been part of a team with pent-up appetite and strategic ambition? And yet the ambition doesn't seem to translate into momentum for its ideas? There is simply more talk than action.

Mental roadblocks can keep organizations from moving forward on something potentially big. They are common when it comes to a strategic project, market opportunity, "big rock," or innovation. The bigger and earlier stage the idea is, the more likely there are several mental roadblocks to cross. Sometimes they are a series of chicken-and-egg questions. Does the idea have merit? What does good look like? Is one choice better than another? Is the idea even feasible? I've found that roadblocks are really forks in the road where ambiguity and uncertainty are high. Lack of visibility can easily lead to inertia.

Complex problem-solving is not the exclusive domain of innovators. In Chapter 1, I shared the pain of a factory shutdown at Volvo from a "systems glitch." The pressure to restore operations made it hard to dig deeper on the root causes. And while we did use a Toyota-like "5 Whys" method to investigate the underlying issues, we had to create space for it. For executives at Volvo to feel comfortable that the problem would not repeat, we needed to put on the table a true understanding of the incident. Only with that could we make choices that would make the future more stable and reliable. Prior to that, many bandages were applied, and the problem festered. The forks in the road were not confronted. That's when coming to a recommendation or common understanding of the best path forward is elusive, and the organization is indecisive.

What are these forks in the road? What makes them hard? This chapter aims to provide concrete ways to identify and cross any fork in the road.

For starters, it's important to recognize when we're likely to face these forks in the roadblock. They occur when vexing questions pile up and a team has a hard time wading through all the unknowns that show up as ambiguity and uncertainty.

Great teams don't wait for questions to fester and become overwhelming before peering into the realities of what they're dealing with. Instead, they quickly recognize forks in the road and find ways to push through the fog. They apply great energy to learning what needs to be understood and avoid premature opinion.

Many industries amid disruption encounter this phenomenon. When Amazon let it be known they were developing a breakthrough e-book device in the mid-2000s, certain questions dominated meetings around the book industry in New York. Would the Kindle be a flash in the pan, and what type of adoption might occur? Could e-books be as profitable as print? Should publishers develop their own device? Had publishers lost the chance ever to collect data on their customers as Amazon was doing? How would brick-and-mortar stores react? What would authors prefer when it came to the new digital medium versus print books? Few publishing houses moved fast enough on these questions, ceding total dominance of e-books to Amazon. They were likely caught in a cycle of inertia.

Looking elsewhere, companies like Netflix and Uber are faced with constant ambiguity as they refine business models as they balance making money and retaining customers. For example, Netflix has attempted to upsell HD streaming as it identifies new features that would make customers upgrade plans. It takes a soft approach on password sharing by nudging customers to migrate their profiles to new paid plans if they're going through life events (like growing up and moving out of the house, or divorce). The need to balance customer expectations while creating revenue growth applies with these ideas. Uber has been for years attempting various ways of creating customer loyalty so it doesn't have to compete on price alone. Years before introducing a membership program, the company went in the direction of rewards. Those are two different constructs for loyalty. A membership program comes with a cost and some differentiated benefits. Rewards are just that—they are earned with each transaction. Uber is full of very bright people. I wonder how they compared these choices when starting with rewards over membership.

Speaking of choices, they are sometimes not the best place to start. A typical strategic framework involves listing the key choices or options so that teams can populate the pros and cons. On the heels of this, they evaluate trade-offs of these pros and cons, and make a recommendation on the best option to pursue. What's wrong with that? Why doesn't it work to identify some choices and then fill in the blanks on their unknowns before picking one? For starters, it assumes the choices are known to begin with. Consumer loyalty programs are everywhere and have been for decades, so Uber can begin with a predefined choice set. But if you're Tesla in 2008 working on autonomous driving, it's risky to define the options before understanding enough of the new territory. Having worked in the car industry during the hype of self-driving cars, I can name several ways this technology has been described. There's levels of autonomy (1 to 5), city versus highway, supervised versus unsupervised, autonomous versus copiloting. Elon Musk has tinkered with how to explain the conditions under which a Tesla can drive itself. When it comes to something pioneering, which Tesla does in spades, it seems to me that we should avoid predefined choice sets. The process of exploration might spur new and more relevant options than what first springs to mind. If we set the choices from the start, before we've explored the unknown, it will be difficult to reset the options that have been previously anchored. New creative options that were not imagined might be suppressed or retrofitted into an inferior one for the wrong reasons. How do we avoid this? Build understanding of what matters, then develop the choices.

If you see or hit a fork in the road, even if you can't describe the choices, that's where exploration comes in.

Exploration gives you the space to avoid the uncertainty of forks in the road from becoming roadblocks. Instead of being stuck and overwhelmed by unknowns that come along with new growth opportunities or critical problems, teams can be empowered to do something about them.

Usually, a significant fork in the road comes with a collection or bundle of unknowns.

Sometimes surfacing the unknowns is a challenge. If you ask several people for input, your head may spin for the sheer ambiguity of it all.

How can a team surface or identify the issues worth understanding in order to make better choices? How does a team get sufficiently deep on an issue? How wide and deep should a team dig for unknowns? You can see how layered a roadblock can be! The difficulty can be figuring out where to start. Any gaps in exploring the fork in the road can be costly when it surfaces later down the road. (See Figure 4.1.)

**Exploration**

**Unclear problem statement**
Weeks and months go by solving for an imprecise understanding of the problem.

**Limited circle of input**
Thinking happens in silos and the collective intelligence of the company is not tapped.

**Missed issues or unknowns**
Important matters are not surfaced until too far down the line.

**Lack of depth on issues**
Important clarifying questions about a matter are missed until too far down the line.

**Difficult to track and manage**
No workflow to organize, track,and make actionable what's being explored (linked to milestones).

**Weak support for recommendations, misalignment and stalled decisions**

**FIGURE 4.1** Common upstream pitfalls

Embracing exploration is a game changer because it not only helps traverse the current fork in the road but trains us to get ahead of the next ones. It's better to see them coming and resolve them through the muscle memory like the workflows you will learn about.

Sometimes, these choices come up as a surprise and turn into roadblocks. How can we be constructive about managing them? We can have only so much foresight.

Give unknowns space, structure, and actionability through exploration.

Viewing exploration as a purposeful but essential action is key to high-performing organizations. It's how we begin Decision Sprint. By the end of this chapter, you'll see how great decision-making starts with exploration. Tap into exploration to problem-solve virtually anything in your organization.

## EXCELLING AT AMAZON

Did you know that what makes an executive more highly regarded at Amazon is the speed at which this person can study the ambiguity in front of them and discern potential paths forward? This kind of learning is akin to the work detectives do in the field. It's the corporate version of crime scene investigation (CSI).

This process starts with asking the right questions; it requires deep curiosity, a good filter for the things that matter, and the ability to connect insights to conclusions. What sets top leaders apart is the ability to do this fast and effectively on a project or objective the company is facing. This approach spreads throughout a company when team members see it in action as part and parcel of culture. It's how Bezos and company built Amazon. And it's how I learned from other leaders around me there. This leadership approach is not documented or explained in any training. Amazon certainly doesn't train people for it. They assess and hire for the people who profile as being able to succeed in this environment. Then it's up to each person to pick it up quickly.

After leaving Amazon, I continued modeling these behaviors and norms one meeting at a time at places like McDonald's, Volvo, and MGM Resorts. At times it could make me seem a fish out of water. It was an onerous and heavy burden to take on because I was also teaching and directing. Let me elaborate on that.

On the one hand, I was in the meetings and engaged on specific topics. On the other hand, I was constantly mindful of how the conversation and the process of developing ideas, recommendations, opinions and decisions unfolded. That could require people to back up and clarify their line of thinking. I coached people to go deep on aspects of their thinking that had gaps or was not reasoned through all the way. Coaching and directing a meeting to bring out new information, connect new information to conclusions, and then collectively develop the next steps is a different mode of leadership. It's not based on authority. It's based on a calibration model. This type of modeling requires more than flowing through the agenda of the meeting. It's about how we think about the subject matter as a collective brain.

I will provide you with a much easier way to bring these Amazon-like skills to your team and organization. Not only will I demystify them, but also you will learn how to make exploration a superpower of your organization.

## WHERE TO START

The need for exploration starts right after a big idea is introduced and continues forever. That sounds strong. We'll touch on the concept of continuous exploration. But let's start at the beginning.

Say there's a new business model, product, offering, or market that may help the company grow. It could bring in new customers, make the products more relevant to customers, or advance the customer relationships or business approach. Let's take two examples, one small and one large.

Put yourself in the shoes of Volvo, which made a massive commitment in 2016 when it committed to selling only electric cars by 2025. That could seem far away when the promise was made. But it was bold and the first of its kind among its competitors BMW, Daimler, Audi, and VW.

As time went on, the company began to see electrification as connected to sustainability. Many companies speak of sustainability as something separate from their products. These companies talk about the power or energy that runs their offices and physical locations but stop short of the supply chains behind their core products.

But sustainability is as much a characteristic of a consumer product as other attributes, whether the design of a car or the taste of a beverage. Sidenote: in my view, all products must be sustainable for customers and the planet to thrive. So the senior team jumped at the potential behind "vegan leather" as sustainability became a priority in the company and the world. Note I'm purposefully using an example I was not involved with as it demonstrates the horizontal reach of effective exploration.

There are many considerations to this opportunity. Let's take a deeper look at the exploration of this concept around "vegan leather":

1. How will customers respond? Vegan is probably a positive notion for a certain age group and demographic. While the average age of a Volvo customer had dropped by about 10 years due to its updated car designs and modern tech, it was still a premium carmaker that sold primarily to affluent people on the older end of the age spectrum.
2. How will vegan leather be viewed from a quality and sense of premium appeal? Volvos are priced like other luxury European cars such as BMW and Mercedes. Will vegan leather add or subtract from Volvo's appeal?
3. What are the unknowns around supply and supply chain? Can Volvo procure enough upholstery material and at what price? Will the incremental price to the vehicle be something the customer is willing to pay? Despite the marketing potential of this idea, the juice has to be worth the squeeze. The bean counters will ensure that.
4. How environmentally sustainable is vegan leather anyway? By what measures? Can the supply be traced for authenticity? Does blockchain play a role in creating trust?
5. What of the cars that have traditional leather from cows, will they be devalued somehow? Will the traditional car buyer be pushed away?

I'm using this example from Volvo to demonstrate how meaningful new ideas will always come with real ambiguity and complexity at the start. It's no wonder innovators can get stuck, and there's no disrespect intended toward other roles in companies. These questions are all valid to tackle.

In the next section, you will see how exploration gives us a way forward and the ability to activate the unknowns.

Later, you'll learn how to build a continuous stream of explorations so that a project stays one step ahead. Not just for a few weeks. But for the months, quarters, and years when it will be active. Continuous exploration is the engine behind initiatives that dominate markets and turn into massive growth engines.

As the post-Covid era begins to unfold, leaders at any organization require this skill. It is teachable as any performance improvement process that shaped the history of business, whether Total Quality Management, Six Sigma, OKRs, or lean management.

# KEY STEPS OF BUILDING EXPLORATIONS

There are three steps to building an exploration: crafting a problem statement, sourcing for breadth, and sourcing for depth. (See Figure 4.2.)

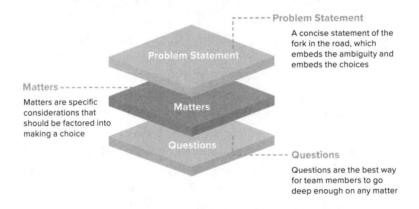

**FIGURE 4.2**  Building an exploration

## *One: Crafting the Problem Statement*

The fork in the road faced by Volvo is really one about serving the past or the future of the car industry. The key problem statement could be written: "Is vegan leather consistent with where our brand is headed?" A problem statement like this incorporates several strategic questions. Does vegan leather fit the big-picture preferences of the customer? Is the idea a fit for the target buyer of the future? Does our brand prioritize more than just the bottom line when making product decisions?

There are other ways to write this problem statement, depending on how mature the opportunity may be. If the company is already convinced the idea is aligned with its North Star, it may want to delve deeper. For example, "Is vegan leather something that will help us win customers and do it profitably?" Or perhaps, "Is vegan leather a meaningful opportunity and feasible to deliver?"

A good problem statement captures the ambiguity of the fork in the road and inspires the choices. Interestingly, we may not know the most relevant choices from the get-go. That's why I don't recommend problem statements where choices are presumed. If we fix the choice set up front, we may be less able to see more creative alternatives. Armed with that, a team can be grounded in what to solve for.

A project may be facing a few forks in the road at the same time. As it relates to supply chain, the core strategic question for Volvo was, can we pull it off? That's a huge unknown because you want to have enough supply and ensure its integrity. A problem statement along the lines of "determine the supply chain feasibility of this idea" might need investigation.

This means several explorations may run in parallel. We want to leverage the time of team members. We can't have everyone working on everything. We need to group people around relevant challenges.

With two distinct explorations, each with their own problem statements, we can determine what kind of knowledge or perspective to include within it. Later on, you will see how properly crafting the problem statement for an exploration will help in selecting the right team members. Indeed, good problem statement definition helps kick off sourcing the right input. It helps people understand what problem we are solving for.

Next we turn to the idea of inputs. *Input* is not a loose, vague, or general concept. The kind of input we're seeking ties directly to the problem statement. And input as we are building an exploration is not the first thing that comes to someone's mind or a stream of consciousness from a team member. Quite the contrary, we want to capture input in two types so that it's easier to lay out all of the input we collect in some structure.

## Two: Sourcing for Breadth

Sourcing input for exploration has two components: breadth and depth. Breadth is the range of (subject) matters that weigh on the choice. Matters are specific considerations that should be factored into making a choice. In other words, we're in a stronger position to choose by raising a matter. Or we're in a weaker position by choosing to stay quiet about a matter.

Let's take some examples from the Volvo case of vegan leather. We mentioned a potential exploration around "supply chain feasibility" with a problem statement like: "Determine the supply chain feasibility of this idea." It's multifaceted and complex to understand. Some of the matters a team might suggest to include in this exploration:

- **Supplier capacity** (getting enough volume given the number of cars manufactured for inventory)
- **Standards** (to define what is vegan material)
- **Incremental cost**
- **Transparency** (to ensure the authenticity of the vegan label)

If determining the supply chain feasibility revolved around one matter, it could be easy to navigate. But there are always several to understand and weigh. How do we come up with the list of the things that matter? We begin by engaging the minds of the working team— the people grouped around the problem-solving effort. Side note: if the working team has not been properly formed, there are some principles for that you will want to read in Chapter 7. I use the term *minds* because a good list will take a range of perspectives. We want to activate each team member's perspective so we don't miss important considerations at the start.

Start by independently collecting suggestions on matters to include. Allow team members to suggest the matters that should be included in the exploration. Give the team members a few days to identify the matters they think are relevant. Set a sourcing period, typically a few days, wherein each team member posts his or her suggestions independently. Ask team members to suggest matters they think are essential factors or considerations in one- to three-word titles. The suggested matters are the input we are seeking at this stage.

Sometimes the human mind will think of matters in the form of questions. In the previous example, if I asked you to name an important (subject) matter, your mind might start with a question like "Can we obtain enough volume of vegan materials from suppliers, given we sell so many cars?" The matter that your question raises is supplier volume or supplier capacity. If this question expands the breadth of what we need to understand, it's really serving to expand (subject) matters. If it were a question that seeks to clarify an existing matter, it's about adding depth and would stay a question (in the taxonomy of Decision Sprint).

Everyone gets to see each other's input on matters—but not until the sourcing period is complete. That way, there's no bias, group think, or second-guessing placed on the input. Even if team members suggest similar or duplicative issues, those can be weeded out easily.

Once the sourcing period is complete, a wonderful list of matters is available to jump-start a team into exploration. Armed with such a list, a team hase fewer blind spots and more clarity on where it should be diving deep. Diving deep is what comes next. The list of matters needs to be scrubbed for duplication and clarity. Is the phrasing of each matter clear and precise, for example?

I encourage teams to look at sourcing matters as a milestone or accomplishment. It's like getting to first base. Share the list with stakeholders, explain the process to get there, and get validation that it's the right canvas for deep diving. I'm willing to bet that 9 in 10 times executives will thank you for bringing effective structure to a major problem statement, and their confidence in the project will grow just by seeing the list. Trust me, executives much prefer hearing about the unknowns at the start versus down the road. You'll learn about the practice of sharing input you've sourced as a discrete workflow in the coming chapters. Decision Sprint will make sure this isn't overlooked.

### Three: Sourcing for Depth

A good list of matters is an awesome starting point for deep diving. We'll need to dig deep enough on each matter, and that's where we turn attention to next. Questions are the best way to spur this.

Too often, teams get caught in meetings with a shallow understanding of something important. This is avoidable if the crucial matters are surfaced early enough, allowing the team enough time to investigate them adequately. The best way for team members to go deep enough on any matter is to develop a list of clarifying questions. *Breadth is about a list of matters. Depth is about a list of clarifying questions for each matter.*

So what is a clarifying question? And how do we write them?

Think of a clarifying question as an attempt to bring out some facts or texture. You're in detective mode. Ask questions that would bring out clues.

Let's take the issue of supplier capacity (getting enough volume given the number of cars being sold) from the Volvo case.

Here are some clarifying questions that might help us dive deeply into this matter:

- How many cars do we estimate will require vegan materials in the next five years?
- When is the desired capacity available, and what is the ramping?
- What is the confidence level in the supplier base?
- What are the raw materials challenges expected in the next few years that could challenge the procurement of what we need, if any?
- What kind of validation or certification of supply will we require?

Like many of you, I'm not a specialist in car interiors or design, but you can see how these questions are obvious to an average businessperson. Good clarifying questions are neutral and open-ended. You write them as when, where, why, or how.

A good clarifying question helps push thinking. Questions don't confirm an existing opinion or a preconceived notion. They accelerate the team's understanding. What kind of question would help us cut through? This is the sole purpose of clarifying questions. And with a good list of them, any matter can be rapidly understood.

How do you improve the chances of getting a good list of questions? And how does a team know if we have a good list of questions? Put people in the mindset of good questioning by reminding them of the problem statement. For our Volvo case, we're exploring supply chain feasibility for good-quality vegan leather.

Let's take an example. The team suggested "standards" (for what qualifies as vegan) as a key matter. Look at this matter through the lens of the problem statement. It might inspire several questions. How would standards be measured? How can they be validated? Who will measure them? Will that generate extra expense for the company? These are all good clarifying questions, with respect to the matter "Standards." Rinse and repeat this process for each matter.

Place people in the mindset of asking questions about each matter that would help inform the problem statement. Answers should be very far away from the mind. Stay purely in the flow of generating clarifying questions.

### Calibrating the Exploration

Now, you're ready for the next steps in building an exploration.

You've given the team a few days. A central point person has collected the questions independently and is ready to share the collective list with the group. How do we know if a list of matters and underlying questions are good enough?

There are several ways to validate. First, at the team level, we can take a pulse. Ask the team in an independent survey to rate the question list for whether the team has captured enough of the right matters and the right clarifying questions for each matter. How are we doing on breadth and depth? Is it 4 out of 10? 8 out of 10? The former is too shallow. The latter is good enough. The 80/20 rule works here.

If our question list is too shallow, consider asking the team what kind of expertise would fill the gap. And then identify people with that expertise within the organization to invite as guests into the exploration."

On top of this, we can validate with stakeholders. Think about the sponsors or more senior stakeholders of the project. They're not in the day-to-day work. And that's a plus. Once questions are sourced, they can be shared. Stakeholders can inform if we're missing something. Or perhaps the list looks good. This step alone has many positive side effects. Stakeholders see the work in progress. They gain confidence and get to make a scalable contribution.

I recommend making this step a specific interaction with project stakeholders or sponsors. Conduct a calibration session to summarize where the team is at with sourcing inputs for both breadth and depth. In this session, we share the exploration's purpose, the considerations sourced, and the clarifying questions for each concern.

Imagine the power of such a meeting. You have canvassed strategic choices, which are full of unknowns, into building blocks. The building blocks are the issues and their underlying questions.

That alone is a tremendous confidence booster. It's a meeting with no answers. No recommendations. Just a canvas of the work to be done. It's a melding of the minds that brings focus. Building the right exploration helps us achieve so much. It's prealignment.

Is this how things work in your organization today? It can be.

## RUNNING EXPLORATIONS

Now for the good stuff. Getting to answers. Armed with the proper considerations and clarifying questions, it's time to get moving on answers. A good list of questions is helpful because it focuses the development of answers. Better questions lead to better answers.

Who should be involved in the development of answers? When it comes to sourcing matters and questions, we can involve the entire core working team (and sometimes delegates who are closer to the action). Getting 5 or even 10 contributors to help build the exploration is helpful. When it comes to providing an answer, that doesn't work.

Good answers stem from combining a lead and a small number of reviewers. Let's walk through each role and how to select the appropriate people. Someone needs to take ownership and put a stake in the ground. That person is probably the "logical owner" to the answer for a question. Let's say our exploration relates to a new feature for a car. Is the question related to consumer demand, consumer marketing, product development, or sales and distribution? Who is responsible to think about that all day long? At the same time, this perspective needs to be shaped and influenced by other team members and/or stakeholders—otherwise, it can be off the mark. We need enough diversity in thought to be integrated within the answer. So we need people who are coming from slightly different worlds than the lead. They play the role of reviewers.

Maybe the lead is in core operations and knows the current marketplace—which is valuable—but we also need someone who lives out in the future and has strong vision. Or it could be the reverse. We want reviewers who're able to raise considerations that stretch the lead. Stretch the answers. When you stretch a rubber band, things may return to the original shape, but you know it didn't break. It's like that with reviewing answers. The shape may not change, but we validate it's made from robust materials. Consider reviewers who are not day-to-day in the matter but who will stretch the thinking. Let me emphasize this again. Don't be shy to add stretch thinkers.

Once a question has a lead and a few reviewers, we can assign those responsibilities. And now we move on to crafting a good answer.

To help illustrate some best practices for answering questions, let's take two from the Volvo exploration. How many cars do we estimate will require vegan materials in the next five years?

I'm going to lay out a hypothetical answer. Again, I am not a car interior designer or procurement specialist, so these answers illustrate how general business acumen is good enough to navigate most unknowns—as long as there's a method.

**Question:** How many cars do we estimate will require vegan materials in the next five years?

**Answer:** We plan to provide vegan as an option for our all-electric lineup of cars. Therefore, this option applies to a fraction of our total production, although that will be the majority by the end of the decade. We expect this to be a standard feature on higher-spec cars or luxury upgrades on other models. If we assume the upgrade behavior is like choosing to upgrade from a standard sound system to an opera quality sound system, that will represent a 25 percent conversion rate.

Considering all of this (see attached model), we expect 150,000 to 300,000 cars will need this material between the early 2020s and the end of the decade. Depending on consumer preferences, a more aggressive plan to cover our product range could be required. Three additional scenarios are provided in the attached model.

I hope this answer demonstrates a few elements.

First start with what is known—any facts, data, or current understanding. Add in reasonable assumptions; explain why they are reasonable and what these assumptions impact. Synthesize a position through a reasoning process. In the preceding example, the answer was straight math from the current plans and expectations, while recognizing that assumptions could change.

In other cases, you will need to spell out your reasoning. Consider the next question in the deep dive for "supplier capacity."

**Question:** When is the desired capacity available and what is the ramping?

**Answer:** This depends. First, it depends on what parts of the interior go vegan (cushions, armrests, headliner, window trims, center console). Second, it depends on our choice of animal-free materials. There are at least five major bio-based and recycled material categories to compare. Plant-based options like apple skin and pineapple are widely available but less durable than recycled plastics, which are more expensive yet more durable. If we assume much of the interior cabin will be animal-free and opt for plant-based, there are no major concerns at this time on capacity. If we opt for recycled materials, there could be a crunch toward the end of the decade as our volume of electric cars grow.

An answer for this question requires a table with some scenarios where the material options are compared and benchmarked. While it's a data-intensive answer, you can see how the response succinctly paints the picture and reasons through the main scenarios. I was a math major in college but readily admit that a few words can summarize a takeaway better than a table of data.

## EXPLORATION @ AMAZON

As someone who's managed almost 10,000 people over 25 years, I can tell you that the best we can expect when dealing with unknowns is collecting the facts and reasoning through the rest of it. This should be a relief to hear. No manager expects a crystal ball.

What makes for a good review of answers? We've talked about stretching the perspective. In running projects at Amazon or anywhere else, I was always eager to share my well-crafted answers with people who could provide stretch to them. Once I took the answer as far as I could, I sought out people who could offer an exciting nugget for me to ponder. I loved it when these nuggets would emerge. We could ponder them and modify our answers. Our answers were strengthened. Looking across the companies I've worked within, Amazon, has a particular habit for this.

Once you've taken stretch perspectives and modified an answer, the reviews have served their purpose.

Let's tap a case from Amazon to bring the superpower of exploration to life.

It's 2011, I am the general manager of Kindle Direct Publishing. If you haven't heard of KDP, it's the self-publishing business of Amazon. And it's huge. Several billion dollars of books are sold each year through this platform, and these books account for over 25 percent of the bestsellers on the Kindle. It's all digital, so the margins are great. And it's reshaped the entire publishing industry. We've become so accustomed to this level of disruption by Amazon. I'm going to share an inside look at how that disruption works. And exploration is key.

I'm leading this business in the early days, and it's turning out to be a rocket ship. There's a few hundred million in revenue, and we are growing 300 percent plus each year. Have you experienced growth at that scale? It's what happens when digital businesses start to take hold.

We want to solidify our position for the long term.

Let's start with strategy. Amazon has tremendous distribution, probably 80 percent of the e-book market. To solidify this, we set our sights on differentiated content. In other words, a world where you could get only certain books on Amazon. Yes, it's Amazon. So they go for the jugular when it comes to competition. In business parlance, it's referred to as a flywheel. So, for example, Prime members get free movies, books, and music. It's how one hand feeds the other. Amazon has many hands that feed each other.

One way to get there: introduce a new program for authors where they could benefit from selling books exclusively on Amazon.

I'm in charge of the new program. We call it "KDP Select." Interesting cultural sidebar: We consider and debated 25 different names. I'm pretty good at product naming, and the top executives agreed to my recommendation.

Here's how we described the program to the world in our press release (which we wrote at the start of the ideation stage—many months before green-lighting the program—to establish our North Star):

> ❝Amazon.com today announced a new membership program for independent authors who use Kindle Direct Publishing. The program, KDP Select, features a suite of benefits that help authors reach new customers, earn higher royalties, and produce better books. These program benefits are available at no cost to any author who elects to work on an exclusive basis with KDP for a one-year period.
>
> Responding to widespread independent author needs, the new program will offer more favorable royalty options, advanced pricing tools, merchandising opportunities, and value-added services that help authors grow their audience and sales. The royalties paid to program members will be up to 80%, representing the highest tier available to KDP authors. ❞

Pretty compelling for authors. We laid out the gravy train. Especially the high royalty rate. It's not common for authors to keep 80 percent of the royalties.

A strategic initiative like this comes with so many unknowns at the start. The PR sounded great. And like I said, we write it months, even quarters, before our ability to go to market. We spend the rest of the time working through the unknowns. As this program developed, we had some strategic choices around how exclusivity works.

We don't call it exploration, but that's what our work boils down to. We spend weeks on the breadth and depth of things. Our team explores matters and questions like these:

### ENFORCEMENT

Will we enforce the policy actively or passively?

Will we enforce the policy for all books or books that sell above a certain threshold?

What will be our response for a violation?

### MONITORING

How accurately can we monitor a book's presence across internet distribution?

Can our monitoring differentiate between a sample and the entire book?

Can we easily flag based on when a book was enrolled in the program and when it was found on other websites?

How costly is it to monitor for 10,000 books versus 100,000 books versus 1,000,000 books?

### COVERAGE

What distribution on the internet will be prohibited?

Are free copies the author gives away covered by the exclusivity?

Are book samples or previews or excerpts covered by the exclusivity?

As you can see our breadth is covered by these three matters (and others). Our depth is covered by the questions underlying each matter.

The exploration helps us find the smartest approach. We want authors to honor the exclusivity but don't want to chase down large numbers of authors, especially when the juice is not worth the squeeze. It would not reflect well on Amazon, as a behemoth. On top of that, monitoring and enforcement can be costly.

In the next chapter on alignment, you will see how exploration makes it easier to draw such conclusions.

After that chapter, you will read about decision-making, I'll come back to this example to demonstrate how exploration and alignment helped Amazon decide on actions. The following actions enabled our team to move quickly and decisively:

- We will use the same tech we use for price comparisons to check whether books that should be exclusive are listed on major websites. We will do this for most books but can't guarantee we will cover all titles. There's not much incremental cost for Amazon.
- We will talk externally about our approach as randomly checking for violations so that authors would certainly think twice before consciously violating. We say monitoring is random, but we are trying to monitor as much as possible. It's better to be conservative about what we can pull off.
- We will talk externally about the consequences of violation. The violating book would be removed from the program (book would not receive the benefits like the higher royalty). It's a fairly direct consequence. In practice, we will send more than one notice and give authors a chance to fix the problem before taking any strong steps.

By taking these decisions, we strike a balance of incentivizing compliance and believe most would make a strong effort toward that given our stance. We carry a big stick in our terms, but in practice are not interested in raking authors over the coals, except for very egregious cases. We try to encourage the right behaviors. We want the authors to be so successful they don't have to think about testing the boundaries.

If you're an author, our decisions are communicated to you on the Amazon website in the form of FAQs. This is one FAQ for authors:

"How do you monitor that my title is exclusive?"

We trust that you have offered your title as exclusive to Kindle. Note that we randomly check a title's exclusivity. Any title that violates our agreement will be terminated and barred from future participation in our exclusivity program. However, your title will be offered on Kindle under our normal terms and conditions.

How did the launch go? It exceeded our wildest expectations. We set a goal for the number of authors who would join the program within the first six months of launch. On the launch evening, I was in the office with our team to make sure there were no technical glitches. We turned the program on around midnight. By the time I left at 3 a.m. on launch night, we had blown past our expectation for the rest of the year.

Our structured approach to exploration allowed us to move with clarity for ourselves and our customers (in this case, authors). Ten years after launching it, the program remains a wild success and functions pretty much on autopilot. It works so well that Amazon gives away $45 million each month (as of late 2022) in bonuses for authors to participate in this program (that's over $500 million annually). And the team has moved on to the next disruption.

## FORMING TEAMS

One of the most common stumbling blocks to even starting exploration is organizational silos. Silos have been around a long time. But there's no longer an excuse for them. Ideally, sponsors of initiatives help bring the right set of competencies or capabilities into the picture during a kickoff. If this doesn't happen, teams should take the self-organizing path.

A properly constructed team for growth is usually cross-functional. Growth strategies and opportunities are not the kind one functional area of a company can tackle. For example, a new business model may take perspective from groups like e-commerce, finance, and various business or business divisions. A new customer offering may require contribution from product management, marketing, engineering, and other groups.

Later, we'll talk about the forums that make sense for a working team to establish for their collaboration. What are the key meetings, their purpose, and cadence? How should the team interact?

A cross-functional working team should include more than the usual suspects. We need to tap the intellectual capital of the company. When forming a team around exploration, ask which perspectives would make us truly strategic about the subject. Integrate the people with these perspectives. Do so as equal team members. Don't allow for existing relationships and comfortable alliances to limit proper team formation and dynamics.

Let me be clear: a high-performance team does not behave like a high school social circle. No camps of insiders and outsiders. Subgroups exist to tackle specific problems. Flatness matters in problem-solving because it generates high-quality inputs. Any silo by its nature limits inputs and perspective. It can drive alignment ahead of exploration.

As you've learned, exploration depends on the quality of inputs. It's a pitfall to align before enough of the right inputs have been sourced.

That's why I recommend kickoff practices that remind teams of Decision Sprint and its components. I will provide details on how to handle such a kickoff in the chapter on workflows.

## WELCOMING GUESTS

Let's say a working team for exploration is making progress. Each member feels high ownership and accountability. But there's still a sense of some missing knowledge.

Will the core team have all the right inputs to build and run explorations? The answer is of course, no. Even a well-formulated team misses things and can be too close to matters.

That's why it's a good idea to expand sourcing efforts at specific points in exploration. In other words, open it up to guests. Guests are other colleagues in the organization who might bring a fresh pair of eyes. They're not randomly selected. Let's go back to the example of vegan leather at Volvo.

The working team consists of people who build the cars and design the seats as well as the marketing and commercial voices who set the sales strategy. But who sells the cars? It's the dealership. And one degree away from those people are the sales managers who manage regions of dealerships. They may not be part of a working team. But when it comes to sourcing issues or questions about commercial matters, they may bring some new considerations to the table.

One might argue that it's the job of the commercial and marketing team in corporate to understand these perspectives. Corporate should always be talking with the field. But it doesn't always happen. And projects can move fast to alignment before this feedback loop is activated.

We can shorten the cycle and avoid missed inputs by bringing in guests to source matters and questions, as well as reviewing answers, in a targeted fashion. By targeted I mean crafting a particular request. Like we are sourcing issues for an exploration about $X$. What should we consider? Or we are sourcing questions to help us understand issue $Y$. What should we consider?

There's no need to bring guests into all the other facets of the project. They will likely feel valued and recognized for the ability to contribute at formative stages. And if their issues, questions, and answers are helpful, they will likely see more of these requests. The project benefits because we shorten the feedback cycle at the expiration stage, we avoid blind spots, and we strengthen it going forward.

Don't hesitate to bring in wider expertise once it's clear what perspective could be missing.

## CONTINUOUS EXPLORATION IS FUTURE PROOFING

Your organization probably engages in planning over various horizons. Companies are very familiar with planning for the coming quarter, a year ahead, and even a few years out.

When in the middle of a project or initiative, it's common to get so buried that planning exploration takes a back seat. A team might be consumed by problems that need to be answered here and now.

Team leaders who want to shift from reactive mode can help the cause by creating space to capture and curate upcoming explorations. Capturing them is relatively easy to execute. It centers on a backlog that any team member can add to. A backlog of explorations is a list of bridges that need to be crossed. Team members might see them coming at random moments, so creating a workspace to collect them is natural.

A better practice is to nudge the team to add to this backlog. Send a reminder each month, for example. Then it will become habit forming.

The way to think about this backlog is what's on deck. We're currently focused on $X$, but very soon we will have to decide on $Y$ and $Z$, which depend on the exploration of $A$ and $B$. What are $A$ and $B$? What is on deck to put the team in a position of momentum and not coming from behind? Add it to the backlog.

A backlog needs curation. This is why a brief monthly meeting with a team leader to scrub it makes sense. Scrubbing is about moving the order of the list around and being more precise in naming the explorations. After curating the list, share it with the wider team so people become aware about what's on the horizon.

Let's face it. To give flight to an ambitious new strategic initiative, we must face a constant flow of challenging problem statements. I offer exploration as a way to raise our eyes to these problem statements so we can innovate into the unknown. It doesn't take a lot of time and it's not rocket science. It just takes a method.

## NEVER TOO EARLY TO START

Let's shift to the entrepreneur's perspective. David Long is the CEO and cofounder of OrangeTheory Fitness, which has grown from zero to $1 billion in revenue and to over 1,500 studios. His company's journey illustrates why it's never too early for startups to be mindful of their innovation and problem-solving systems.

## Excerpts from an Interview with David Long, CEO and Cofounder, OrangeTheory Fitness

### Growing from the Garage into a Major Consumer Brand

**Atif:** Can you elaborate on the core innovations that helped the company get going?

**David:** My cofounder Ellen had come up with the concept of a group environment with a motivational coach that could help move people on their journey at their own pace. It was very organic, raw, and special.

That was really the starting point. I think there were a couple of key innovations coming out of that. First, we quickly realized we need to systemize the actual workout programming in a very scientific way and deliver it to the coaches (which now number about 8,000). I created a program to capture how a coach would be able to engage with a group and still make the individual feel part of the process, integrating technology and the science behind it. That we started right at location one.

Second, we were technology lite as far as a way for people to understand how hard they were working physically as part of the class. Remember the Polar or Garmin? People could do it, but it was triathletes and runners that were training on their own. We developed a system to, for the first time, monitor heart rates as part of class. The coach can see it. We can start teaching customers about it. And it was really the cornerstone of the program. When people think they are killing themselves for an hour, nobody wants to sign up for that. But if they have to push hard for, say, 20 percent, that's a lot more achievable and digestible. That set off dominoes for us because that was such a huge unlock. Other people tried to do it, but we just made sure that this was going to be the core. We were able to grow on that.

**Atif:** What is the core insight that has created product-market fit?

**David:** I think the core premise, and what science proves is that people don't stick with a fitness program without accountability, like showing up to something. It's difficult to have good long-term adherence. Even though, if you look at the at-home solutions, it's obviously gotten a lot better with the interface, yet that hasn't moved the needle on adherence to exercise. People need some sort of studio, a place to go, and all the psychology behind people going in a group to work out. Even if you don't know another person in the class, there's a lot of horsepower behind that.

**Atif:** How did things evolve from the early days, when everybody's involved in innovation?

**David:** In the early days of only 20 to 30 people, we could talk about things on a regular basis about what people are seeing when they're out launching a new studio. This included franchisees with their voices that were really connected, too. Together we created this culture of a lot of communication, which can become really cumbersome and overwhelming later on. Organically, we managed that.

For about three years it was just a constant cycle. And then we hit a much bigger growth path. That's when we started a more typical organizational structure. I still think we did a pretty good job keeping that innovation spirit going and circulating a lot of information. We were very connected with the franchise owners and out in the field so much.

**Atif:** What could have gone wrong as the company scaled?

**David:** Things could have gone wrong if we went off the rails on core product. There was pressure to expand focus—let's do kids' programs, let's launch yoga, let's launch all these different things. And I think that's a natural tendency when there's white space in the schedule. Let's do more.

We stuck to one workout type a day, just over and over again. We stepped to the core fitness product, knowing it was the best thing to deliver to customers in that hour. So how do we tweak it and make it better? We didn't try to add a bunch of other products at that time. It was really improving everything around it to make that even better.

**Atif:** Shifting to innovation when you're already at scale, obviously you're trying to do that by setting up the right structure while providing autonomy to people to figure things out. How does that work?

**David:** At some point, some functions became more defined. Our key functions—fitness, technology, product development teams—were still very much always innovating.

In the last couple of years, we launched an innovation team that focused on what's two, three years down the road. They end up pulling in people from a lot of those functions.

Our connected fitness road map is one example. Our fitness, innovation, analytics, and digital technology teams formed a working group. That group went off and spent probably 25 to 30 hours over a course of six weeks to deep dive and produce a preview to share with me. I don't think I changed a thing. It was pretty exciting to see that body of work.

The goal should be having a group of people that are a lot smarter than you. I feel like I've achieved that piece, which is pretty exciting.

Talking about an idea is great, but talking about how to get it on a road map and deliver it with resources and measure an ROI against it—that type of discipline. Evaluating the layers below—how does it impact the functions—and being able to put that on two pieces of paper was pretty amazing. Other groups within the company are taking a similar approach. That's super exciting because I can just continue to riff and talk about ideas and be part of the process.

In the early days, we missed out on half the things and half the things worked. Today, the stakes are higher. We need to make sure that if something needs to go in production to 1,500 studios or more down the road, we have got to be way more disciplined.

# Alignment

**D**o you have a robust (and I hope inspiring) sense of why exploration matters, and how to go about it? The purpose of high-quality exploration is to make it easier to draw conclusions. Conclusions are clear positions we can take on strategic choices. Action comes on heels of this flow.

It's not surprising for an initiative to get stuck when people arrive at different conclusions. As if that were not enough, it can be challenging to understand how people arrive at their opinions, and to do it efficiently. Stakeholders, sponsors, and working team members may reach conclusions based on partial information and different assumptions. Have you ever seen this come to life in a meeting? Time can be lost backing up to understand the reasoning and then redirecting them It's a very complicated maneuver.

Your company's most important initiatives cannot afford such misunderstandings and schisms; they are kryptonite for taking action. Things get slowed down. There are fits and starts. Collaboration struggles; trust may even erode. Yet the pitfalls are too common. (See Figure 5.1.)

Explorations drive tremendous value as they are being designed and built way upstream. The passing of time tends to work against shared understanding. Sorting through unknowns and building understanding in the process is a big deal for that reason. It puts everyone on the path of convergence.

**Alignment before exploration**
Wrong sequence of alignment before enough issues are understood leads to stalled progress down the line ("faux alignment").

**Weak links uncovered**
Connection between recommendations and conclusions to underlying issues can be weak links.

**Limited transparency**
Lack of visibility to the work leading up to alignment and work in progress.

**Overhead for preparation**
Pre-reads and pre-meetings can require bespoke preparation of content and continuous effort.

**Alignment meeting overload**
Alignment is overly dependent on check-in meetings, email summaries, messaging overload.

Alignment can become a burden and bureaucratic.

**FIGURE 5.1**  Common pitfalls of alignment

Teams achieve alignment when they work from the same context (exploration) to draw common conclusions. It's about like seeing the breadcrumbs. It's an unforced mind-meld.

I talked earlier about the episode where I banned alignment at McDonald's. That wasn't the right call. Instead, it's better to give alignment the correct meaning. Alignment based on exploration is useful and constructive. Alignment before exploration is a serious pitfall.

Alignment is not just a state of affairs, like a traffic light that is green, yellow, or red. It is a dedicated space to (1) test how much shared understanding there is about the strategic choices; and (2) capture a range of complementary conclusions about the path forward. That's why I will elaborate on several workflows that comprise the work of alignment in Chapter 7. After completing exploration, several conclusions can likely be drawn. Conclusions are much more than "greenlight or not" or "choose option *A* over option *B*." You'll see how conclusions typically have layers.

I'll explain ways to make alignment data-driven, identify where it exists or is lacking, and show how to resolve alignment gaps. When it comes to shared understanding, rather than just trying to read the room, seek out ways to make it data-driven. Many of us with corporate backgrounds can relate to back door alignment, which can work against building a culture of trust. Data-driven approaches allow a team to zero in on where people see the same direction or not. Making this specifics of alignment or lack of it more visible will speed up the resolution. Provided it's known where alignment is lacking, we can do something about it. We can investigate the objections and bring others on board or modify. When it's too broad and can't be articulated, the chances of a resolution fall.

In the end, effective alignment always feels the same in the organization. It gels a team. It gels teams and their sponsors. It gels an organization. It doesn't matter which function, department, or level of the organization team members belong to. True alignment cuts through boundaries and silos. They simply melt away. It's the ultimate feeling of co-creation.

## HOW TO RUN AN ALIGNMENT PROCESS

Once you've completed an exploration, it's time to take some positions. Start with the working team, the people closest to the day-to-day of the initiative. I will elaborate on how to involve others, including stakeholders and the highest-level sponsors or executives. The process is like scaffolding. We start with the core and build out from there.

There are four steps to the process. (See Figure 5.2.)

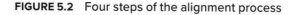

**FIGURE 5.2** Four steps of the alignment process

## Step One: Collect Conclusions

Set a period of time to collect independent conclusions from the core team. Assign team members to reflect on the exploration and submit their responses.

The prompt can be as simple as, "What conclusions would you draw from the exploration?" When doing this, encourage participants to review specific exploration content like a set of FAQs. I personally love FAQs as they are succinct and easy to produce. Ask members to suggest several conclusions. Why? Because strategic direction usually contains layers. For example, when it comes to vegan leather for Volvo, one conclusion may be it's feasible to source enough supply. Another may be that Volvo could offset the incremental cost by cutting back some other aspects of the interior that consumers no longer value. These would be two very positive realizations for the company, and advance the momentum of the idea. We would want to make sure to action tasks related to both conclusions.

Independent input is key, so collect conclusions individually. In Chapter 7, I will elaborate on the workflow that helps collect input on conclusions independently. A few days should be enough time for reflection. The lightbulb can pop on in our minds during a late-night cereal binge or in the shower just as much as in a work setting.

Who receives them the call to provide this kind of input? Teams sometimes have the luxury of a program manager to herd the cats. This is the ideal person to administer the process. Later on, in Chapter 12, you will see how digital tools can take the headache out of herding cats and provide automation. The workflows will be automatically moved along, and everyone will know their action items.

Once suggested conclusions are collected, the team leader will likely need some scrubbing to merge duplicates or close cousins. At this point, a lot of the work within alignment has been asynchronous. You're familiar with asynchronous work. We do it all day long with Slack, teams, texting and apps. We collaborate on calendars, documents and so much more but on our time.

There is no need to gather the team in a meeting to collect conclusions. This is a time saver.

## *Step Two: Vote on Conclusions*

There's a role for meetings, but one more activity can be done asynchronously before holding them. It's voting on the conclusions.

Why vote on conclusions? Well, the results can shed light on the level of alignment. Voting cuts through the fog of perception and the role of various personalities. It promotes a data-driven approach for more focused conversations. How does voting work? It's most valuable when presenting team members with a list and asking them for two inputs:

1. Stack ranking conclusions. Say there are 4–5 conclusions collected from the team. Rank them compared to each other, starting with the most important.
2. Level of agreement. How strongly do you agree or disagree with each conclusion?

When we stack rank, we are looking for which conclusion is most important to align, whether we agree with it or not. Importance is another way to talk about materiality. We want to be extra sure about the more material items. Collecting input on the level of agreement tells us whether support is present, how widespread it is, or how divergent it may be.

In other words, the votes give the team a heatmap of alignment. The heatmap tells you where alignment is good, in which case no discussion is required. It's where there is strong divergence in alignment where dialogue needs to happen. The heatmap of voting results helps us put the finger on those facets of the project.

Let's take some examples:

1. One conclusion makes it to the top of the stack rank. It's the most important one because nearly everyone ranks it as the most material item on the table. More than that, everyone agrees with it. The data is a meaningful endorsement of the conclusion. The opposite could also save us much time. The feedback about a conclusion is widespread disagreement. In a meeting we can quickly validate this and move on.

2. One conclusion has some members who strongly support and others who strongly disagree. This is gold in terms of focusing the dialogue. It's clear there is a lack of alignment; you can use meetings to figure out why. Compare that to most workplaces where often we conduct meetings assuming everyone is aligned because the direction is clear in our minds. We discover the lack of alignment during the meeting, and it's hard to resolve. Even worse, silence during meetings could lead to having to deal with a hidden misalignment.

3. Looking across conclusions, we see high levels of support on essential items, but some lower-ranked items are not as clear. We don't need to slow down projects to deal with these because when the big picture is aligned, the less material conclusions can be routed into deep dives for resolution. Voting takes out the personality factor and gives us actionable data.

Armed with this asynchronous work, a team can meet to review the voting results and heatmap. It's an excellent source of validation to see people across a team reaching common conclusions. That builds confidence. When there is divergence, this meeting can be used to identify why. The discussion should focus on what takes place in today's workplace. For example, team members may not agree with the assumptions in one of the answers. We can pinpoint the issue and the team can develop an action path to revisit or rework it.

## The Role of Testing

Questions being addressed in an exploration may be answered to the best of a team's ability but sometimes that falls short of the mark. It's best when reviewing answers for this gap to be identified. Sometimes we don't capture such a gap until we're trying to create alignment. Consider the example where an assumption is questioned and a test is crafted to get real data from the marketplace. While this may add time to the project, it might also provide the evidence needed for convergence. Evidence is a great tool for alignment, and if our heatmap tells us we lack it, consider what tests can be constructed to reduce ambiguity.

Hyatt Hotel's former Senior Vice President and Global Head of Digital Julia Vander Ploeg shared in an interview how using data to test assumptions is a way to encourage organizations to embrace the unknown:

## DATA AND CHANGE AT HYATT

"It's hard for organizations to change meetings from a pre-packaged, pre-aligned PowerPoint where everybody knows exactly what questions will be asked to meetings where assumptions are challenged and tough questions can be discussed thoughtfully. What don't we know? Why don't we know that? How could we figure that out? How are we going to test this?

"Take Hyatt, for example. We were able to shift an initiative from affirming what we already knew to one to where we didn't have all the answers. And we were OK with that—having unknowns. We piloted a relatively standard change on our website to how users search for properties, which in and of itself is not that crazy, but it provided interesting data. There was a conversion lift on desktop, but it went the other way on mobile. We celebrated the fact that the data showed it did way worse in mobile because we learned something new and valuable and it provided us with a path to make positive changes. Previously, we might have blended all the data together to show it was an overall success."

### Step Three: Preparing Content

Alignment is a process of scaffolding. It starts with the team and extends out into the organization. Once conclusions are apparent to a working team, it's time to prepare the content that helps engage the layers in our scaffolding metaphor. Before expanding the circle, we have to prepare something to bring to the table. That's why step three is focused on building content.

Preparing content usually means creating the dreaded Power-Point presentation. I'm not outright against it for use in business. It can be a good medium for pitches to investors or storytelling with a board of directors. But when it comes to management activities in a company, it can do more harm than good. Presentations are a shallow, imprecise format for the fact gathering, reasoning, and thinking that sits behind the alignment for a strategic project. The written word is a better starting point.

PowerPoint is "banned" at Amazon; instead, the company has standardized a six-page written narrative as its primary form of content. Bezos believed the naked word forces us to explain how we are thinking and reasoning through something. The written word forces clarity of thought in a team setting, so every attendee can follow along, intensely examine, and provide feedback. When the narrative is on the table, there is nowhere to hide.

I'm comfortable with these six-page narratives. I've written dozens while at Amazon. I have used them earlier in my career at other companies, writing product strategy documents, investments memos, or even term sheets for partnerships. I like writing (hence this book), but not everyone does or can grow the skill.

That's why I believe you don't have to go about it exactly the way Amazon does.

I prefer the idea of FAQs, written answers to a list of related questions.

FAQs are easier to develop and don't introduce the same hurdle. They don't give you PTSD, like you're writing a college term paper. Most people in the workplace get stuck in place when faced with the idea of writing a cohesive narrative in the spirit of Amazon. Since leaving Amazon, I've tried to introduce its six-page narrative at multiple companies, and even people with Ivy League degrees struggled to catch on. In one case, I provided an outline and example, yet a talented MIT grad could not get it over the finish line.

FAQs are the same building blocks of information, yet are more approachable. They're bite-sized. To build more comprehensive alignment you'll need some content to share. Assemble content with these sections:

1. **Description.** Describe the topic of the exploration, the underlying problem statement, and why it matters. Two or three paragraphs will be sufficient. The audience is probably not new to the initiativet but it's always good to reinforce the big picture.

2. **FAQs.** Assemble the questions and answers from the completed exploration. Organize the FAQs by matter. That will make them easier to consume.
3. **Conclusions.** After collecting and voting on findings, the team will hold a validation session to review them. During this discussion, the group enters an open revision process where folks can change their input or their votes. From that session, you'll have updated information to use for content. Then you can list conclusions in three categories based on their status: agreed; open; removed.

The list of agreed findings is where most of the group has voted strongly agreed or agreed. Open conclusions have a difference of opinion to resolve. Removed conclusions were raised initially but decided by the team as irrelevant. Think of the document as context plus a set of recommendations. Decision Sprint provides much of this information. As we flow through Decision Sprint, we may not realize it's generating the content we need down the road (like this point of building content).

## *Step Four: Socializing Conclusions*

Step four is socializing conclusions, now that an overall narrative for the problem statement has been put together. Now we execute on the scaffolding. A team may be ready to move ahead to action but to do so, will likely need to get two to three functional leaders in the organization onboard. Remember, these sponsors may not be in the day-to-day. Even when working members keep their leaders abreast of the latest progress and thinking in a project, it's natural for those leaders to seek to understand and shape these projects. The good news is it's not a fresh start. Recall, when building explorations, we likely calibrated how those explorations were built with these leaders. So they should be pre-aligned to some degree. They are aware of the substance of the exploration. Now that exploration has been run and completed, it's time to show how the car looks on the other side of the carwash.

Now it's time for the team to go on a roadshow to meet with executives about the initiative. Think of meetings with functional leaders as focused on knowledge sharing. "This is what we learned" through exploration, and "this is what we reasoned through based on what was learned." "It produced these conclusions. What did we miss? Would you modify anything? Does it make sense?"

This approach tends to make alignment ridiculously easy. Leaders see the difference compared to initiatives where these methods are not in place. Teams working in the legacy manner are coming with perfectly packaged plans looking for a rubber stamp.

When I taught exploration work to teams, especially how to socialize knowledge coming out of it, alignment became easy for them. Not always, but most of the time. It's all because of the upstream focus organized by Decision Sprint. That effort begins to pay dividends because you've done the upstream work.

Socializing knowledge for alignment could vary depending on the size of your company. If you're a large behemoth company, things can get more formal. There may be an official "steering committee" chaired by 2–3 leaders who are peers. In this case, I recommend teams do an individual meeting with each leader ahead of the official steering committee.

Place senior leaders in a position to become advocates through this approach. Why? The higher up you go and the more formal the culture, the more likely leaders value the space for individualized briefings. They often have a ton of pride, and want to appear on top of things. Overcome this by providing them space to understand the work behind recommendations. As long as the team is socializing the same knowledge across its sponsor group, doing individual sessions can grease the wheels for the committee meetings.

Don't lose sight of the big picture. Even if you don't get new input from socializing the completed explorations and conclusions, you will achieve something greater. Shared understanding. Support. Commitment. Advocacy.

That's why socializing knowledge is so thrilling. It's where the team gets to build momentum. It spreads understanding when done well, solidifies buy-in, and creates advocates for the initiative at hand.

People will thank you for investing the time to catch them up and build their understanding. Get people working from the same information on the back of high-quality learning before decision-making. It's rarely attempted—yet so essential and effective.

# FOUR SAMPLE FAQS

In the prior chapter, we dove deep on Amazon's self publishing business. I've created these questions to illustrate how Amazon would explore important facets of a program for authors where they would choose to publish exclusively in exchange for benefits. There's a lot to this exploration, but these four FAQs provide a good representation of how a team might think about the idea. After reviewing these FAQs about launching an exclusivity program for authors to publish on Amazon, I will demonstrate how they can be used to draw conclusions. Note: this content is for illustration only and not the official FAQ's of the program.

## *Matter: Enforcement*

**Question:** Will we enforce the policy actively or passively?

**Answer:** Word of mouth travels quickly across the internet. If we don't actively enforce our policy this could become easily noticeable. Bloggers will write about it. There is a strong community around self-publishing. That's a good thing, but it also means that ideas and practices are shared and spread quickly. Even a few examples of violations that are not acted on could become a signal that we are okay with them. It could encourage more of that behavior.

Just as importantly, if we intend to make a customer claim or promise around books that they can't get anywhere else, we have a commitment to actively enforce. To stay true to such a claim, there cannot be widespread violations and we should be actively trying to minimize them.

## *Matter: Enforcement*

**Question:** What will be our response for a violation?

**Answer:** We must tread carefully in responding to violations by giving authors every reasonable chance to address them. Many independent authors are new to the field, and not savvy about the intricacies of the process. Mistakes can happen unintentionally. For example, managing listings across different e-commerce sites or handling smaller channels like book giveaways. Our response should clarify the terms as described in our FAQs, provide evidence of the violation and provide a reasonable amount of time for the issue to be fixed. We would continue to monitor the issue's status, provide second and third notices (if applicable) and then delist the title from the program.

## Matter: Monitoring

**Question:** How accurately can we monitor a book's presence across internet distribution?

**Answer:** Our web crawlers, utilized for price comparisons across sites on the internet, are both comprehensive and accurate for finding items such as books. When it comes to accuracy, we can match the title and the author name to determine that a book may be listed somewhere else on the internet. We may struggle with sequels and how they are named. We will need to flag these for manual review to address this accuracy issue.

We will crawl frequently across the top [x] sites to find matches, and less frequently across the wider internet (such as the author's own website). Therefore, a daily report for top sites and a weekly report for the wider internet is realistic.

## Matter: Monitoring Costs

**Question:** How costly is it to monitor 10,000 books versus 100,000 books versus 1,000,000 books?

**Answer:** The manual steps introduce variable costs for us to monitor. Web crawling is already built for very high scale and use across the company. Applying it to this program has some incremental cost but the difference between monitoring thousands versus hundreds of thousands of books is not material.

Manual work is introduced when: (a) for each flagged book, a person needs to verify it; (b) for each violation, a notice needs to be generated; (c) responses for authors need to be reviewed; (d) follow-up is required when a violation is not resolved. We estimate that over [x]% accuracy in flagging books for violation. We estimate a cost of $[y] per title to handle a violation. Over year one of the program, when the number of enrolled titles is expected to be [z], this implies a year one cost of $[ABC] to support the program.

What conclusions would you draw from the answers to these questions? Here are a few that a team might suggest:

1. We should actively enforce the policy.
2. Enforcement should be constructive.
3. Enforcement should not be overly strong except in extreme cases.
4. Manual reviews will be necessary to accurately determine and validate violations.
5. We will need to build automaton tools to scale the manual review.
6. Tools will be important for this program to scale.

How do we draw good conclusions? A conclusion backed by solid reasoning is what we're seeking. In business, we won't have perfect information and we need to move quickly. High quality exploration should provide sufficient reasons to draw good conclusions.

When collecting suggested conclusions from a team (via the asynchronous methods shared earlier), we might also collect their reasons. People can share their reasons verbally when these conclusions are discussed or write them down ahead of time.

In any case, to illustrate the idea of reasoning let's share the thread behind the conclusions listed above. These are merely examples of how I would go about stating reasons. There are probably many ways to communicate the same ideas. The key is whether the reasons would justify the conclusions in the mind of anyone with common sense (based on contents of the exploration). It's more about logical conclusions and less about any particular genius or expertise.

**Conclusion:** We should actively enforce the policy.

**Reason:** Word of mouth is so strong on the internet that lack of enforcement will create a big mess.

**Conclusion:** Enforcement should be constructive.

**Reason:** Amazon should not be seen as using its weight to be forceful in enforcing rules with independent authors.

**Conclusion:** Manual reviews will be necessary to accurately determine and validate violations.

**Reason:** Our technology provides a good starting point to identify books but to be sure we will need to manually review them. It's important to be extremely accurate before making any claim around a violation.

**Conclusion:** We will need to build automaton tools to scale the manual review.

**Reason:** Once a title is flagged for review, there is a manual process to validate the match and this comes at the cost of $[x] per title. To cut this cost down by [y]%, we will need to develop tools to make the review more efficient.

**Conclusion:** Tools will be important for this program to scale.

**Reason:** Tools will reduce the cost of reviewing each title and speed up the process. We cannot afford an army of reviewers and potentially face a huge volume of books to review. Assuming [x] mins for a completely manual review and a volume of [y] inbound books per day, it would take [z] days to complete a review with a team of [xyz] people. While we will grow the team, we must also speed up their review time to meet any reasonable SLA.

As you can see, more than one meaningful conclusion could surface. That is often the case with high-quality explorations. The conclusions can be quite layered. Each layer will inform some concrete actions in the project execution.

In the next chapter, you will see how even when we get to project performance, there is always a next frontier to explore. In this example from Amazon, you can see how the need for tools or automation could make sense, but we need some definition before building them. That would spur a future exploration.

How did our exploration come together into a cohesive direction at Amazon?

We wanted authors to honor the exclusivity but didn't want to be heavy-handed with it. We actively enforced the commitments but allowed for several opportunities to correct violations. For noticeable titles we took a stronger stance. Scale was a major issue to address. At the time we thought the program would vastly expand because it's so enticing for self-published authors to make higher royalties.

On top of that, we realized that precise monitoring and enforcement was costly. We accelerated the build out of a content review team and their technology platform to scale the program.

All of this is spelled out in a six-page narrative that went up the chain to Jeff Bezos. We held two sessions with Jeff where our exploration, conclusions, and next steps were shared. Sound work allowed us to proceed. Ten years on, the program survives and thrives. Upstream work is paying dividends over a decade later.

Let's talk about the elephant in the room. When a current exploration doesn't allow conclusions to be definitive, then we need to identify what issues were missing from the exploration. The exploration can be extended to fill in these gaps. The team will have to come back to drawing conclusions when that work is completed. Yes, this happens at Amazon, a lot. Amazon doesn't hesitate to hold or shelve ideas when that's the right call. Sometimes the right call is to wait and see or even kill an idea (for example, an idea I led at Amazon focused on a social network for writers did not fly). You'll hear more about that in the next chapter on decision-making.

# Decision-Making

**W**e're reaching the boldest phase of Decision Sprint. Now that your team has explored the critical aspects of an initiative, drawn conclusions, and gathered support for those conclusions, you're primed for decision-making. Decision Sprint transports us from a messy pile of unknowns to decision points. (See Figure 6.1.)

Decision-making is a process of connecting our drawn conclusions to action. A decision is a choice to take certain actions or decide against those actions. Actions are not ambiguous. The need is to be specific and concrete.

Some decisions require the courage to hold or fold projects that have failed to gather momentum. It's not always about green-lighting new actions. I will touch on this issue of more challenging choices as well.

## PREPARATION

In a decision-making setting, a team will often present to stakeholders with the authority to give the green light. These stakeholders may have a few touchpoints with the team over prior weeks or months. So they will often need a recap of the upstream work. Decision Sprint radically

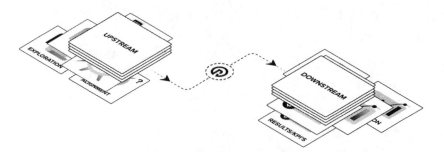

**FIGURE 6.1**   Decision points connect upstream to downstream.

simplifies this. We can follow a breadcrumb of questions to answers to conclusions produced through our Decision Sprint workflows. Some of the work you might include in a review includes:

- How was the exploration built? When building the exploration, the team arrived at well-defined matters and questions underlying each matter.
- What answers were developed through the exploration?
- These first two items can be shared in a pre-read or shared in the meeting with time set aside for reading at the start of the meeting. Here we tap the FAQs, which include the matters and underlying questions with their answers.
- What conclusions were drawn from the exploration? If presentations are the norm, you might begin the interactive part of a meeting at this point. Put a stake in the ground by sharing the conclusions. Go through each conclusion and connect it to the reasoning process. The FAQs developed in the exploration will provide the basis of the reasons. Refer to specific FAQs to support a conclusion.

Decision Sprint makes all this information available, a no-stress output. It makes content easy to tap into. The form and timing of sharing the content is going to be company specific. It depends on the norms.

Once the conclusions are shared, there's likely to be dialogue. Open it up for clarifying questions. The exploration may be strong, but perhaps there are new considerations spotted. Dialogue is a good way to think through these considerations and determine if any conclusions should be modified.

Let's return to our example from Amazon. We explored the opportunity for Kindle to create a program to secure books exclusively from authors and drew several conclusions. One conclusion: our team would need to develop tools to scale the review of books that might be violating the terms of the program. Our customer promise of books that can be found only on Amazon would be watered down if these books were listed across other e-commerce sites. The potential for a high volume of books to review and the cost of hiring people to do it could become prohibitive. Assuming there was alignment on this conclusion, we need to figure out the key actions.

We make a list of actions to consider. In this case, they could include:

- Schedule a brainstorm to identify a minimum viable product (MVP) scope for the automation tools.
- Reallocate engineering resources from other things to build the automation tools.
- Develop a forecasted volume of books that we will need to review so that we can hire the right number of contractors while Amazon is developing the automation tool.

It's even better if the actions have some specificity on who and when. Who will take the actions? What will happen when?

Taking this into consideration, we can revise the action list:

- Schedule a brainstorm to identify an MVP scope for the automation tools, including the engineering, content review, and legal teams (next week).
- Reallocate engineering resources from within the direct publishing team to support a development of the automation tools (end of month).
- Work with the business team to estimate a forecasted volume of books that will need to be reviewed so that we can hire the right number of contractors while the automation tool is being developed (two weeks).

# TIME FOR ACTION

Let's return to our proposed list of actions. The actions are the decisions.

If you're part of a team seeking approval for decisions, try to go beyond the directional alignment. When decision-making meetings take place, be specific. Decision makers are primed for action once they are in alignment. Rather than wait for another opportunity to drive into execution, take advantage of the moment. Be ready with the specific actions that put things in motion. That's how we build strong momentum in projects. Witnessing decision makers support the recommended direction *and* underlying actions will catapult the team into execution mode.

Put a list of actions on the table, and invite input. For example, a team might inquire with these questions:

- Are these the right actions?
- Have we missed anything?
- Do these actions have any dependencies that need to be factored in?

A team might collect more comprehensive actions by opening the door to this input. Time with a set of sponsors is precious. Seeking input while the right people are around the table is a quick way to build in comprehensive actions.

Are all actions necessarily approved together? No. Some are clear to execute. Others might be fine-tuned through dialogue in decision meetings. Sometimes a proposed action goes too far and needs to be revisited in a future decision meeting. Another possibility is "yes, but needs to be further understood." This last possibility is a good transition. There will always be the next batch of items to explore.

The main takeaway is this: when the work leading up to decision points is strong, there's a desire for action. That's why a good decision-making process will bring together the potential actions with the exploration and alignment work that sit behind it. This is the realization of Decision Sprint. It's a powerful elixir when it comes together.

# CONTINUOUS EXPLORATION
## (AKA MAKING THE DEAN'S LIST)

So your team completed Decision Sprint. Great. You have reached the next fork in the road for implementing your innovation or initiative. Other teams may implement the first set of actions from Decision Sprint. Now you are preparing to run ahead to the next layer of the initiative. Ride the momentum from the first sprint as the ideal transition to the next one.

The way to think about this is to ask, "Given that we have decided *X*, what should we explore next?" An example from my own experience: I helped Volvo develop plans to offer a subscription to cars. Let me explain this very strategic initiative. You could get a car sight-unseen from your phone at a transparent, no-haggle, national price. The new business was green-lighted as one of the company's big bets. We made our intentions public—to have one-third of the cars we produced sold through subscriptions versus the way cars had been sold for the previous 100 years. Huge stake in the ground! A key pillar of our growth strategy.

Then we arrived at the next big fork in the road: What's in the offering? Many questions need to be addressed to define the offering. What would make a compelling subscription, and could that be achievable? For example, bundling insurance and maintenance into the subscription seemed very compelling. Or the ability to return the car after a year? Or the ability to swap from one model to another? And which cars would be available? Would it be our entire lineup or just the most coveted new models?

There would be a lot to explore in developing the offering.

Turning to which cars should be available, as you know there can be thousands of configurations of cars even when Volvo's car lineup is basically 8 to 10 cars. Volvo offers large, mid-size, and small SUVs, large and mid-sedans, and several cross-country models (wagons). When you start to configure a car, there could be hundreds of thousands of variations. That's not a good thing when you're trying to create a predictable flow of vehicles that can get into consumers' hands without sitting on lots. What made more sense for the subscription business was something more like iPhone options. Within this, comes another layer of considerations. Should the cars be high specification (leather, sound system, sensors, tires) so they're desirable? Just a few colors and trims? Should we start with our newest cars, such as the millennial friendly XC40, with the latest tech and design? Perhaps pairing a cool car with a subscription model would fit the target customer.

Once we created this new business, it was a deep well of unknowns. As soon as we make some decisions, the next group of unknowns came to the surface. Exploration becomes part of life when you're working on a big bet.

Is there a way to make the situation less overwhelming? The answer is yes. Accelerate momentum by being ready with the next batch of things to explore. Let's say a decision meeting ends with key actions approved. An even better outcome is to give a preview of where the team will focus next. Pair successful decision-making with a taste of the explorations that are up next. After deciding, bring the focus to the next set of relevant unknowns—and exploration as the way to make those unknowns actionable. This is the heart of continuous exploration and making it a deep ritual in your organization. The superpower of exploration gets well entrenched when a team builds a habit of reviewing explorations that are completed and previewing the ones that are "up next."

## THE PAUSE BUTTON, FOR GOOD REASON

At the resolution of a Decision Sprint, smart managers must also consider the sometimes unpopular option of not taking action. Taking action is not always the right call. If the show is moving too fast, or there are too many unanswered questions, you may need to push pause.

We know intuitively that "no action" is sometimes the best course. This can happen even when teams have done a great job of the steps leading up to decision-making. But I note two principal reasons why holding on an initiative makes sense.

First, there could be a higher-level dependency. It may need to be sorted before the project being reviewed can proceed.

What are examples of higher-order dependencies? They include:

1. The ability to fund a project among alternatives in the portfolio
2. The capacity for the organization to give the project the right mindshare
3. Something external that needs to fall in place first

Let's cover each one. A company may have several high-merit projects it's considering. Some must take a backseat. But let's move beyond this.

When the initiative is core to company strategy, the funding path may not be an issue. Even when securing funding, the logical owners and stakeholders have only so much bandwidth. That's the second kind of dependency. If they're knee-deep in something that requires deep problem-solving and brainwork, the potential for distraction could introduce risk. This dependency needs to be managed; it should never be an excuse for dragging the feet on innovation.

To mitigate the risk of "kicking the can down the road," a good filter is velocity. Look at velocity to see if the people who claim to have limited bandwidth have a more fundamental issue in their organization. The real issue can be the organizational pace. It may not be keeping up. In this case, we must challenge it.

A third dependency is the external marketplace. Something in the ecosystem may need to take hold before the idea can fly. We might love building metaverse applications, but if consumers aren't taking to the hardware, a less aggressive path might be in order.

Most of these situations are not deal killers for an idea with good merit. They influence "when" more than "if" an initiative will be green-lighted. At Amazon, there are countless times when we hustled to produce explorations and strategic plans only to hold on them. Sometimes the wait was a few weeks. In other instances, it could be months. In nearly every case, we understood why once we saw what else the company was focused on with management time and company resources.

Management is not about green-lighting every initiative of merit. It can be about juggling them so they don't lose steam while working with constraints of resources and bandwidth. If we take a wider view of time, most ideas at Amazon received the vetting and commitment they deserved. Teams did not feel deflated in the process of iterating over promising ideas over months and quarters. Teams know the volume of ideation is so very high, as is the quality bar.

In an earlier chapter, I mentioned a project I initiated at Amazon that did not get off the ground. It was a social network for content creators to share their work in a serialized format. While the product was launched, it didn't get strong traction and Amazon hit the pause button. Years later, a different group of people returned to it, nailing the product-market fit. The product is now thriving and growing.

In a high-performance environment, teams get used to a temporary pause. At the same time, management needs to demonstrate to teams that ideas with merit have a chance to proceed even when paused. A pause is not a "no" and does not dilute the ambition behind the project.

I have found that incumbent companies (typically Fortune 500) struggle with projects of this type. They are accustomed to "yes" or "no" and not comfortable with the middle case. When asked, "Are we moving forward with a certain initiative?" they seek a black-or-white answer. As we've shared, there are reasons why the time for proceeding may be "not now." We need a method for keeping these opportunities warm.

To do so, companies can adopt a "pipeline" mentality. And a decision pipeline process is a good way to bring structure to it.

## DECISION PIPELINES, ALWAYS READY

Decision Sprint promotes a pipeline of vetted opportunities. This pipeline is quite strategic. Even if the pipeline consists of completed explorations alone (i.e., they have not progressed into alignment or decisions), this can be huge. A set of completed explorations will help a company stay current instead of falling behind. Companies can find themselves several steps behind innovation in the marketplace. We've all seen it. While others enjoy growth, our organization is still trying to get its act together. It needs to go through exploration, alignment, and decision-making very quickly. Without methods like Decision Sprint, the quality of the process can vary, stealing time and adding confusion.

What if our organizations were not caught by surprise? What if we had a pipeline of explorations that we bring through the process of alignment? And what if a company could refer to a set of decisions and recommended actions based on this work? In other words, we have a significantly advanced the starting points when the time has come for execution mode. We don't need to start all the way upstream.

These initiatives that have advanced through the upstream process yet are in a holding pattern make excellent additions to the pipeline. In Chapter 7, on workflow, I will walk through where the pipeline process is reviewed and evaluated (hint: it's right after the previous batch of upstream work has been completed and reached decision points). The pipeline process will help us start new sprints for new ideas to complement the roster of initiatives that have graduated from the "Decision Sprint academy." This becomes easier to achieve as you encourage teams to embrace the idea of continuous exploration and discovery. You'll see how teams committed to the continuous exploration of their initiatives will quickly populate a meaningful pipeline for senior executives.

## TWO HEADSPACES OF GREAT EXECUTIVES

High-performance organizations hold themselves accountable to strong pipeline development.

Opportunities on the front end and back end of Decision Sprint, and their pace, should matter to senior executives just as much as those in deep execution mode. It's not a luxury to explore what's next when today's uncertainty is so high. A business never knows when it will need it. And there's never a perfect time to make space for it. In Chapter 13, you'll learn about the role of AI in measuring whether it's enough.

## Excerpts from an Interview with José Cil, CEO of Restaurant Brands International

### On Decision-Making:
### Balancing Execution and Innovation at Scale

**Atif:** How do you get your teams working together on transformative innovations? What is the most effective process for making decisions as a company embarks on a big leap?

**José:** You get as many voices and viewpoints as you can when you are making decisions. The ultimate filter is that you do the right thing for the people who are going to be impacted by the decision. You don't start with the bottom line in mind. You start with the people affected in mind. Then ultimately, if you do that consistently well, it will drive the bottom line in a meaningful way.

On innovation and my management style, I think it's essential to have clear big goals that everyone understands. In our business, we have a very significant baseline to operate. You need to effectively manage your day-to-day business, which is all about execution, experience, and ensuring that you consistently deliver the promise you make to your guests. In our case, we do that through our digital apps, drive-throughs, and the restaurants with curbside pickup. That is less about innovation than being great at customer experience, a highly undervalued quality in management.

I think it's important to underscore that execution and delivering on the promise of the brand or the business to the guests is most important because without that positive and memorable experience, you are unlikely to have repeat business, which ultimately drives preference and loyalty in our space.

Aside from that, we do think innovation is critical, and our brands, Burger King, Popeye's, Tim Hortons, and Firehouse Subs, are among the most innovative on the product side. On the digital front, our app for Tim Hortons has become the number one food and beverage app in Canada in three years.

We have been able to grow our digital business tremendously because of the innovative mindset that our team has. We have clear goals, we set big targets, and then we follow strong routines in terms of the enablers of those targets. We have short-term milestones to achieve that help us conclude that we are on track, keep going; or we are way off track, stop and let's make a pivot.

We tested some conveyor systems for the Tim Hortons business in Canada to add a lane. We were able to develop and test having a drive-through window serving customers through a conveyor belt. We could see it in action very quickly because we had a clear goal: expand off-premise capabilities of our restaurants when we had limited real estate space. Then we had close management routines to track progress. I saw it in Windsor, Ontario, a few short months after we had first tabled the idea. Though not all ideas wind up in every restaurant or market, this is something that we wanted to at least test and validate.

**Atif:** Sounds like the company started with a strategic objective or problem statement. Would you say that the team was given the space to solve the problem or meet that objective? Can you talk a little bit about providing space?

**José:** Yes. You must have high-quality people who are motivated and enthusiastic and excited about the prospects of being able to provide solutions to problems that our consumers or our operators in the restaurants are dealing with.

When we started talking about expanding our off-premise capabilities at Tim Hortons, we clearly didn't come in and say, hey, we should do a conveyor belt. Can you guys go and figure that out? We talked about the problem. We talked about the need to find more off-premise capabilities in our restaurants. We set some timelines for when to have these discussions, and then the team went out, researched, benchmarked, looked at what's out there, and thought about it with specific resources internally and externally. They shared several options, some needing a lot of capital and others needing less. Then we went out and put a number of these ideas into tests and validated those financially against the guest impact that it had, and that's how we make these types of decisions.

**Atif:** Is there anything this team did that helped make it easier for you to agree with their recommendations? For example, an approach to problem-solving that boosted your confidence to keep going?

**José:** The way that I gain confidence is by going through the details of the operation. I like to spend some time hands-on looking at every aspect. We do some research as well and some concept testing with consumers. And some focus groups validate that the product or the feature we are proposing to provide would be something that a consumer would consider as a positive benefit for their interaction with the brand. So the more touchpoints we have with guests and franchisees in a restaurant, the more confidence we will gain that it will have an impact.

Many executives struggle to juggle the mindsets of execution and "upstream thinking." That's why it must become habit-forming through workflows. They are different modes, different headspaces. Day-to-day pressures compared to open-ended thinking about the next frontier. The day-to-day can often win this tug-of-war. Executives tend to clear the deck of "distractions" and solve for the here and now. Of course, there are times for this mode. Like my first day at Volvo when production had stopped at the company's main factory due to a software glitch. It wasn't the time and place to think beyond the now. Forget disrupting the automotive industry. We needed to save our quarter.

While these situations can take weeks to resolve fully, there's a specific period of intensity after which you have the right actions in motion and can step back. When we manage the crisis, not the other way around, that creates space. At Volvo, I knew we needed to act with urgency on innovation with so much disruption in the automotive industry upon us. We solved the factory glitch and began to tackle our strategic opportunities with similar intensity over the next few months. I speak from experience when saying readiness for your next frontier is not something you will always have the space to pursue. When the window is open, lean in without hesitation.

And don't take out day-to-day frustrations on teams that are working explorations. This can sometimes take place when the "here and now" isn't performing, and teams charged with innovation efforts somehow face a sudden scrutiny. You'll wish you had enabled and encouraged them later when the company has the headspace for solving bigger problems and craves their potential. Avoid falling into this cycle of love-hate within innovating into the unknown. Be steadfast.

# PASSING

The decision to pass on an opportunity is always better if we know why and can cascade it within our organization. Decision Sprint provides a way to do that.

This might unfold in the following sequence. We build a good exploration. After we run the probe and look at the content it produces, we see things more clearly.

We might be unable to draw solid and confident conclusions. Maybe the business case will only make sense with the optimistic assumptions. Maybe there isn't solid data or reasoning to support the upside. Having sourced the right matters and questions, building an exploration has served its purpose. We have canvassed the opportunity adequately. As the team begins to address the questions, the answers tell us there are too many holes.

When teams are encouraged to explore using Decision Sprint, they will likely kill most weak ideas without burdening senior management. In this respect, it's a way for teams to self-regulate and vet ideas. That saves everyone time. In other cases, ideas or opportunities may be more top-down. Maybe the CEO had what seemed like a brilliant idea or a curiosity. The details do not check out. We can share findings of the exploration and the conclusions that were drawn.

Whether the impetus was top-down or bottom-up is less important. What matters is giving us a way to confidently pass on an idea, in a way that is transparent. Put another way, Decision Sprint is not a marathon.

In the realm of digital transformation, data provides an objective way to facilitate nimble decision-making. "It's being able to work with data and take bias out of it in terms of what business outcomes are happening," Hyatt Senior Vice President and Global Head of Digital Julia Vander Ploeg said.

> ❝What you and I learned is how to adapt an experimental mindset where you can quickly figure out what's going to deliver the business outcome you are looking for versus theorizing endlessly and what it might be.
>
> The faster you can test that out, the faster you can move to the next iteration. That's the beauty of what attracted me to digital commerce 15 years ago: you can make it scientific. You can test things quickly. You could see what worked. ❞

Julia sees this as a leadership skill:

> ❝The leaders of business in the future are people who can bring everyone around them to act that way too. It's tricky, because often there is so much emotion in business—for example, who gets to make a decision on something. Leaders who come in and say, "Let's not even argue about that. Let's figure out how quick we can figure out what the data will tell us really can bring organizations along to the next level." I see those as being really essential skills to whatever it is a leader is developing.
>
> At Hyatt, we recently partnered with Apple to move room keys into Apple Wallet. Everybody in hospitality right now has a thing where you can open up the app and you can unlock a door with it, but there's all this friction in that process. In practice, it didn't really make a difference for anybody because the amount of time it took to go through all those steps was more cumbersome than taking out one of those plastic cards.
>
> What Apple was solving for was, hey, put that right in Wallet so you don't even have to wake up your phone. It's like a boarding pass. If you wear an Apple Watch, you can use that, and you don't have to set anything down either. I can hold my Apple Watch up to the door to open my door. The data showed that it will get a lot more usability that way, just taking unnecessary friction out. So again, the theory of how cool something is may or may not translate to what somebody is really going

to do with it. I have always been shocked by how just the littlest bit of friction or hurdles can make everybody "fall out," so to speak. 🙷

When we "pass," that does not mean we wasted time. If you're a venture capitalist, the job is to pass on eight or nine out of ten things you see. Pick the one home run. Running a business is different. Most of what comes to the attention of senior decision makers should stem from the strategy and strategic pillars they've set. The nature of the ideas and opportunities should be relevant to realizing the North Star.

At the same time, we want to encourage stretch thinking. That's not happening if all ideas sail through and some are not being passed on after exploration.

It's important to treat a pass as a normal part of the decision-making fabric. Exploration serves a purpose just as much with a pass as a green light. Make sure leaders communicate this to the teams involved. The pass is not a failure.

### Excerpts from an Interview with Julia Vander Ploeg, former chief digital officer, Hyatt

#### Influencing Leader to Leader

**Atif:** You are comfortable unleashing teams to have a hypothesis and test it, and be in a better position to know more in a week or two or three weeks. Can you tell us more about that?

**Julia:** Yes. It comes down to the conversation in the room with the business stakeholder or product owner, where we agree to peel back the layers about why you think we should build this or that feature. I ask, What is it that you, as a business stakeholder, assume your feature will do? Yes, you want to grow revenue as a business, but what things need to happen to help us grow revenue? Incredibly, this question often doesn't get asked.

When we have identified the assumptions and the changes in behavior the business stakeholder wants to see, we can have the team look at different hypotheses for what could happen. Maybe it's changing the button color. Perhaps it's putting choices in a different order in the flow. Maybe it's calling it something different, whatever. Let's have them test a bunch of things. If we can boil down the choices with data to identify that change in behavior that you assume or are seeking to have happen, we're now all working on evidence and objective reality.

**Atif:** Is it challenging, considering the rush to ship and build things and execute, to give teams the space to be in learning mode? To provide space to be a lot smarter about a matter in a few weeks? How hard is it to give teams the space to do that?

**Julia:** It shouldn't be that hard. The challenge becomes that much of corporate America is built around certainty. Here is my road map. I know what I am going to get. I know when I am going to get it. I know what it's going to cost me. What we're talking about is kind of a 180 on that. That goes back to this cultural change that you are putting into place that embraces uncertainty.

If most of the time is being spent reaffirming what everyone feels good and comfortable and safe talking about, the team will not crack new territory. You're not learning, you're not pushing the envelope. Leaders have to rethink what their role is. It's the difference between leading through authority versus real coaching.

## CASCADING DECISIONS

Most organizations forget one of the easiest wins they can make is moving initiatives forward. This win is so overlooked yet so powerful. It's easy to do. And it's low-anxiety, high-satisfaction for all involved.

It's the cascading of decisions. Let's say Decision Sprint is completed. The actions decided are ready to be rolled out. What happens next?

Many people involved in execution may not have been in the room with the decision makers. Typically, they are subsequently called into meetings and next steps are discussed. What does the group need to deliver, and how will it go about it? There may be a debrief on the decisions. But we often skip socializing the complete Decision Sprint elements. Take the team through the elements of Decision Sprint from exploration to alignment to the conclusions. Spend 30 minutes conducting a full debrief when holding a next steps meeting. Or share the content beforehand.

Socializing this content is more than a victory lap. First, those who were involved in building and running explorations will see their impact. Closing the loop with the decisions these explorations enabled is positive reinforcement. It helps spread the practice of explorations and the use of Decisions Sprint. Don't leave this opportunity on the table. Second, people may not see the whole path to decision-making. They may not have been involved in all aspects of Decision Sprint. Share the full extent of Decision Sprint so that people have a richer and fuller context. Team members will be involved for weeks and months in execution.

## WILL YOU BE MY LAUNCH PARTNER?

Let's shift gears to talk about rapid decision-making. Circumstances may not allow a formal Decision Sprint to unfold. Here's a story that illustrates such a case.

It was the *dead of winter* in downtown Chicago. The lake was beautiful, but the bitter cold and wind had us rushing from the parking lot into the lobby of the Four Seasons. We were there to meet executives from Apple related to a top-secret project. Apple is known for shrouding new product launches in secrecy, and we were experiencing a taste of it. One week earlier, the company phoned an executive on my team and said, "There's something we want to show you. If interested in hearing more, we can meet at Four Seasons next week but bring only your CEO and your boss."

I was the boss they were referring to. There wasn't even a clue as to the subject matter. Thankfully, we had set up a team in San Francisco, and this move started paying dividends very quickly. The executive in charge of the office, Zaki Fasihuddin, had within months placed McDonald's on the map for big tech from Google to Apple. Zaki was the vice president of innovation and business development.

As our meeting at the Four Seasons began, the Apple team pulls out a black briefcase. There's a code required to open it. But they don't have it. They phone a number to receive it. It's all structured and orchestrated. The people we are meeting with have only certain permissions. You get the feeling they have a team dedicated to "how to protect secrets."

One executive opens the black briefcase, and inside is the next iPhone. It seems similar to the then-current iPhone version, so my gut reaction was muted. Maybe I was expecting a big leap like a folding phone, more cameras, or a surprising form factor. The Apple team explains this is the first iPhone with an NFC chip. If you're not familiar with NFC, it's how two devices can talk to each other and pass information. For a retailer, this could be huge. Today, you can tap your phone to a payment terminal and make a cashless payment. That's what Apple was about to share with us. Apple Pay was about to become a real thing.

Everyone knows Apple Pay or Google Pay today, but in 2015 this technology was not mainstream. Apple getting into the game was a major step. But they needed partners. In some categories of innovation, Apple can go it alone or carry the market. It can make the market through its product genius alone. But in payments, it needed to partner with the places people make payments, like major retailers. And who better to turn to than McDonald's? McDonald's is a very frequently visited retailer. It's more frequently visited than Walmart or Target. It's intended to be a fast experience so contactless payment could be an excellent time-saver. And it's global, with a presence in over 90 countries.

The ask from Apple is to upgrade our payment terminals to feature NFC readers. That way the iPhone can pass credit card information to the terminal. Today this process works seamlessly. Many people trigger Apple Pay with a touch, authenticate with Face ID, and hold the phone near the reader. We do this now at convenience stores, gas stations, and even mom-and-pop stores. But for this level of adoption by consumers and retailers to be reached, you have to start somewhere. Apple would love to launch with McDonald's and other major category leaders in brick-and-mortar retail as partners.

"One more thing," as Steve Jobs used to say. Apple would like us to be ready on launch day. That implied all 14,000 restaurants in the United States would need to be able to support this new way of paying. With just a few months' lead time, meeting this deadline would challenge our normal pace.

I loved the idea of being an Apple launch partner and could imagine our CEO, Steve Easterbook, sharing a stage at Apple's launch, announcing our partnership. Many possibilities were racing through our minds about how far this could go. Unique promotions when you pay with the phone, brand marketing through Apple's channels, and other powerful collaborations. You begin to shift the positioning of a company by being a first mover. The initiative would help our objective to make McDonald's a more digital, forward positioning experience. Being a laggard here would produce limited impact. At some point, major retailers would support Apple Pay as they update their payment terminals, and consumers would not give us credit for differentiation.

After our meeting, I recommended we jump on this opportunity, and Steve, our CEO, was inclined. He gave us the green light. The ball was now in our court.

There were many unknowns. But our challenge was even greater. Apple required that we limit the number of people involved with McDonald's. We must disclose each person to Apple. It was a need-to-know project. There were obvious challenges to going about exploration when the participants were restricted. How would we get our arms around the key issues when we could not be open about it?

Zaki took the lead on a day-to-day basis. There were two major forks in the road. First, could we make it happen? We had only about four months to ready every McDonald's in the United States. This meant upgrading technology, training crew, and other operational considerations. Second, how would we get the partnership right? That mattered to us. It was not enough to share the limelight with Apple on launch day. We needed to be able to justify our investment of time and resources, hastening them ahead of other things we could be doing.

Zaki spent time discreetly teaming with operational experts. He didn't have the luxury of Decision Sprint nor the luxury of forming a working team to flow through one. They explore the first fork in the road—could we make it happen? It was a rapid-fire exploration.

The key issues surfaced pretty quickly. The underlying questions were not easy ones to address, but the team developed some hypotheses and tested them in restaurants. The partnership between Zaki's innovation squad and the operational veterans was key. Operations and IT teams rose to challenge by helping rule out or rule in certain solutions to the rollout.

Some of the matters, questions, and answers:

## *Matter: Drive-Through Experience*

**Question:** In the United States, drive-through is a huge part of the business. How will the customer bring the phone in proximity to the payment terminal without dropping it?

**Answer:** After testing various options, we believe the payment terminal can sit on a metal arm that can be extended through the drive-through window with special extended cabling. This will bring the terminal within the customer's reach, and allow the customer to comfortably tap. We have implemented this approach in our test restaurants and continue to improve its form factor for ease of use.

**Question:** How would crew members support this customer experience without increasing operational time?

**Answer:** Contactless payments are much faster than handing a credit card to a crew person and safer as well. With contactless payment, a few steps are simplified than when paying with a credit card in the drive-through. These include transfer of a card from customer to crew and insertion or dipping of a card into a reader.

That said, training and awareness are key. It could be a problem and add time if the crew member needs to consult with a manager, as well as risk the disappointment to the customer if the crew cannot complete the task. The solution is to ensure hands-on training for anyone staffed at the drive-through window. Operating instructions placed at the station are a second line of support or reference.

## *Matter: NFC Coverage*

**Question:** What percentage of payment terminals are NFC enabled?

**Answer:** We scanned the payment terminal network topology in each regional market to make sure that the minimum payment terminal standard per last upgrade cycle has been met. The minimum spec would ensure that a payment terminal is RFID-enabled, meaning it has the requisite microchip and a radio antenna to conduct the wireless tap-and-go experience with a mobile phone. In our scan, we discovered that $x$ percent were enabled. It will take $y$ weeks to cover the remaining, and it's our intention to accomplish that by launch.

**Question:** What is the effort and timing to upgrade nonenabled, missing or disconnected terminals?

**Answer:** We created a test plan to be executed across all US regions for the in-store IT technician to be able to inspect if a minimum terminal spec has been met. A rush procurement procedure was established to quickly release funds to order and install new terminals. In addition, certain terminals were offline because of damaged cabling or were disconnected altogether. A new cabling bundle was designed and specially packaged for this particular initiative. It could be ordered and installed to bring dormant terminals back online. These would be shipped to restaurants with enough lead time to make the launch.

## Matter: Software Readiness

**Question:** How will we ensure the new iPhone can communicate with the payment terminal to enable secure contactless payments?

**Answer:** A special "safe room" could be established within internal IT testing lab under complete secrecy and strict access restrictions. Apple agreed to send a test version of the new iPhone human-delivered via a lockbox to headquarters. This would ensure the secure element within the iPhone containing encrypted payment information in token form could be securely transmitted via an NFC tap to a payment terminal for successful payment.

**Question:** Could the software communication between the iPhone and the payment processor via the terminal scale handle the demands of a production environment?

**Answer:** A high threshold of successful transactions, meaning a very low transaction failure rate, has to be met to be considered production ready. Various simulations and stress tests were conducted to ensure the large volume of throughput and expected settlement times could be achieved. In addition, the software mechanism on the processor side was being modified to ensure transactions would be routed down the proper payment rails and that a reporting mechanism existed to be able to specifically tag a payment as contactless. We would need this for metrics and troubleshooting.

When it comes to the bigger picture, Zaki and his crack team brought their Silicon Valley experience to bear. There's much more involved here than feasibility. Now it's about the creative side.

Looking back, these were the issues we faced at the time.

How could we make "payments with your phone" bring more customers into McDonald's? It may not happen on day one, but could it be a needle mover over time? There are comarketing promotions between Apple and McDonald's. There is opportunity to integrate Apple Pay into the McDonald's app. There is opportunity to tap into Apple's channels to brand McDonald's as a leader in digital experience.

While we had a tight deadline, we had some time to explore these frontiers. But early on, we calculated it made sense for us to be a launch partner.

For Zaki's closeup description of this historic and rapid Decision Sprint, see the following interview.

## Apple Pay and Innovating in the Unknown at McDonald's

### Excerpts from a Conversation with Zaki Fasihuddin, former VP of Innovation and Partnerships at McDonald's

**Atif:** What did McDonald's bring to the table in helping put Apple Pay on the map?

**Zaki:** Apple recognized McDonald's had three main strengths. First, a standard point-of-sale (POS) technology that could be turned on overnight for Apple Pay. Second, the scale of 14,000 restaurants across the United States. And third, many McDonald's customers were iPhone users.

In 2003, McDonald's started to make the move to accepting card payments and made a salient decision to invest in a POS system nationally that was NFC-enabled. This technology allowed a customer to simply tap an NFC-enabled card or device to make a payment. That was probably one of the reasons why Apple was pursuing us, because they saw that upon launch we would instantly become their biggest network of acceptance.

To become their launch partner, there was still a lot that had to get done. So, for example, not all the software in all these POS systems were upgraded to the same level, and not all had NFC turned on. The main pain point for McDonald's was that the drive-through lane was not designed for a tap-and-go payment. Our ops guys were concerned that we would add an additional 60 to 90 seconds to the drive-through experience. We had to design a solution that didn't slow down our drive-through experience because it is pretty much the lifeblood of McDonald's.

This required operational innovation. We didn't want to add additional time to the drive-through experience, but we were creating a new behavior for the customer sitting in the car as well as the McDonald's crew member. The customer had to reach out the car window holding their phone to tap onto the POS device. The POS device, however, was attached to the register and needed to be extended by the crew member out of the drive-through window to the car. This is something that had never been done before in the history of commerce. We had to design special cabling or extend the existing cabling to allow this to happen.

This required precision of execution on the back-end operations. Our operations people are critical to McDonald's because McDonald's is all about consistency and speed of service: you place your order and within a few minutes, you are out with your food and drink.

**Atif:** Drive-though is what built McDonald's.

**Zaki:** Exactly, the more cars you push through that drive-through lane, the more money the franchisee makes, the more money corporate makes. That's where sponsorship from operational leaders was really important. We said, look, this is part of our digitization journey. We are undertaking this path. It's going to feel uncomfortable. This is the first of many things we are going to introduce into the restaurant experience that are new. We just need to figure out how to optimize and fit it into our system. That kind of system involvement and development conversation hadn't happened in several years.

**Atif:** What kind of innovations were required?

**Zaki:** We had to figure out how to extend the cabling and how to test the software. So we put together a tiger team. We had this little crack team in POS. We had a crack team in IT. We had a crack team in digital. Every week we would check how we were doing in terms of our plan to be live on day one so when Tim Cook was on stage and introduced Apple Pay to the world, we would be ready.

So we came up with a number of innovations. First, we created cabling in a box and we shipped it to every restaurant. And every restaurant had an IT person who was in charge of making sure that was installed. Then to solve the drive-through problem, one of our team members came up with this innovative idea to design a metal arm. Think of it as like a metal tray on an extendable arm where the POS system sits on top and you bolt the metal arm into the drive-through window and the attendant pushes that out. The POS unit moves close to the car window so that the customer can easily tap their phone.

**Atif:** Ultimately it reduces time once you have that setup. Obviously, it's just a tap as opposed to giving change or fumbling with a card?

**Zaki:** That's right. A big concern was that we couldn't have customers hand us their phones because that creates all kinds of liability. It could fall to the pavement and crack. So we designed this elaborate swivel system. However, we then realized when we actually fabricated it in the lab, in a restaurant lab, we couldn't produce and install them within four months in 14,000 restaurants. So what we did was a bit of a hack where we created a stick with a tray on the top. The drive-through attendant would extend this out. They would hold out this metal rod, this flat tray, with the POS system. And the POS system was cabled down. Cables had to be able to extend back and slowly extend out the window. So that's essentially the innovation created for the drive-through.

We were able to get those fabricated and shipped to all restaurants in time. We had to tell the restaurants that they couldn't talk about this prior to day one. It was super secretive. Of course, the press is always snooping. We didn't want this story to break that McDonald's was preparing for phone tap payments. So there was a cultural element of having a small crack team inside McDonald's working in secret. The team was convinced it was worth doing and secrecy was key. Then having that C-level sponsorship (CEO, CIO, and CDO) was vital. Without that, this would not have happened.

**Atif:** How was the feeling within McDonald's at launch?

**Zaki:** It was a euphoric day when it launched. The CEO announced the milestones to all the employees. We are innovating with the most innovative company in the world.

While there was euphoria, there were a number of leaders in the company that didn't know about it and were caught off guard. So we had some damage control to do.

What I learned is that to be a true change agent, you have to give the glory to the others who you are taking along on the journey, because if you are not doing that, then you are not doing your job as a transformation agent. Your job is to win hearts and minds, to get people to change their mindset, to get people to open up to new things, to get people to be OK with trying and failing. With innovation work, failure is part of the process.

**Afit:** Then you had Covid.

**Zaki:** Yes, with the pandemic, contactless payment became front and center. We had to rely on mobile ordering, mobile payments, and mobile delivery. My team did the first pilot partnership with Uber for food delivery on UberEats at McDonald's.

It's now a significant percentage of a turnover of franchisees of McDonald's, where it was zero back then. We are talking about Door-Dash, GrubHub, and UberEats. At the time, internally some felt "nobody is ever going to want their food delivered by some stranger," but we know that it's quite the opposite. Co-creation with these partners set up McDonald's for the next decade.

# PART THREE

# INSTALLING DECISION SPRINT

# Workflow

By now, you understand the big-picture elements of Decision Sprint and what they are all about. Now I'd like to delve into the practitioner mode. Practitioner mode is a more concrete altitude. It's about activating and applying Decision Sprint for something you are working on, right now.

Earlier I promised that Decision Sprint would not require "clean sheeting" today's common processes, or starting from scratch. If you're on a team, there are likely some standing meetings and steps that are in motion to progress your initiative or project. How does Decision Sprint connect with today's meetings and steps? That's where workflow comes in. In this chapter, you'll learn how to put Decision Sprint into practice through 13 workflows. And you'll see how they simplify and streamline existing collaboration by design. The meetings and interactions you are holding today live within the 13 workflows that we will cover. I will demonstrate the benefits of shifting and simplifying today's approach and how to accomplish that. You will learn how to put Decision Sprint into practice through 13 workflows:

**Workflow #1**    Initiating an Exploration

**Workflow #2**    Sourcing Matters

**Workflow #3**    Sourcing Questions

**Workflow #4**    Calibrating the Exploration

**Workflow #5**    Sharing the Canvas
**Workflow #6**    Answering Questions
**Workflow #7**    Calibrating Answers
**Workflow #8**    Drawing Conclusions
**Workflow #9**    Preparing for Alignment
**Workflow #10**   Conducting Alignment
**Workflow #11**   Identifying Decisions
**Workflow #12**   Preparing Content
**Workflow #13**   Conducting Decision Meetings

# WHY SHIFT FROM MEETINGS TO WORKFLOW

Workflow is a step in a sequence with a defined purpose, set of collaborators, and precise inputs and outputs. The work that gets done in each step can take several formats. An alternative to meetings is possible. Format is the fifth element of each workflow. Decision Sprint contains 13 workflows (steps), each with these five elements. I will spell it out in great detail as you progress through this chapter. Figure 7.1 summarizes the key elements of each workflow.

| 5 elements of a workflow | |
|---|---|
| PARTICIPATION | Who are the core participants, and in what roles? |
| PURPOSE | What is the purpose of the step? |
| INPUTS | What are the minimum conditions that need to be fulfilled before starting? |
| OUTPUTS | What are we aiming to produce? |
| FORMAT | What interactions are most effective and efficient to achieve the purpose? |

**FIGURE 7.1**   Five elements of a workflow

Thinking in terms of workflow is better than thinking about meetings. For starters, a step in a workflow can take place without a meeting, as in another format of interaction. That's the obvious part. Second, meetings often lack purpose. I will walk you through how purposeful interactions occur when designed with specific inputs and outputs in mind. These inputs and outputs vary as an initiative is developed or as a team gets into deeper stages of problem-solving. Decision Sprint provides the distinct inputs and outputs you need to have in mind to make each interaction build on what comes before it. Imagine a chain of interactions that *truly* build on each other—everyone understands the fit of the current, prior, and coming interactions. Workflow provides this "build" effect. Kelly Campbell, president of Peacock and Direct to Consumer at NBC Universal, refers to it as a "snowball effect" as you'll read about in this chapter.

Now let's zoom out. We get a bird's-eye view of Decision Sprint and its 13 workflows through Figure 7.2.

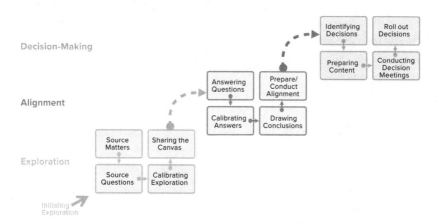

**FIGURE 7.2**  Bird's-eye view—Decision Sprint workflows

Why does the bird's-eye view matter?

Think back to Chapter 1, where we discussed input versus output meetings at McDonald's.

During my first executive review, I focused my questions on inputs, while my colleagues had organized the meeting to present outputs such as recommendations. I didn't have the language to describe the step in the workflow I sought to validate or better understand. Moreover, the team probably lacked the methods to perform that step properly. My team and I could benefit from working the five elements of each step and seeing the steps in sequence. Seeing the collection of workflows would be like hand-holding us as we sorted a giant puzzle. Imagine if I could inquire about a particular workflow. When did it take place? What were the inputs, outputs, and collaborators? A collection of workflows would make it easy for me to calibrate and keep the team progressing.

By shifting to workflows, I believe you get a two-for-one punch. Existing interactions are far more effective and less error prone. Less rework and fewer blind spots. The combination of a bird's-eye view and detailed elements of each workflow help avoid these pitfalls. Streamlining becomes an added gift as teams figure out how to progress work with fewer meetings while remaining collaborative. Work gets done in new and better ways, reducing meeting counts.

Now let's walk through each workflow and delve into the unlocks. You will acquire a strong sense of how each workflow adds value and how it feeds the next. If you're collaborating on something important in your role today, it's likely you will find an immediate application of these workflows.

## START WITH A PROGRESS BAR

Before walking through each workflow, let's start with a critical hygiene factor. Imagine a progress bar that anchors a team, a bird's-eye view of workflows and where we stand now. Which workflow is active, what have we completed, and what's on tap? And how about essential milestones such as executive reviews or decision meetings? How can we time each workflow with respect to important milestones such as executive reviews or decision meetings? Many refer to that as "working backward." How do we feed essential milestones with the workflows of Decision Sprint and keep them in sync?

I've crafted Decision Sprint as a collection of workflows to enable this anchoring. The anchoring makes it easy for everyone involved to know where we are and what remains to get done with respect to readiness for milestones. But it's much more than a checklist of steps. These workflows are steadfast on their purpose to ensure quality. There's less room for cutting corners on quality because the inputs and outputs of each workflow are well defined. We cannot give them lip service. Instead, they help us avoid cutting corners when it comes to sourcing and synthesizing input, drawing strong conclusions and recommendations, and preparing for decision points.

Let's turn to Decision Sprint workflows and define them in detail. As you have seen in Figure 7.1, five things are defined upfront for each workflow:

1. **Participation:** Who are the core participants and what are their roles?
2. **Purpose:** What is the purpose of the step?
3. **Inputs:** What minimum conditions need to be fulfilled before starting?
4. **Outputs:** What are we aiming to produce?
5. **Format:** What interactions are most effective and efficient to achieve the purpose?

## INITIATING EXPLORATION

We've covered why exploration starts with a clear problem statement. Often the problem statement starts with the following question: What is the major fork in the road facing the project?

Initiating an exploration is about crafting the problem statement and grouping the right set of competencies around it. Competencies are the know-how or perspective that are relevant to the problem statement. If we identify the competencies, then we can bring the right people into the exploration (i.e., the working team based on relevant roles). (See Figure 7.3.)

When it comes to sponsorship, I'm inspired by how Kelly Campbell, president of Peacock and Direct to Consumer at NBC

Universal, describes peak workflow as a snowball effect that starts with a "champion":

> ❝ People are more successful when they feel they are part of something or when they feel real ownership in it. I start by finding the leader who has genuine energy for the idea or project. ❞

I encourage this person to run with the idea, then to come back in a week and tell us how we can make it bigger. The champion establishes the starting point and next steps, including who the right people are to bring into the problem-solving. I want the champion to operationalize the workflow quickly, because if you let something be intangible for too long, then it will struggle to gain momentum.

I believe in the value of champions bringing people together to build upon ideas with new perspectives. It's like building a snowman. You start with snow, and as you keep rolling, you add more snow as well as other things like ice and dirt, and your snowman base gets bigger and firmer until it just works. Then you move on to the next one. It's particularly critical for functional leaders who think through a particular lens to bring various viewpoints and people together to build an initial idea into something bigger.

## Workflow #1

### Initiating an Exploration

| | |
|---|---|
| PARTICIPATION | Project sponsors + project leader + sprint administrator |
| PURPOSE | Validate problem statement and identify working team members |
| INPUTS | Several different and related competencies reflected in the working team + an exploration with a problem statement |
| OUTPUTS | A list of working team members |
| FORMAT | Brainstorm meeting or time-bound independent submissions (no meeting required) |

**FIGURE 7.3** Workflow #1: Initiating an exploration

Let's say our business is considering entering a new market. We must think about the market, consumer behavior, partnership opportunities, marketing plans, technology, product experience, and more. It goes well beyond any one function. The champion needs to bring cohesion to the idea building and carry this throughout the formation of the business plan and strategic approach. Having a champion who will take an idea and bring together the right people to build upon it and make it bigger is key to the exploration.

Before launching into problem-solving mode, it's a good idea to validate how the exploration is framed with sponsors and decision-makers. In Chapter 4, we walked through the art of crafting a problem statement. When initiating an exploration, it's a good idea to place three to four variations of the problem statement on the table. It's likely to take some dialogue, debate, and input to refine and select the most appropriate one. It does get easier from there. After validating the problem statement, it's time to tap into the right competencies or core team members to involve. It's not about involving an army of people or making sure no one feels left out. It's about identifying the competencies most relevant to the problem statement and determining where in the organization they may reside. Sometimes it's obvious who to involve, and in other cases, thinking about competencies helps us develop the most relevant group. With a problem statement and the competencies grouped around it, we are on our way. But don't miss the opportunity to set expectations around the full Decision Sprint.

In this chapter you'll learn how interactions with sponsors and decision makers are an opportunity to create transparency and build trust in the methods.

At the initiation stage, we have an opportunity to share a bird's-eye view of Decision Sprint. The team can demonstrate the elements of Decision Sprint (see Figure 7.2), including exploration, alignment, and decision-making.

Like any good workflow, it's helpful to clarify "you are here" among the several steps involved in the flow. Remember my point about anchoring. The team might even choose to go one level deeper by sharing what goes into building the exploration and how that produces a canvas of the problem space even before detailed work has begun.

Focus on the front end of Decision Sprint. I would highlight workflows 1 to 4 so sponsors and decision makers can see the more immediate value of Decision Sprint. They may thank you for shedding light on previewing the work to be done and the method for it. In fact, you can even set an expectation on progress (e.g., within two to three weeks the canvas will be ready for review).

## BUILDING AN EXPLORATION

It makes sense to start with the sourcing of matters. You've learned that as part of exploration, we are looking to canvass it with the right matters and underlying questions behind each matter. To do this, a team needs a central coordinator to collect suggestions from across the team. Once the coordinator captures those, they may have to scrub the inputs to group similar suggestions, improve wording, and determine which suggestions fit the exploration.

Let's bring Workflow #2 to life. As you can see in Figure 7.4 under "Format," there's no need to hold a meeting, but often to keep team members engaged on a request for suggested matters, we bring people together. If a brainstorm is the chosen format, it must be structured to avoid groupthink. To promote independent thinking, use the typical sticky note approach. Give each group member a few minutes to independently jot down suggestions and only then reveal the input across the group.

I'm sure you've been in plenty of these design-thinking workshops where one works individually or in subteams, and then the whole group comes back together to look at the collective ideas. Ideas are clustered based on similarity, and the group can see individual work in the context of all input. Patterns are more clear that way and so is independent thinking. The group is prompted for any missing ideas to continue the extraction of ideas.

Using this approach for sourcing matters is effective, though living in a post-Covid era, where digital tools are pervasive, you can collect suggestions in myriad ways without gathering a group. I dedicate an entire chapter to digital tools. We'll talk more about what's called asynchronous work later on in this chapter.

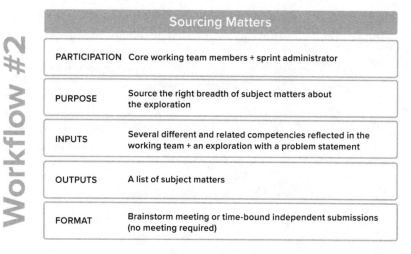

**Workflow #2**

| Sourcing Matters | |
| --- | --- |
| PARTICIPATION | Core working team members + sprint administrator |
| PURPOSE | Source the right breadth of subject matters about the exploration |
| INPUTS | Several different and related competencies reflected in the working team + an exploration with a problem statement |
| OUTPUTS | A list of subject matters |
| FORMAT | Brainstorm meeting or time-bound independent submissions (no meeting required) |

**FIGURE 7.4** Workflow #2: Sourcing matters

Moving on from matters to questions is what further builds out the exploration. As a refresher, we value matters because they help us cover the breadth of the exploration. They help us ensure we don't miss an important consideration that needs to be understood. But breadth is not enough. That's where questions help. Questions are a way to go deep on any given matter. These clarifying questions are how we dive deep enough into a matter. We want to source questions that cover the meaningful contours of the subject matter. Don't just window shop; go inside and feel the texture of the fabric.

Space out the sourcing of questions from matters because breadth and depth require different brain spaces. Our brains may float between breadth and depth, and a facilitator would have to capture input within a structure. That's why a single brainstorm to handle both can be tricky. Is the suggestion about the breadth of the exploration, or is it helping going deep about an aspect of it?

If we fail to separate them, the result may be mediocre for each. A resilient solution is to make each its own workflow. That's why sourcing questions is its own workflow. (See Figure 7.5.) All that said, it's powerful to collect suggestions when people are in a stream of consciousness. In Chapter 4, I elaborated on how people often start with a question in raising a matter and how to spot the difference between a clarifying question to a matter and a matter masked as a question. A matter raised in the form of a question can be handled by the tips in that chapter.

| Sourcing Questions | |
|---|---|
| PARTICIPATION | Core working team members + sprint administrator |
| PURPOSE | Source the right depth of considerations for each matter through clarifying questions |
| INPUTS | A list of subject matters pertaining to the exploration |
| OUTPUTS | A list of questions for each matter |
| FORMAT | Brainstorm meeting or time-bound independent submissions (no meeting required) |

**Workflow #3**

**FIGURE 7.5** Workflow #3: Sourcing questions

Question sourcing tends to go fast. Curiosity tends to come alive once we anchor the mind to a specific matter. The quality of questions is another matter.

Let's say that the team has meeting fatigue and uses time-bound independent submissions to manage this workflow. When it's done, the coordinator may have to scrub the suggested questions as was done for matters. This effort is more than removing duplicates and editing wording. It's about sharpening questions to make them more precise.

Once we build an exploration, it will run, and team members will spend real effort reasoning through answers. So it's key that you formulate the questions as precisely as possible. How can this be achieved? How can this question be written to help peel back the onion layers? Does it give the person assigned to answering it pause for thought? Yes, we want to help the people assigned to answer questions by promoting thought and directing thought to the most relevant tracks.

That's why scrubbing questions (beyond the hygiene factors) should be a collective effort even if just two or three people are involved. The next workflow will start with this.

Before moving on, let me be realistic about the strict separation of sourcing matters before questions. We need a way to capture questions whenever they happen to arise in our minds. For example, the team may be sourcing matters. What if while suggesting a matter, a team member gets a spark on some underlying questions? Don't lose the opportunity to capture this—keep a backlog where these questions can be submitted. Otherwise, they may never be recalled. A backlog is a place where we capture suggestions for matters or questions before that workflow is active.

Workflow #4 is more of a working session for the team. (See Figure 7.6.) It starts by collecting feedback on the question list. A list of questions organized by matter can be evaluated for two things: (a) the priority of the matters relative to the problem statement; (b) how comprehensive the question list may be for each matter. To make the second point more clear, I'm referring to whether there are enough good questions for each matter. It's beneficial to capture feedback on both items in order to identify possible gaps. For example, a high priority matter may fall short of enough depth (not enough questions). Identifying this gap "upstream" allows us to do something about it. What can be done? It starts with asking what kind of expertise would help fill in the knowledge gaps. Refer back to the notion of "vegan leather" as an idea Volvo has explored in its push for sustainability and to innovate on the next generation of cars. Let's say that traceability in the supply chain was an important matter when it comes to vegan leather. And let's further assume that no one on the working team is a real expert on the subject so intuitively they feel blindspots could exist. The team might identify expertise gaps like blockchain as being relevant to developing more important questions for this matter.

It's now time to run an iteration on question sourcing. Yes, it's worth spending the time to repeat the sourcing activity you learned about in Workflow #2.

And it's likely to produce results because Workflow #4 provided insight into potential blindspots. A team can do a more focused job in its second iteration of question sourcing once it has a priority to the list of matters, and insight into the level of comprehensiveness (or lack of it) which may exist in the list of questions for each matter. It can focus the team's efforts on adding more questions where depth is lacking and where it's critical. Bringing in guests into this second iteration of sourcing questions based on missing expertise is a great way to address blind spots. It's a targeted expansion of the sourcing process.

**Workflow #4**

| Calibrating the Exploration | |
|---|---|
| PARTICIPATION | Day-to-day sponsor + sprint administrator |
| PURPOSE | Review matters and questions; assign questions |
| INPUTS | A list of matters and questions |
| OUTPUTS | Shareable canvas of the exploration (matters, questions, and assignments to answer questions/review answers) |
| FORMAT | Planning meeting, or collaborative editing tool |

**FIGURE 7.6** Workflow #4: Calibrating the exploration

Next comes assigning work. There are two types of assignments. First, a single person is on point to answer a question. Second, there may be one or more reviewers for each answer. The role of a reviewer is to comment on the answer, typically bringing up considerations that should be integrated. A reviewer typically has a specific perspective on the answer but is not as close to the entire picture as the point person.

Having a point person and reviewers is like a check and balance. It's also about avoiding blind spots. It's about teamwork because the point person and the reviewers must agree. A reviewer ultimately has to approve an answer for it to be submitted (we'll go into this interaction under Workflow #7).

So where does this leave us? What have we achieved calibrating an exploration?

Imagine a working team has completed the sourcing process for matters and questions. It's a strong canvas for the exploration. There are not yet answers, but we have good breadth and depth to the problem space behind the exploration. On top of that, we have connected the competencies within the organization to question and answer levels. That's powerful and a milestone in and of itself.

It positions us for a kind of prebuy from senior executives. That's why our next workflow is sharing. Before anyone answers a question, sharing the exploration canvas will unlock massive trust and buy-in.

Executive decision makers can often wonder what is the status of a key project? What is the team up to? When will we next review the progress?

Decision Sprint provides engagement between the team, sponsors, or decision makers at optimal intervals. These intervals develop shared understanding while making good use of everyone's time. For executives, this means leveraging their time (bang for buck); for team members, it means avoiding meeting overload (bureaucracy or micromanagement). Workflow #5 is one of the optimal intervals. (See Figure 7.7.)

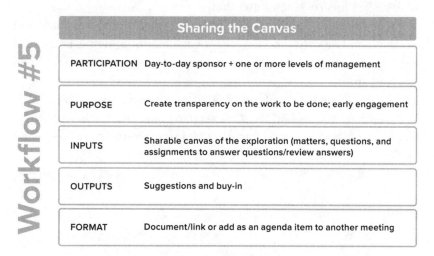

FIGURE 7.7 Workflow #5: Sharing the canvas

The exploration canvas is where we engage decision makers to move forward. It's how teams can build confidence before any recommendations, conclusions, or decisions are even on the table. The simple act of laying out an intelligent canvas for the exploration builds trust. Put yourself in the shoes of a busy senior executive. There may be a lot riding on an initiative, and the executive may have visibility only every few weeks. An intelligent canvas is a good sign for a person in this situation. It builds confidence that recommendations, conclusions, or decisions will come on the back of strong understanding. None of that has yet happened, but the foundation is strong enough to believe it will. Implement Workflows #1 to 5 to change the game of how problems are solved, ideas are pursued, and projects are run in your organization.

Now that we've built the exploration, it's time to run it.

## RUNNING AN EXPLORATION

A useful exploration helps our end game of making alignment and decision easier. The team must flow through the exploration within a timeline. For example, content from an exploration needs to be available for key meetings or interactions.

An exploration could take a couple of weeks, typically not days and certainly not months. You'll see how each matter and question in the exploration involves deep dives by more focused groups of people to develop answers.

The building blocks of the exploration are question-answer pairs. Let's refer to these as FAQs. FAQs are great in my opinion because they imply succinct answers that get to the heart of things. (See Figure 7.8.)

**Workflow #6**

| Answering Questions | |
|---|---|
| PARTICIPATION | Answer lead + answer reviewers |
| PURPOSE | Put a stake in the ground answer for each question using reasoning and data |
| INPUTS | Assigned question, data sources, forethought to key considerations |
| OUTPUTS | A collection of draft answer (or FAQs) |
| FORMAT | Deep-dive meeting and/or digital collaboration tool |

**FIGURE 7.8** Workflow #6: Answering questions

Assign one person to write an FAQ answer and one or more people to review it. Some questions are straightforward enough that someone can take a stab at the answer. Others require discussion to acquire input before the first draft can be crafted. We'll refer to that as a deep dive.

Some questions require data collection (e.g., running a test). A group may meet to develop the test—and set aside time to conduct the test and gather data to answer questions. In the previous chapter, you've read about the Apple Pay launch at McDonald's and the operational tests that clarified the best customer experience for tap-and-pay in the drive-through. It required test-and-learn. You've also heard from the Hyatt executive who is not shy to sponsor a pipeline of customer tests to fuel decision-making. A continuous pipeline of testing is highly complementary to Decision Sprint. If we know the data needs that are coming from our pipeline of explorations, we can develop a prioritized list of tests to run. Coordinating these two pipelines saves time, as there could be natural dependencies.

The timeline for answering a question might need to be adjusted based on the lead time for tests to acquire data. For example, a customer survey or A/B testing. Coordinating pipelines is a more proactive approach.

Answers need to go through a few iterations (See Figure 7.9.) That's where reviewers come in. A draft answer is shared with reviewers for their feedback. Feedback can stem from asking what's missing, what part of an answer is hard to follow, or which links are weak.

Feedback loops can take place over email, messaging, and collaborative apps. A dialogue in one sitting may also do the trick if those interactions are looping.

One of the most exciting signs of progress is when answers begin to stream in. People assigned to answer and review questions have completed their work and submitted them. For each matter, we may have several underlying FAQs. With these FAQs we hope for a well-rounded understanding of each matter in our exploration. The team will use these FAQs to come up with recommendations, conclusions, and proposed decisions. That's why a round of calibration for answers is important.

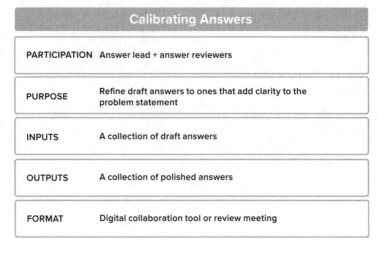

**Workflow #7**

| Calibrating Answers | |
|---|---|
| PARTICIPATION | Answer lead + answer reviewers |
| PURPOSE | Refine draft answers to ones that add clarity to the problem statement |
| INPUTS | A collection of draft answers |
| OUTPUTS | A collection of polished answers |
| FORMAT | Digital collaboration tool or review meeting |

**FIGURE 7.9** Workflow #7: Calibrating answers

## DEVELOPING ALIGNMENT

Building and running explorations has prepared a team to develop specific recommendations for the initiative or problem being tackled. After reviewing the exploration, the team will likely see with more clarity the right direction to propose.

It's a pivotal point for the initiative and opportunity for buy-in if we get it right.

Workflow #8 is about drawing conclusions based on high-quality exploration. (See Figure 7.10.) With the content from the exploration, we want to probe the team for all the meaningful conclusions they can draw. There could be several important conclusions. Some may be more strategic, and others more tactical. We want to capture a range. We also want to probe the group for the level of conviction behind each conclusion. I refer to this as a heat map that captures how intense the level of agreement is for each conclusion.

To start, I like the idea of capturing as many diverse conclusions as possible across the team. It's a rare opportunity to source fresh input.

To do this, we need some way to collect conclusions independently.

An excellent mechanism is a purposeful brainstorm, in which the working team jots down their input independently, then clusters them for the whole group to see. At the same time, I'm a big fan of modern digital tools that enable the same thing to be done without calling a meeting.

| | Drawing Conclusions | |
|---|---|---|
| PARTICIPATION | Each member of the working team | |
| PURPOSE | Source meaningful conclusions through a process of independent thinking | |
| INPUTS | A collection of FAQs | |
| OUTPUTS | A list of conclusions or recommendations | |
| FORMAT | Brainstorm meeting or digital collaboration tool | |

**Workflow #8**

**FIGURE 7.10** Workflow #8: Drawing conclusions

This may require two parts. First, ask each team member to share the conclusions drawn from exploration directly to the coordinator. Once everyone has a period to do this, the coordinator can collect the results and scrub them so that similar items are reduced to single options. Often conclusions are complementary as they address different decisions. For example, you can make a new sandwich very saucy or not, and make the bun very toasty or not. Whatever you conclude on each decision is somewhat independent of the other. Opposing conclusions can be combined because of the next step you will hear about.

I recommend using a survey tool to poll the collective list of conclusions and ask people to share their *level of agreement* on a scale. It's like voting on each conclusion in terms of the scale of agreement you have with it. Survey results provide some aggregate level data that could be eye-opening. If there is high level of agreement on a conclusion, then alignment is achieved. It's the disconnects that need more discussion. I've talked about a heat map as a way to summarize where the disconnects exist.

Turning to format, what's the advantage of digital tools versus having a standard brainstorm?

It comes down to whether the brainstorming meeting will have the collaboration dynamics you seek. Will everyone be in the right headspace? Will they adhere to the process? Do you have a good facilitator who will keep things on track?

Digital tools offer a more structured approach that gives back a little time to people. On top of that, they surface data on where the collective thinking stands that is sometimes hard to quantify in a meeting.

We will see much more of this in the future, especially as younger generations define how we work. They will see it as a preferred mechanism. It produces what we're looking for and does it with more flexibility.

In Chapter 3, I shared with you a point of frustration that led me to ban the word "alignment." It was a case of alignment before exploration. Alignment was feeding bureaucracy and command and control. By now, we've learned that committing to exploration changes the game. It cures alignment and makes it a tool to accelerate. Think about the power of heat map data that is laying out conclusions and the level of agreement.

It's the team's collective thinking, which is based on understanding the right issues in the right way. It helps us avoid drawing conclusions from other factors, such as the department we belong to, social pressure, or the personality mix of who's involved. It comes from high-quality exploration and independent reasoning based on having done the work.

After Workflow #8, the focus of the team shifts to getting stakeholders on board with what the team members see. (See Figure 7.11.)

What do we need to get started, given that we have clarity on our direction? How can we get into action mode? First, we need to socialize the work we've done with key leaders in the organization.

A working team may be accountable to the next level of leaders. For example, a member of a cross-functional team for a project may report into a functional leader. Let's say you have several VPs who are functional leaders, and they have assigned or contributed team members to a cross-functional project. These functional leaders at the

VP level may not be involved daily with the project but are important stakeholders. They need to be aligned to the initiative's direction and ability to provide input. They need to feel ownership. We can do that without creating bureaucracy.

| Preparing for Alignment | |
| --- | --- |
| PARTICIPATION | Project sponsor + sprint administrator |
| PURPOSE | Connect the dots between the recommendations on the table and how this was arrived at through the exploration |
| INPUTS | Exploration content + recommendations sourced from the group |
| OUTPUTS | A content package that can be shared with the next level of leadership |
| FORMAT | Document |

FIGURE 7.11  Workflow #9: Preparing for alignment

A working team will likely have been in the weeds sorting through the unknowns and running explorations. When it comes time to lift our heads and engage with leaders, we need a CliffsNotes version of the work behind the work, the conclusions we've drawn, and recommendations. How we got there is just as important as what we recommend. Only then will leaders around the table be able to feel real ownership. Team members must put them in a position to have understanding and conviction.

How do we do this without creating bureaucracy? That is the beauty of Decision Sprint. Decision Sprint allows the team to compile the work into consumable content. Content becomes a real time-saver and speeds up everything because it's a living version of how the team went about problem-solving.

Putting content together shouldn't be a chore. The work of exploration and drawing conclusions from explorations gives us the content we need.

Here are the key elements of such a compelling content package:

- Problem statement
- List of key matters explored with their underlying questions
- FAQs group by theme
- Key conclusions
- Recommendations

Other companies use content to speed up alignment. Amazon, which is perhaps the best example, requires each meeting to start with a narrative. Amazon's narrative is based on preference for the written word in essay form that is fueled by a culture of detective work, which is not documented or taught. Decision Sprint gives you something less quirky and easier to produce because it's an output of workflow that guides a team from *A* to *Z*.

Workflow #10 attempts to solidify alignment. (See Figure 7.12.) The idea is to get leaders nodding their heads and getting their hearts and minds behind the few key recommendations that matter. It's an important milestone to achieve.

| | Conducting Alignment |
|---|---|
| PARTICIPATION | The level of leadership above the working team (typically functional leaders) |
| PURPOSE | Buy-in and sponsorship of the recommendations |
| INPUTS | Content package |
| OUTPUTS | Refinements to recommendations and suggested actions to bring them to life |
| FORMAT | Meeting |

**Workflow #10**

**FIGURE 7.12** Workflow #10: Conducting alignment

A good interaction for this is a monthly project review with functional leaders. Share a pre-read from Workflow #9 to set the tables.

During the interaction, slow down and walk through the content from Workflow #8 at the pace the leaders are seeking. Remember, they aren't in the day-to-day and their ownership matters. So expect a round of clarifying questions. While you should allocate a third of the meeting or more for this, often the clarifying questions are limited because the FAQs have hit all the key unknowns and curiosities. Now onto the main event.

Focus on these questions:

- Do these recommendations make sense?
- Are we missing anything?
- If they do, what actions do you suggest the team take?

Once alignment is achieved, you will feel a shift in the energy in the room. People around the table transition into action mode. It's the idea of acceleration. Acceleration of commitment and conviction is one of the most elusive things to achieve in business. Congratulations. You've just arrived there.

What if the alignment session does not unfold smoothly? What if key stakeholders are not onboard with the recommendations? What if they introduce new considerations that really sway things away from the team's recommendations? What if they simply do not make the connections?

For starters, it's better to know at this stage versus further down the line. Imagine the pain of realizing the disconnect at a later stage like a decision point (Workflow #13). It's better to go back to the drawing board now and do an iteration of the exploration. The team needs to know what specifically was missing. Was there a blind spot? Is the blind spot confirmed or one that needs to be validated? What are the implications of the blind spot?

## DRIVING DECISIONS

As we've shared in Chapter 6, decisions come down to specific *actions* a company is willing to commit. On the heels of alignment, a team can prepare for the actions they will be proposing. The alignment allows the team to define these details. Without this level of buy-in, planning would be premature. Connect decisions to the work behind them to make the decisions stick. Imagine the power of proposing these decisions with the work that has preceded. The audience for these decisions will be able to see the entire flow of exploration, conclusions, and recommendations. Decision Sprint provides a way to accomplish this. (See Figure 7.13.)

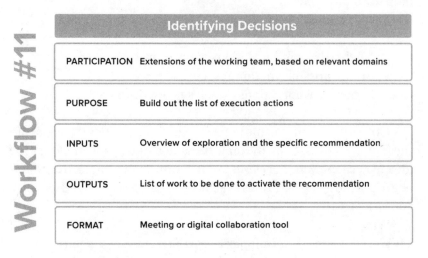

**FIGURE 7.13** Workflow #11: Identifying decisions

When it comes to identifying decisions, tap the people closest to day-to-day execution. Convene them to suggest actions for each recommendation. Let's say there is buy-in around a recommended feature of a new product. Before meeting with decision makers, the team will want to gather specifics like the timing, cost, and a more specific business case. Decisions typically involve resources, timelines, road maps, policies, and customer messaging.

A good way to accomplish this is to extend the circle of participation. For each recommendation, canvas the people who would drive the execution. Give thought to execution against the recommendations. Who would be involved? Share recommendations to gather input on the necessary actions. Remember, a decision is nothing more than a commitment to necessary actions. To identify decisions, figure out what actions unlock execution.

# PREPARING FOR DECISIONS

Content is the hero when preparing for decision-making meetings. You can source it from the exploration phase of Decision Sprint. Content matters because decision-making forums are very binary. They need to conclude with "yes" or "no" concerning a list of decisions. There's not enough time to explain the many layers of context. And yet decision makers need to follow the trail of how a team works through matters to arrive at recommendations and their underlying decisions (the actions that make sense to take if the recommendation is deemed sound). Content is the most effective way to do this. (See Figure 7.14.)

**Workflow #12**

| Preparing Content | |
|---|---|
| PARTICIPATION | Several core working team members + project sponsor |
| PURPOSE | Develop succinct background materials to set the table for decision-making |
| INPUTS | Exploration content + recommendations that have been aligned + actions list |
| OUTPUTS | FAQ document, narrative document, or presentation |
| FORMAT | Digital collaboration tool + review meetings |

**FIGURE 7.14** Workflow #12: Preparing content

Pulling content together can come in a variety of forms including:

- FAQ is perhaps the most efficient format because it's text-based and mainly a list of questions and answers organized by theme. Because our explorations consist of matters, think about grouping matters into a common theme.
- Narrative offers the short-story version of the problem being explored and investigation of the key matters organized into a business-case type format. That means an introduction,

explanation of the key issues, options, solutions, and recommendations. The narrative takes more work than an FAQ because it introduces the need for writing skills, such as organizing the flow of information, writing transitions, and creating a single cohesive document.

- Presentation. I'm a huge fan of the visual representation of concepts, mental models, and frameworks. As a great shortcut to communication, you should evaluate if you can generate a few key visuals to illustrate concepts. But presentations are not great for the written word. That's why I'd rather produce or consume FAQs with built-in visual representations of information. A full-blown presentation is not ideal for decision-making.

- Demos are the best representation of what a team may be proposing to do for a customer or to solve a problem—particularly for digital products. I recommend using a demo if your team can present it in real time. You need to pair the demo with the right context on exploration and the recommendations coming out of it.

## CONDUCTING DECISION MEETINGS

Decision-making forums vary by the size of an organization. For a larger company, the audience of decision makers may be entirely different than the functional leaders who've had the benefit of alignment. If that's not the case, you can think of decision meetings as a follow-up with the same audience that has been through the alignment process with the working team.

Whether it's the first meeting with the audience or a follow-up, a decision meeting goes further than a meeting focused on alignment.

These meetings get down to concrete "yes" or "no" on specific decisions. Execution directly follows these decision points. When decisions are approved, people start to take actions by a wider set of the organization. Resources are committed, people may be hired, and project plans roll into motion.

Decision meetings need to follow an efficient format, as the highest-level stakeholders in companies typically have a vast plate. (See Figure 7.15.) Decision meetings for senior executives may cover several different initiatives. Your team could be just one item on the agenda. A working team may have just 15 to 30 minutes to cover a lot of ground. This includes starting with any clarifications about the exploration and recommendations (this content is typically shared in advance—though not always). The meat of the dialogue typically is about the decisions themselves, rather than the recommendations, which are at a higher level. Because the working team has conducted alignment, the chances of the recommendations being on target is much higher.

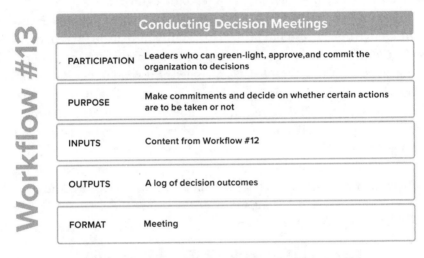

**Workflow #13**

**Conducting Decision Meetings**

| | |
|---|---|
| PARTICIPATION | Leaders who can green-light, approve, and commit the organization to decisions |
| PURPOSE | Make commitments and decide on whether certain actions are to be taken or not |
| INPUTS | Content from Workflow #12 |
| OUTPUTS | A log of decision outcomes |
| FORMAT | Meeting |

**FIGURE 7.15**  Workflow #13: Conducting decision meetings

When it comes to decision-making, the audience seeks to understand each decision and help fine-tune the specifics. For example, a recommendation on the scope of a new product may be approved in terms of key features and capabilities. When deciding on the budget to make these happen, the group may want to vet the numbers further. Before committing, the audience may want to see what could be done with less money or stage the commitment in some way.

Decisions often involve trade-offs above and beyond the project. An idea may be very compelling, yet the funds need to come from somewhere. You can expect a group of senior leaders to discuss in real time the trade-off possibilities from much higher levels than the remit of the working team. This is a good dynamic because it means things are getting awfully close to commitment.

The best possible outcome in a decision meeting is when leadership transitions into a mode of linking to more significant decisions they need to make to support specific decisions your team may be proposing. Sorting these higher-level dependencies are how leaders seek to support your work. They may not get resolved in a 30-minute strategic briefing and decision meeting on your initiative. But when leaders take ownership of these higher-level dependencies, they are doing their part to pave the way for execution. These are some of the best meetings you will experience as a working team. It's when each level of the company contributes at its highest impact. With Decision Sprint, we enable the most senior leaders in a company to be in this zone.

Catalog the outcome of each recommendation and the underlying decisions as part of the decision meeting. Recall from Chapter 6, a proposal may have several decisions packaged with it. That's because several actions could be required to follow a particular recommendation. When decision meetings end, everyone has to be on the same page. Which decisions were approved? Which were fine-tuned and how so? Which are conditionally approved pending resolving another dependency? When will that take place and who owns it? And what about decisions that are not approved? What are the reasons?

## CONTINUOUS EXPLORATION

There's one more opportunity to leverage a gathering of decision-makers. After the current decisions have been sorted, give a preview to the next exploration. Explain the next fork in the road the team may be spending time on and examples of matters that would be part of it. This creates an ongoing appetite for explorations. After successfully deliberation on the current fork in the road, provide visibility on the next one.

Doing so roots behaviors. We are training the organization to connect the dots between living in the upstream (building exploration) and benefiting downstream when the time for decision-making comes. Continuous exploration is the heart of decision-making. Good decisions start with exploration. These are more than slogans. They come alive in the workflow.

# Tap Workflows to Express Culture

This chapter will show you how to pair the workflows of Decision Sprint with taglines. Taglines are like shorthand communication that represent the meaning of the workflows and their value to the organization. The combination of workflows with this form of communication is a powerful mover of culture.

*Culture* is an ambiguous term, often boiling down to slogans that represent ambition more than day-to-day reality. Decision Sprint takes the opposite approach. It starts with workflows that bring out the best in the organization. It uses these workflows to impact the day-to-day experience of employees. It's my contention that employee experience is the real indicator of any culture. That's why Decision Sprint does so much of the heavy lifting for culture. It's rooted in workflows, not words.

## THE WORKFLOW LEXICON

Speaking of words, in this section I provide a set of taglines leaders can use to move a culture in the right direction. Because the workflows back them up, they are not empty ambitions. As employees adopt the related workflows, these taglines will summarize the desired behaviors and mindsets. They are shorthand expressions to capture the spirit of the underlying workflow. You are likely to see the taglines become part of company language. Common language is a real asset because it can speed up understanding. Pair workflows and taglines for accelerated shifts in company culture. If you're a newer company, this is a great opportunity to establish rituals and behaviors. You have the luxury of building the right culture from the start.

Let's look at some taglines, their meanings, and the workflows that reinforce them.

## Workflow #1:
## Initiation (of the Exploration)

**Frame the Problem** is how to talk about concepts such as "identify what to solve for," "put words to the core challenge," "simplify this huge opportunity into what matters," "what will make or break our success," and similar nudges to distill problem-solving. At the initiation stage, we want to bring out the challenge of the problem-solving effort. Framing a problem statement that brings out the ambiguity of the central challenge or opportunity is key.

**Exploration Before Alignment** is shorthand for "don't rush to opinions," "seek to understand first," "suspend judgment," "don't be a know-it-all," and similar nudges to avoid closed mindsets. With a problem statement in hand, it's critical to anchor the value of exploration and how people will approach it at the initiation stage. A good problem statement will make people grasp the need for exploration. That's why both these taglines complement each other.

## Workflow #1:
## Initiation (of the Working Team)

**Group People Around Challenges** is shorthand for "build the brain trust," "break silos," "empower the team," "gather the right know-how," "focus on contribution over position," and similar nudges to assemble the appropriate competencies based on the problem being solved.

As we're forming teams, we can design them around the people most able to contribute to addressing our problem statement(s). We avoid bloated teams and participants just for the sake of it. The general rule of thumb is Amazon's "2-pizza" team (two pizzas should be enough to feed the team).

## Workflows #2 and #3:
## Sourcing Input for Exploration

**Input Obsession** motivates us to "avoid blind spots," "surface the right matters," "tap into the power of clarifying questions," "ask why five times," "source diverse perspectives," and similar nudges to canvass a problem statement with the right breadth and depth.

**Embrace Unknowns** comprises "get out of the comfort zone," "identify what needs to be understood," "learn and be curious," "don't be frightened not to know the answer," and similar nudges to promote a learning mindset.

Sourcing input deserves space and is often shortchanged as we rush to create solutions and plans. By now, you can see it's hugely valuable to properly canvass a problem statement, and getting people to see the value of inputs to create better outputs is essential.

## Workflows #4 and #5:
## Calibrating and Sharing the Exploration

**Preview the Work** captures "what road is the team headed down," "how has the problem been framed," "show us the canvas," "provide the thought process," "share the inputs that were gathered," and similar nudges to promote early alignment. Workflows #5 and #6 are where we can share a meaningful milestone—the exploration canvas—and start to build understanding and trust with sponsors. When we preview the "work to be done" and sponsors agree, the tables are being set for future interactions.

**Calibration over Control** is a tagline most synonymous with my leadership track record. It suggests a way of engaging with teams that is active yet still provides autonomy. You will hear more about it in

Chapter 10, but let me introduce the idea. In this new world, leaders need to think about team enablement. Enabling teams is not a passive exercise for leaders. It doesn't devalue leadership work. Let's say a team is asked to develop a plan for a new idea or solve a new problem space. Leaders play a role in actively shaping inputs the team is sourcing and the conclusions being drawn from these inputs. I refer to this as calibration. In a calibration model, a leader doesn't wait for finalized thinking to provide feedback. By then it's too late to calibrate whether the right inputs have been collected to canvass the problem. When calibration goes well, it provides leaders with evidence to provide teams with space. With this space, teams can run ahead with deeper work. In a control model, a leader may share the objective and wait for well-baked plans to be presented. That leaves a ton of problem-solving activity in the middle. As executive reviews near, teams feel they need to have the "answers." Tolerance for ambiguity shrinks. Expectations for answers are high as time elapses. It can lead to micromanagement.

## Workflows #6 and #7:
### Answering Questions and Calibrating Answers

**Dive Deep** frames "get into the messy unknowns," "do great detective work," "jump into the deep end and make sense of it," and similar nudges to develop a firm grasp of the underlying matters. It's no wonder this tagline is one of Amazon's leadership principles. You often feel overwhelmed when starting to get into hairy details. When the puzzle begins to come together, the rate of progress picks up quickly. My goal for teams is they have a strong command of the problem or opportunity they've been exploring and that is a direct outcome of diving deep.

## Workflows #8 and #9:
### Drawing Conclusions and Preparing for Alignment

**Show the Breadcrumbs** is shorthand for "connect what was explored to what is being recommended," "draw the line of thinking," "show the work," and similar nudges to make alignment less subjective and more based on objective exploration.

**Content Matters** reframes "prepare succinct content," "put time into documenting what was learned," "provide a thoughtful narrative," and similar nudges to promote translating upstream work into easy-to-follow information. Sponsors and executives have limited time. And this requires teams to think about their audience. It's essential to make information consumable and express it as puzzle pieces that fit together. I'm a big fan of FAQs as a form of content. Less a fan when it comes to PowerPoint for decision-making. Well-constructed illustrations, visuals, infographics, or tables are a great complement to FAQs.

## Workflow #10:
## Conducting Alignment

**Make It a Binary** is shorthand for "put a stake in the ground," "take a stand one way or another," "what does your gut tell you," and similar nudges to cut through where people stand and why. A forcing function helps get a pure signal from the people involved. Tapping into the raw instincts of the people involved is essential to surface. It helps us isolate where there is common understanding and where it's missing. We need a heat map of where the level of agreement on an important recommendation is falling short, so we can have dialogue around it.

## Workflow #11:
## Identifying Decisions

**Socialize Knowledge to Grow It** denotes "start thinking about execution," "make the rounds," "grow and build on what we know," "expand circles to the next layer of input," and similar nudges to surface relevant actions once a direction is set.

This tagline helps build on knowledge coming out of exploration. Rather than being satisfied with high-level recommendations, it's important to identify detailed actions once these recommendations are aligned. This often requires expanding the circle of people involved to those closer to execution (e.g., in the field or operations). By making the rounds, we uncover new details on what it takes to execute and be able to refine our recommendations or direction for the better.

### Workflows #12 and #13:
### Preparing for and Conducting Decision Meetings

**Commit to Action** encapsulates "be all in," "avoid second-guessing," "take ownership," and similar nudges to look ahead, not backward once a decision is made. We spend time on the upstream to confront the unknowns and make sense of them. Once we transition from upstream to downstream, all the energy should go to execution. Second-guessing based on personal agendas over the substance of the work is a nonstarter. It's toxic and should never be tolerated.

## THE ROLE OF LEADERS

This is a taxonomy of upstream work. Of course, downstream work needs to be motivated as well (it typically comes in the form of accountability for results). Culture should speak to both realms. If you're reading this book, I'm guessing your organization has more work to do motivating excellence upstream. It would be powerful to combine what works to promote today's downstream performance with some of the upstream taglines.

How can leaders roll these out? Let's talk about the micro and macro here. At the micro level, it's about using the meetings and interactions with team members to role model. For example, if a project is recently initiated, and the problem statement is being defined, nudge people back from opinions on the answer. Carry the mantra of "exploration before alignment."

One of my favorites is "socialize knowledge to grow it." This is an important reminder once teams and their sponsors have aligned. They agree on the recommended direction and the mutual understanding behind it. What typically happens at this stage is complacency. Teams can see the approvals on the horizon. But it's not the time to stop. Consulting with the next layer of collaborators, the people closest to execution, will help translate recommendations into potential actions. This action list is necessary for the decision stages. By socializing knowledge, the team makes the leap from recommendations to detailed actions.

At the macro level, there are opportunities to share leadership principles in the course of providing business and strategy updates. Let's say initiatives are highlighted in various company forums. Leaders can cherry-pick one or two cultural ingredients that a team role models exceptionally well. Highlight the project wins and build in the cultural wins as well.

I invite you as a leader to pick a few of the taglines and embrace them as part of your personal brand. Which ones resonate the most? Which ones call you? Which would impact the company the most? Here's where company needs and your professional growth intertwine. The world needs more upstream leaders. How are you showing up to be the kind of leader the world needs?

# Hack Today's System

In this chapter, I will situate the workflows you've just learned about with typical processes and meeting types we find in companies. I'm sure you are curious how Decision Sprint works with brainstorms, deep dives, and review meetings that are today's norms. Workflows are a great way to think about streamlining meetings and what meetings get replaced or migrated to asynchronous work. Asynchronous work takes place when team members can effectively collaborate without the need for meeting. We'll talk more about that in the chapter on digital tools.

My promise is there will *be fewer and more effective meetings* for everyone at all levels. I know many of you will appreciate this. We're talking about making more progress in half the time. But it's much bigger. It's about orchestrating milestones with calm, instead of constant drama and painful twists, as a team navigates milestones related to decisions, getting people on board, and approvals. Most of this chapter spells out how to use Decision Sprint to navigate milestones in this way. You can apply Decision Sprint to navigate milestones across any big bet, innovation effort, strategic initiative, or problem-solving activity. (See Figure 9.1.)

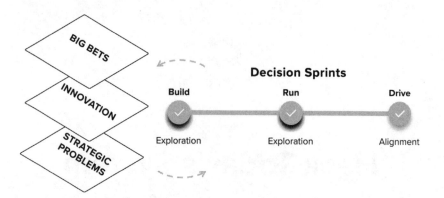

**FIGURE 9.1**   Where Decision Sprint is a game-changer for business

We will address eight common meeting types:

- Kickoffs
- Brainstorms
- Planning
- Early project reviews
- Deep dives
- Ongoing project reviews
- Strategy sessions
- Executive reviews

## LET'S TALK FLOW STATE

Decision Sprint makes this possible because it places your project in a flow state. You may have read about the flow state for humans. What is the flow state for projects or team-based problem-solving? It comes back to unknowns. Once you initiate a project, the clock on expectations starts to tick. As more time elapses in the initiative, we expect to reduce uncertainty and tackle unknowns.

At the kickoff, we expect the unknowns to be high. After a few weeks, the team is expected to have pieced together a direction. We expect more clarity with time. The ratio of knowns to unknowns needs to increase quite a bit. And this expectation continues to build for each milestone (e.g., phase of a project). By the time of an alignment session, we expect polished answers from the collaboration efforts of the team.

But what if the rate of moving things from unknowns to knowns doesn't match the expectations of the milestone? The milestone may have a particular label, like "finalize project strategy" or "review content for the steering committee," and these labels (often referred to as "gates" in project management lingo) carry expectations. The rate of moving unknowns to knowns needs to keep up. Otherwise the labels we give to the milestones of the project are just ideals. It's a sign the underlying activities (workflows) didn't deliver. Teams know when this is happening but don't have a language for it. They experience anxiety, stress, fear, and frustration. When in flow, each step builds momentum for the next. The pace of moving from unknowns to knowns is keeping up with expectations. The team's emotions are safety, confidence, motivation, and trust. I measure flow by the pace at which disambiguating the problem, or solving for unknowns, is happening. If you've worked on projects or major problem-solving activities in a company, you will probably nod in agreement.

The right workflows should produce a flow state. Otherwise, they are just impostors, steps on a chart that don't help and that mislead. We've all been there. The milestones look good on paper, as does self-reported status, but the reality is less confident.

## Today's Meetings

Let's discover how to experience momentum that comes in a flow state. It starts with the meetings you might already have. You probably have these types of meetings: kickoffs, brainstorms, planning, deep dives, project updates, strategy sessions, and steering committees. Your process may not include all these meeting types, but they likely include many. In this chapter, I will share how to improve these meetings with the workflows of Decision Sprint and how to achieve a flow state. I will demonstrate how Decision Sprint both streamlines and makes them smarter.

# THE KICKOFF

Most projects feature a kickoff. This is where a team is looking to clarify its purpose and get organized. You can use Workflow #1 as a guide for the kickoff. The main difference between what most teams do and Workflow #1 is:

- Agreeing upon a concise problem statement (which we've elaborated on in Chapter 4) gets the team in a discovery mindset, elevating their thoughts to unknowns rather than known commodities.
- We provide an overview of the overall process to get from uncertainty and ambiguity to concrete recommendations and direction. In Workflow #1, we introduce the end-to-end aspects of Decision Sprint. It's a map of how the team will navigate the unknowns.

The problem statement could lead to some "OMG, how will we tackle this?" moments as our brains instinctively flood with meaningful and relevant uncertainties. Decision Sprint is the detailed step-by-step way to deal with the messy pile of unknowns that come along with kicking off new and meaningful projects. *It creates space for them.*

With a layout of upstream work (exploration, alignment, and decision-making), the team can see a potential way forward at a high level. Don't miss the chance for this powerful one-two combo to set a high bar for problem-solving and while providing a map for navigating the process.

When Workflow #1 has been executed, we've set similar expectations with the senior levels of the company. At multiple levels of the company, we should consistently explain how project exploration fits into the picture of creating alignment and driving decisions.

The absence of this can leave a team with mixed feelings. Teams often leave kickoffs with fear or concern about the magnitude of what needs to be solved. It can feel like a mountain, which instantly places us out of flow state. It doesn't have to be that way. You can be in flow state knowing there is complexity and uncertainty ahead, provided the methods are there to enable the team.

Here's what you should do differently:

- Review the problem statement and recognize the degree of unknowns
- Provide an overall view of upstream work (exploration, alignment, decision-making)

# BRAINSTORMS

By now, you know exploration is the first phase of Decision Sprint. In this section, I will explain how to effectively use a brainstorm to build out an exploration.

One common pitfall of a loosely defined brainstorm is expectations. Everyone is on a different page regarding "where things stand" and therefore what needs to be brainstormed. So the question is, what are we brainstorming? Where does our exploration stand?

Workflows #3 and #4 make clear what is being brainstormed.

We've all been in these shoes. A brainstorm wavers among solutions, uncovering issues that need to be understood, trying to understand them, and drawing conclusions. That's a lot to load on a brainstorm—we come out with a mix. The team may not be able to do an adequate job. Maybe some creative options are missed because that kind of brainstorming got pulled into the weeds. There may be some preconceived notions about barriers, which may be surmountable. A list of essential considerations was not fully developed because the team went into a deep dive on one of them—the "rabbit hole," so to speak. Maybe understanding a vital consideration was shortchanged because the room accepted a conclusion without allowing space for it.

That can lead to confusion, weak links, and conflicting understanding. The typical solution: schedule another brainstorm!

How do we avoid these pitfalls? How do we error-correct loosely defined brainstorms? How do we create a mind meld so that our working team is not so divergent on what kind of brainstorming they are doing in their minds?

Here's the first tip. Avoid the pitfall of vacillating between building an exploration and running it. What's the difference? Building an exploration is about calibrating what needs to be explored (breadth and depth, as you've learned about in Chapter 4). Running an exploration is about filling in the canvas and answering questions. These are incompatible in a single setting.

They shouldn't mix. A more purposeful approach is to break them into two distinct steps. That's why brainstorms to *build exploration* (Workflows #2 and #3) come before brainstorms to *run explorations* (Workflows #6 and #7).

If a team holds a single meeting to source matters and questions, the input should come in that order. Brainstorm Workflow #2, and then move on to Workflow #3. If you can do both in a single session, don't shortchange the time allotted. Plan for 90 to 120 minutes.

A good step following Workflows #2 and #3 is sharing with sponsors. Do that rather than moving directly from a brainstorm to build exploration to *actually* running the exploration.Between building the exploration and running it, is a good opportunity for sharing.

### Conducting the Input Brainstorm

As we discussed earlier, sourcing the right matters and questions is key to building exploration. Matters describe the breadth of a problem, and questions are a way to go deep on each matter.

A typical brainstorm or design thinking workshop format would be appropriate. That's one where participants use sticky notes to jot down their ideas individually, and the group-level discussion takes place to elaborate these ideas in the collective. Similar suggestions are clustered, surprising suggestions are explored, and patterns are observed. From there, the participants develop a list of the top suggested matters (and later questions for each matter). It's collective work. Participants understand how the list was arrived at because they were part of the process and saw it unfold.

As you will read about in Chapter 12 on digital tools, we have several ways to accomplish the brainstorm without having to hold a meeting. Digital tools provide us the means to source input and collect suggestions faster and more efficiently. There will still be the opportunity for gathering people to review the collective input, while giving team members more time and flexibility to provide their perspectives.

Change leaders from the very top, such as Kelly Campbell, know it's vital to move beyond getting credit and cast a wide net for sourcing and vetting ideas. Kelly said:

> 66 I appreciate people who have no fear of their idea getting counted as someone else's idea or of another team taking it and doing something with it. In sourcing input, it's clearly important to ask good questions and listen. It's also important to throw out ideas for others to react to. This is a great way to gather feedback and perspective that can further shape your thinking. There is value in doing this with obvious sources of information—people on your team or in your industry, as well as those that may not always feel so obvious—people outside of your company or industry altogether.
>
> In my view, the people who tend to move ideas forward into tangible plans and outcomes are those who take an open approach to sourcing input, who share their best ideas with belief that this will help the idea. That to me is part of the process of building ideas that drive change and value. 99

Digital tools make it easier to cast a wider net (and you'll learn about that in Chapter 12).

---

**Here's what you should do differently:**

- **Move away from chaotic brainstorming.**
- **Do this by clarifying the input the team needs given the stage of the exploration. Canvass the breadth and depth of the exploration (build the exploration) in a dedicated session. Stop short of developing answers and drawing conclusions.**

---

## PLANNING MEETINGS

A working team relies on a few key people to coordinate the overall work plan. Coming out of a brainstorm, this typically comes in the form of summarizing meeting notes and creating a list of action items.

It's a list of who's accountable for what. Decision Sprint enables planners to know if the collection of inputs is adequate enough to proceed.

The measure is one of precision and completeness. If the brainstorm hasn't done a great job of sourcing input in terms of breadth and depth, follow-up actions will suffer. For example, suppose a colleague raised a matter in a way that is not neutral. There's already a bias, so the follow-up action (exploration) won't give it a fair shake. The exploration of the matter may confirm the initial bias. Perhaps clarifying questions (as a way to go deep) were shortchanged. Sourcing input is such a rare window to activate curiosity and bring out the contours of each matter.

There's a sinking feeling when you're planning an initiative and the substance seems lacking after looking at notes from the brainstorm (or the pictures of it we take on the phone). The team makes a dent into the exploration, but it still feels shallow, incomplete, and at risk of blind spots.

What do good planners do in this case? They reassemble and reflect. If a brainstorm has been too chaotic and hasn't hit the mark, the best move for core planners is to place the current outputs into the exploration framework and rerun the workflows as a more structured brainstorm. Explain or introduce the method to the team so they can help fill in the gaps efficiently. You might prompt the team in a direct fashion. "We have only a partial list of the key matters to explore. What other considerations make sense? What could go wrong that we need to grasp? What are the risks? What do we need to solve for to make things go well?" Build out the breadth of the problem statement in terms of matters. Then go deeper on each one through clarifying questions.

Planners also have the role of scrubbing input from the working team. After brainstorming, the work of planning is to prepare the team for deep dives. A brainstorm is great, but it often produces a messy list of matters and questions. Matters may be duplicates or need some wording refinement to clarify their meaning. Questions could be on the right track but need similar refinements. Workflow #5 provides for all of this and covers the task of assigning questions.

As part of assigning collaborators to investigate each matter, it's important to ask who in the organization can lend a meaningful perspective. An organization has an entire pool of people who could be knowledgeable or enthusiastic about a specific matter. We certainly cannot make a working team so large that it gets bureaucratic. But we can identify extended collaborators to include on particular matters. It's a more specific level of involvement, like a guest you invite over.

Workflow #6 helps us socialize the current exploration with senior stakeholders. Before going too far with the plan for exploration, we have a round of calibration with the executive layer. I will elaborate on that in the executive review section.

---

**Here's what you should do differently:**

- **Convert brainstorm content into exploration content using the matters and questions framework.**
- **Adjust timelines if the exploration appears incomplete and use workflows to fill in gaps.**

---

## EARLY PROJECT REVIEWS

It's likely a working team holds regular check-ins on the project status. A typical cadence is biweekly or weekly. If the project or parts of the project are upstream (not yet moved to execution), it's typically very hard to ascertain the status. It could be along the lines of "the teams are meeting to understand the issues better." In the best cases, it may be expressed as "we are deep diving on topics *A, B, C.*"

But what's underneath the hood?

### AVOIDING WATERFALL INTERACTIONS

**Interview with Clarice Strong, former VP of Strategic Initiatives, MGM Resorts**

A huge pitfall is that top management often lacks a way to calibrate exploration before the team runs ahead. In other words, transparency into how exploration has been built is necessary even before the exploration can be effectively run. In our interview, here is what Clarice Strong has to say about the subject:

*What should happen in the initial exploration phase is gathering inputs, and sharing them.*

That process is so broken at most companies. Often teams work for two to four weeks at a time in a vacuum. They do all their analysis and thoughtful work and then spend lots of time creating a bunch of slides and putting together recommendations into a pretty deck. Then they go sit in a stuffy conference room with the senior leadership team and begin the process of getting executives on the same page. It's incredibly difficult because the team has one meeting to convince a bunch of leaders on the recommendations in a single hour. Any monkey wrench that is introduced, let's say a blind spot, can set the team back. The rework can add weeks.

As Clarice points out, sharing is beneficial for all levels of the organization.

*It goes both ways. The senior leadership group doesn't have transparency into what's going on in this broader workstream while it's in process, like before [a major steering review] meeting happens. And the team doesn't have transparency to the evolving perspectives of the leadership group. The solution must be to create a steady state of transparency and create a mechanism for decision-makers to inject input throughout the process.*

With Decision Sprint, we know exactly what the matters are, and how they are being explored (via the questions). It's easy for teams to share status through these building blocks. Whether that's a numeric value, progress bar, or some other visualization, it's more precise and clearer where things stand. The matters and questions allow us to share exploration status in early project reviews. They give us real texture for work in progress.

> **Here's what you should do differently:**
> - **Report on exploration status using the building blocks of matters, questions, and answers.**
> - **Survey the team for data on the quality of these building blocks.**

# DEEP DIVES

Deep dives at the team level often start with creating smaller teams to investigate specific matters. A relevant matter was raised in the brainstorm, and now it's time to understand it better. At this point, hopefully, the matter has been curated so that the underlying questions are neutral (not leaning negative or positive).

Recall that the core planning team is charged with going matter by matter to identify potential collaborators for each. It's not practical to hold a deep dive for each matter, so they will likely be grouped into key themes. Include the extended collaborators in the deep dives where they fit best.

Neutral questions are a team's best friend in a deep dive. They help us rework assumptions or hypotheses that are limited or biased. Starting with neutral questions, allows deep dive participants to channel their contribution quickly. Because of their expertise and knowledge, they can reason through questions quickly.

Neutral questions also help us avoid coming to conclusions too soon during a deep dive. As leaders, we've been on the receiving end of a deep dive where the team did not give a fair shake to the possibilities. What's possible becomes what is easy. That will not support the organization's growth ambitions or potential. Going deep means going deep into the question-and-answer process.

Deep dives are also a place for creative problem-solving. Bringing together a core group that has a great deal of so much perspective can spawn new ways for improving existing processes or operations.

Deep dives may need to spin off some action items of their own. For example, the group may want to initiate test-and-learn activities. This is a great step when things are not obvious, and a test takes low to moderate effort. When the answer is "it depends" and we can construct a test to inform a hypothesis, it's often worth it.

The implication of testing is that deep dive work is layered. It may not be completed in a single session. Some aspects of the deep dive may take a few weeks to complete based on the testing activities.

---

**Here's what you should do differently:**

- **Start with neutral questions, and use them to go deep on key matters.**

- **Include guests to avoid blind spots and fill in knowledge gaps.**

# ONGOING PROJECT REVIEWS

As project exploration hits high gear, team members conduct deep dives, answer questions, and pursue tests or supporting data.

A typical biweekly project review calls for an update on how things are going. The key is to build from the exploration canvas that was built and socialized with executives earlier. What's different in Decision Sprint is the transparency of where the owners for various matters stand in bringing clarity. Imagine seeing a list of completed FAQs (answers to questions organized by matter). It's like seeing a picture get filled in. This goes beyond status. Knowledge and insight are being socialized. When that happens, we make it easier for the group to achieve mutual understanding. Everyone is working from the same insights and working knowledge. Don't lose the opportunity to embrace this game-changing project review approach.

---

**Here's what you should do differently:**

- **Shift from status readouts to concrete knowledge sharing.**
- **Level up the working knowledge of the team at every opportunity.**

---

# STRATEGY SESSIONS

Gathering a working team to develop the direction of a project is often referred to as a strategy session. It's when there is enough information to start drawing conclusions and recommendations.

One problem is not treating this as a discrete step (meeting or interaction). Often teams rush to prepare presentable materials for an executive review, and one or two members take a lead on a deck. There's nothing wrong with a lead or two. The issue is by the time they produce a packaged draft of the strategy, it can be hard to unpack. It's better to avoid packaging before collecting raw suggestions. We're referring to suggested conclusions that draw upon a completed exploration. And it's essential to run that process in a collaborative session to get a wide lens on conclusions and derive some alignment data.

How does this save time? A crack in alignment will show up later. There will be many side meetings to address missing consensus. Alignment within the working team will speed up by conducting Workflow #8, as the working team is often representative of everyone else.

After discussion has allowed the working team to converge on recommendations, the time is appropriate to move ahead on content preparation and packaging.

---

**Here's what you should do differently:**

- **Use Workflow #8 in a dedicated session of the working team to derive recommendations based on exploration.**
- **Avoid packaging the "answer" too early, as it could lead to weak links and restarting the effort.**

---

## EXECUTIVE REVIEWS

We may think the primary purpose of time with executives is to achieve buy-in, commitment, and decisions. We want approval for strategic direction, funding, resources, and execution plans. Don't shortchange the role of upstream interactions that can help move a project from ideas to action.

When a project team has time with executives, there are one of three purposes:

1. Previewing (which we've already covered)
2. Strategic alignment—Workflow #10
3. Decision-making—Workflow #13

Let's start with meetings to align on recommendations. This interaction should include both the exploration work and the team's recommendations. What's different is the team spends far less time showing "how you got there." Start by recapping the exploration canvas (matters and questions). It's a recap of where things were left in the prior interaction. Then flow through workflows where recommendations are presented and linked to the exploration content (completed FAQs).

There will be less time on "show us the work behind the recommendations," and "show us how you got here," and "take me through the thought process." What will replace it?

It's the strategic dialogue. It's fine-tuning of recommendations to improve them or racing ahead to supportive actions like dependencies these executives can address.

Depending on how available executives may be, a team may need to share recommendations and decision-making information in one review. A single interaction may need to cover the strategic alignment and the decision-making. Ideally these are spaced out. With alignment on recommendations, the team will go about preparing decisions (Workflow #12) and come back to the next executive review with those details as well as a related execution plan.

When this time comes, the team should be ready to meet the action orientation of the executives. Executives will be in that mode as they have already strategically aligned. Context can be recapped in a pre-read or in a document that's reviewed at the start of the meeting. The team should be ready to start with concrete actions grouped by recommendation. The audience will seek to understand each decision and help fine-tune the specifics. Detailed decisions are part of Workflow #13. That's what makes it different. We don't leave executive decision-making sessions with ambiguity. The actions should be able to roll.

---

**Here's what you should do differently:**

- **Start previewing exploration with senior leaders before it's launched but after it's been built. This will create prealignment.**

- **Draw connections between recommendations being made in an executive review and the exploration content that is the basis to reduce the "show me how you got here" dynamic.**

- **A good practice for decision meetings is to catalog the outcome of each recommendation and the underlying decisions.**

---

# EXAMPLES

Let's zoom out to the big picture.

We've reviewed how Decision Sprint workflows fit with various meetings that are common in projects or initiatives. Let's take a few examples at how Decision Sprint workflows can power milestones.

## Example 1: Workflows Power Alignment

Figure 9.2 is a use case for how Workflows #2 to #5 can feed a milestone like an alignment meeting.

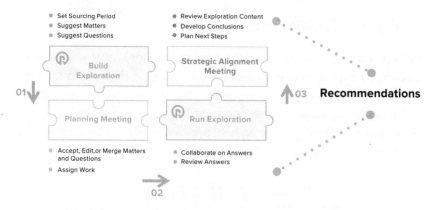

**FIGURE 9.2** Build and run exploration to feed alignment

The first box is a brainstorm to source input for the exploration. The second box is the work of a small planning group to organize the inputs from the brainstorm into action. They prepare the exploration. The third box is running the exploration. These workflows will power a milestone such as a project review with key stakeholders, as shown in the fourth box.

If we know the alignment meeting is coming up in a month, we can work backward to be prepared.

How so?

Work backward from the milestone with a reasonable lead time for each step of the workflow. A few days for sourcing input, a few days for organizing it, and a week or more to run the exploration. Include some buffer beyond that to convene the working team with the completed exploration to determine the key findings or conclusions or recommendations they will want to make in the review.

Teams often need to work backward from milestone dates determined by executive calendars. But it's not always like that. The executives might ask the team when they will be ready for such an interaction. Use this opportunity to meet based on lead time. Consider the lead time of key workflows to determine the timing.

This milestone is one that a team can enter with confidence knowing that the sequence of activities worked in their favor. It will produce the best possible ground to stand on.

## Example 2: Socializing an Exploration

Let's take another example. In this case, we are looking to socialize an upcoming exploration with executives, knowing that weeks later we will delve into recommendations coming from this exercise. Again, in this case, no answers or recommendations are provided. It's simply a canvas of the exploration. It's a preview of where the team will be spending time and energy. (See Figure 9.3).

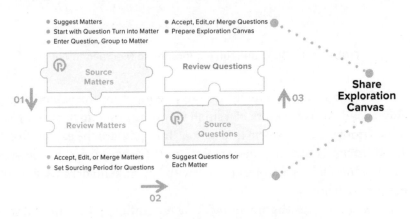

**FIGURE 9.3** Build and share exploration

It starts by sourcing matters. If input comes in the form of a question, ask the person suggesting the question to group it to the matter its referring to. After allowing a period of time for the suggestion of matters, it's a good idea to review the list for duplicates. It's then time to source questions. Ideally, the team will suggest enough questions for each matter. If not, another iteration to source questions can be run with a focus on matters where there is not confidence in the question list. After completing this flow (See Figure 9.3), it's time to preview the exploration. Bring together the problem statement, breadth and depth of the exploration as defined by matters and questions, and expected delivery date for completion into a single view.

I am a huge fan of working backward with workflows to power milestones. Every company is a little different, but we can reach milestones with smarter and more streamlined collaboration with the right workflows.

---

**Here's what you should do different:**

- Tap into the opportunity to share an exploration once it's built for pre-alignment.

- Work backward from milestones. Use these workflows to orchestrate your milestones with greater simplicity and ease.

---

# Roles and Personas

I hope in this chapter you will find your role and persona represented. Most people can describe their role in an organization. A persona is more nebulous.

A persona is more than a list of responsibilities. It defines how you show up in your role. It's how you see your purpose and choose to act and behave to fulfill that purpose.

I've held multiple personas in my career, as I've evolved from a team leader known for innovation to an operational C-suite executive and now a board member of public companies.

I've also interacted with every persona in my work, from enforcers of existing norms to free-spirited thinkers who can struggle to find rhythm in a broader company culture. This brings me to the topic of personal growth. Any new methodology is an opportunity for personal growth, especially if it provides one of the key success factors for managers in the emerging era.

Decision Sprint provides a way to move initiatives along better while also growing the individual. That's why it is a win-win system. After reflecting on various archetypes, I will share how your persona taps into Decision Sprint for personal development. I'm so excited about the potential Decision Sprint holds for the individual.

# STARTING WITH ROLES

Let's start with a discussion of roles and how they relate to Decision Sprint. I hope to clarify how your role can reap new benefits from Decision Sprint and help your organization in the process.

For simplicity, a key initiative will usually have three groups of roles:

**C-level.** The most senior level of the company, responsible for approving plans and decisions that put the plan in motion.

**Sponsors.** A collection of leaders the working team reports to as part of the broader remits of these stakeholders. The sponsors have several areas of responsibility beyond those who represent them on the working team.

**Working team.** The people with the skills and competencies to develop, plan, and execute the initiative.

Think of these roles in concentric circles, as opposed to layers. The size of a company could simplify this concentric circle of roles, as in the case of a startup (where the sponsors may be the C-levels). Expansion beyond three rings would only make things unwieldy. In a large global company, forming three groups means setting limits. Management needs to actively curate the groups.

I will touch upon the specialized roles within each group.

## Working Team

Let's start with the working team. Its responsibilities are primarily to:

- Source input for explorations
- Build explorations based on the input
- Run explorations to feed recommendations
- Conduct alignment sessions
- Prepare for decision-making sessions
- Plan workflows to meet deadlines and milestones with sponsors and C-levels

The working team manages a bevy of duties, but forming the team and setting up the problem statement are not among them. That's the work of the sponsors, which we touch upon next.

As a working team member, you need to leave silos behind. You've been grouped around a common purpose, challenge, or problem statement. Avoid viewing your role as a representative of the function you report into. Let me say that again: you are not representing your function. You represent the company around the problem statement. This frame of mind will bring out the collective intelligence of the group. You're solving a puzzle from the overall company perspective.

The working team could have a spectrum of members, from those involved in current operations (who tend to be pragmatic) to those looking out into further horizons (who tend to favor innovation). This spectrum strengthens the range of inputs.

At the same time, avoid being predictable or limited to having a perspective defined by your role in the organization. Be more broadly curious, and process new inputs from others around the table before forming opinions. Don't be a know-it-all. The critical point is to transcend your job description. Play the role of one of many working team members grouped around a common purpose.

Like most projects, there is typically a day-to-day project leader or owner. The project leader or owner develops the strategy and brings the initiative to life. I fully recognize that a project leader can carry many titles depending on the organization (such as product manager, general manager, head of function X or Y, etc.). Decision Sprint makes this person's life much easier. If you're in this role, get familiar with the workflows of Decision Sprint (Chapter 7) and how to tap them to simplify the experience for everyone.

The project lead's responsibilities include:

- Ensure the proposed exploration meets a high bar of breadth and depth
- Validate the timeline for Decision Sprint workflows and project milestone
- Ensure the completed exploration drives the project recommendations

- Drive the alignment session
- Ensure a high bar for decision-making content

The project admin holds another specialized job within the working team and plays a vital part. The project admin will:

- Plan out the workflows in relation to broader milestones
- Initiate the sourcing period for input
- Curate input to make it actionable for exploration
- Assign tasks for exploration
- Report on exploration status in project reviews, as well as timelines for various workflows in Decision Sprint
- Work the project lead to resolve any gaps, bottlenecks in the timeline
- Develop usable content from exploration work for alignment and decision-making

## Sponsors

Sponsors are at a higher level than working team members. Like the working team, there could be a lead sponsor—the person who is most capable to drive the new growth or innovation initiative. What makes one leader more capable to lead versus another?

A curious leader with a learning mindset is essential. This leader can articulate the North Star and "what good looks," which is another way of saying this person has a vision to inspire others. Always pick the person most out in front of ideation to be the lead sponsor. The one who is most comfortable with unknowns and the ability to work through them.

At the same time, it takes a certain level of maturity for this person to be effective. The lead sponsor has peers who roll up major workstreams related to the planning and execution of the initiative. They must be onboard. That's why alignment matters, and we've discussed the entire set of workflows to achieve it. These workflows provide an enthusiastic sponsor with the means to work effectively with peers.

If you're a peer in the sponsor group, don't be passive. The lead may have more heavy lifting, but as a co-sponsor, you're equally responsible for the essential contributions of this group.

Sponsors have these essential responsibilities:

- Form the working team by identifying the relevant competencies
- Clarify the problem statement
- Clarify the milestones and manage them to create space for Decion Sprint
- Validate the proposed exploration meets a high bar of breadth and depth
- Engage in the alignment process
- Evaluate the recommendations
- Calibrate decision-making content

The lead sponsor should carry these additional responsibilities:

- Keep the C-levels abreast of the timelines and set expectations for their engagement
- Craft the specific interactions with the C-levels and make the calendars align
- Help the project lead secure the formation and participation of the working team members

## The C-Level

Decision Sprint is a way for the most senior levels of a company to provide autonomy while being engaged actively. You might see these as conflicting to achieve. So how is it accomplished?

"Calibration over control" is one of my catch management phrases, and it's the best way to describe the mindset shift Decision Sprint enables for the most senior levels of a company. As we've discussed earlier, leaders play a role in actively shaping inputs the team is sourcing, and the conclusions being drawn from these inputs. I refer to these as calibration points. In a calibration model, a leader doesn't wait for finalized thinking to provide feedback. By then it's too late to "calibrate" whether the right inputs have been collected to canvas the problem. When calibration goes well, it provides leaders with evidence to provide teams with space. With this space, teams can run ahead with deeper work.

In a control model, a leader may share the objective and wait for well-baked plans to be presented. As executive reviews near, tolerance for ambiguity shrinks. Expectations for answers are high as time elapses. Without the mechanism for leaders and teams to spend time with the ambiguity, there's a lot of guesswork and blind spots we can introduce. If the leader senses these gaps deep into a project, it could trigger an urge to control, and that's not good for anyone. Many teams have experienced a level of command and control where the autonomy is stripped away. That's why I emphasize working "upstream" with teams. It protects against reactive control behaviors.

The idea of upstream work is to provide a better way to give teams the space to do their best work—while creating the right points of engagement "up the chain."

In Decision Sprint, C levels can expect these points of engagement:

- Preview of the exploration before it's run, and the overarching problem statement
- Timeline of milestones from exploration to alignment to decision-making
- Review of decisions and recommendations linked to underlying exploration

Note that the first two points of engagement take place in the very upstream stage of work. Before providing teams with high levels of autonomy and leaning on the sponsor group to support them, there is transparency at the most senior levels.

It's based on this that the C-levels' main responsibilities are:

- Provide "quick and dirty" input on the exploration before it's run (including matters, questions, and working team members)
- Perform robust calibration (agree/disagree) on the proposed recommendations and decisions coming out of the alignment stage
- For approved decisions and direction, shift the conversation into action mode, including identifying and solving for more comprehensive organizational dependencies

- Support the rollout and communication of decisions into the organization

It's the visibility from the very start of what is being solved for, and the methods to get there, that C-levels can rely on for confidence. When they reengage with the initiative, the consistency of the content and methods are noticeable. The C-levels know the context is set, and teams can use time to go deep on the merits of what's being proposed as recommendations or decisions.

# FINDING YOUR PERSONA

In this section, I introduce the concept of personas—eight personas to be precise. I hope you can identify with a persona that represents how you experience working into the unknown. Every persona has some watch-outs. I won't be shy in pointing them out. At the same time, I will share perspectives on overcoming these pitfalls that could limit your growth as a leader and how you show up for the organization. Simply bringing awareness to your tendencies can help a lot. That's why this section centers mostly on personal development and growth.

Note that more than one persona might be relevant to you. Many of us are hybrids.

## *Standalone Innovators*

People can be collateral damage in an organization, and often these people are standalone innovators. It's a type of innovator who idealizes full autonomy from the mother ship, yet fails to see how the expertise in the mother ship is required to develop a powerful idea properly.

Much of this book is about developing explorations and recommendations based on high-quality input that crosses silos. I've seen many standalone innovators, people whose ideas are compelling wind up ineffective and disheartened. You can wind up as roadkill even if your ideas point the company in the right direction. I wrote this book to help you avoid becoming roadkill.

Use Decision Sprint to channel the organization in a way that embraces unknowns. It's better than a model where you're very accepting of unknowns, but the mother ship is fighting them. You won't win that battle.

Show the organization a way to deal with unknowns that is constructive. It's better than running shadow projects and tests that don't consider the practical matters related to your big ideas. Recruit a senior sponsor to help form the working team you'll need to cover the scope of the initiative. As an innovator with a compelling idea, you deserve sponsorship. If the chances of this materializing are low, move on to an organization where your ideas will have a fighting chance. Find some tethering.

**Takeaways.** Keep pushing the organization with your vision but get them to see the value of exploration and commit to it. Find sponsors who will commit the organization to form working teams to run explorations. Source input on issues and matters to solve for, and build high-quality explorations. Once more people in the organization get a feel for how to innovate into the unknown, they will want to get on board to push the problem-solving and innovation.

## Intrapreneurs

You're wired for unknowns, new territory, and crafting the North Star. You see the vision right away. It's likely you mix with industry innovators and bring ideas from outside into the organization. At the same time, you deliberately work through the organization to build support and create momentum for an initiative. That's a rare combination. Most people with vision have little patience to bring others along.

If an intrapreneur were an athlete, they would hold the distinction of being both an offensive and defensive all-star. But let's be real. Having been one myself and then hired others to do it when my role expanded to a much broader scope, this work is exhausting. You cannot scale yourself to the degree required for each new initiative that arises. That's why you must establish a method to do the heavy lifting.

Find ways to scale yourself; otherwise, the burnout factor will loom large. You must find a way to channel skepticism, doubt, and alignment before exploration. The effort must become more scalable with each attempt. That's what Decision Sprint offers.

## THE SERIAL INTRAPRENUER

Zaki Fasihuddin has excelled at the intrapreneur persona for years, working as a VP of Innovation at MGM, Volvo, McDonald's, and Pay-Pal before that. A digital innovator who has consistently delivered big initiatives, Zaki knows how to build a protected space for ideation while engaging and informing stakeholders.

Zaki explains that the intrapreneur persona must commit to building alignment:

> *What comes to mind is that number one, you cannot view your role as purely one thing. Yeah, I was the digital guy. I was the partnerships and innovation guy. But at the end of the day, you must think across the entire cusp of the experience, and you must figure out a way to problem-solve across that entire customer experience. Though you might not own other key cross-functional pieces that have to come together, you must find a way to drive problem-solving.*

You must wear a few different hats. You need to think holistically about that customer journey and doing whatever it takes to work cross-functionally inside the company, to stitch that journey together. Typically, companies are not organized like that.

Zaki soon realized that while startups are constantly developing the minimum viable product (MVP), the intrapreneur needs to sharpen communication to motivate people to contribute: "So, you have to go out and recruit and convince people to join this new project which may or may not be sanctioned, number one."

And as an intrapreneur, Zaki agrees you need to do a lot with a little.

> *Number two, you won't be resourced. You must be able to be extremely efficient with very few resources or you must*

*be proficient at being able to cobble together resources. When I brought this idea of Apple Pay to the Point-of-Sale team at McDonald's, they said, "Hey, our roadmap is defined for the next two years. We have no room in our road map to help you. That required a lot of persuasion, internal selling, and things like that."*

As I've noted, intrapreneurs naturally take to a Decision Sprint because it creates clarity and that paves the way for action. This is the third attribute: "We often rely on bias for action in big companies to start from the top. A successful entrepreneur doesn't need that dictated or mandated from the top. So in a big company teams need to create the case for action by problem-solving the hard stuff—like the unknowns."

In other words, the intrapreneur rolls up their sleeves:

*You must be great at problem-solving. Everybody is going to give you a hundred reasons why something is not going to work. You must be engineering around problems, engineering around blockers constantly. You have to be good at storytelling because if people don't understand why you are doing this, then they will not support you. You must articulate a clear vision of why you are proposing a certain thing.*

Zaki knows there is upside in playing the intrapreneur role.

*Every time I joined a traditional organization, that choice for me is clear. I want to be the innovator. I want to be the agitator. I want to be the person that when people say, oh, that's a new and hard thing. Who should we have work on that? I want them to think about my team as the right people to kick-start it.*

**Takeaways.** Scale yourself by establishing methods for problem-solving. These activate the organization and you will need the help. Invest in explaining and establishing the process and running efforts through it. Train and evangelize the organization in these new methods until they are adopted and stick.

## *Analyticals*

If it can be explained as a hypothesis with reasons behind it, this describes the analytical persona. Within a group, you could be unique. You might be most deeply committed to synthesizing the hypothesis, reasoning, and data.

People might seek you out in the company to better understand how to think about an initiative, especially more operational players who are less intuitive regarding new ideas. That's why your contribution can help a number of the other personas. You can quickly help a pragmatist overcome doubt or concern. You can complement a standalone innovator with the content to land ideas. Otherwise, the standalone innovator is riding on vision, demos, or conviction alone. You can be a great pair with an intrapreneur, though the best intrapreneurs are deeply analytical too.

Clarice, a former VP of Strategic Initiatives at MGM Resorts, fits the analytical persona. Clarice is able to toggle between macro aspirations and data obsession. She demonstrates the power and purpose of the analytical persona:

> At MGM specifically, my team supported strategic planning because there was no corporate strategy function in the organization.
>
> Thinking about how big organizations approach strategic projects, there's a macro level of work and a micro level of work. At the macro level, the best case is that the company is starting with a clear articulation of strategy. They are clear around goals and vision for the company. At this macro level, when done well, companies canvass all the opportunities they have in the organization, create a portfolio, and align on the things they're going to move forward with. That set of opportunities all clearly tie back to the strategy.

Clarice's leadership in analytics helped find the signals in the noise:

> We put a consistent scoring mechanism around them. We ensured the portfolio tied to the strategy and aligned

project teams around big opportunities. You must figure out the right measurement criteria so that you're making investment in the right things.

At the micro level, we had strong project managers who made sure we were getting all the relevant inputs from the different stakeholders, thereby creating clarity for the team on the key issues and how they would be addressed. You build that clarity focusing on the problem and how it is explored—it must start there. That's what good looks like. Of course, we also would set up tracking on the progress of projects once in flight and KPIs to ensure ultimate project success. But all of that was built on the back of strong inputs. **"**

**Takeaways.** Find the gaps in the organization where your ability to distill and influence is necessary and can make impact. Partner with these personas, especially innovators who find it difficult to translate their ideas into the language of the organization. Do the work missing from an analytical standpoint to plug gaps between big ideas and what the mother ship may need to understand to provide support.

## *Pragmatists*

You tend to see why something will not work at first but can be open to supporting solutions if they are put on the table. Unknowns are uncomfortable for you at the onset.

Be careful who you surround yourself with. If your team contains pessimists with influence, they will often convince you the unknowns are bigger than they are in reality. They will constantly raise the specter of risk before giving much space for the unknowns to be understood. At the same time, your instincts for pragmatic issues are a real strength; provided you can stay neutral about them, they can serve a significant purpose.

As a president in the Fortune 500, I would always want a pragmatist around the table. My team of C-suite executives weren't clones of me. It was my job to ensure pragmatists felt included just as much as the visionaries. This paid huge dividends for me at a company like Volvo. Once we built trust, the pragmatists within my management provided valuable counsel—where would we hit headwinds in this 90-year-old organization? Why? And what could overcome them?

**Takeaways.** Lean on your instincts while keeping them neutral until the right domain experts can explore them. Build a culture of "truth tellers" who will let you know when pessimism and concerns are getting the better of you. Avoid the tendency to be "glass half-empty." Surround yourself with "solution-oriented" staff, open to finding reasonable ways forward with new ideas.

## Pessimists

I won't sugarcoat this. You tend to believe that any idea or initiative has a shelf life that is less than your tenure at the company. So even a burst of enthusiasm for a new initiative is not enough to mobilize your support. You'd rather wait and see what sticks. You may have outlasted one or two CEOs, so you have seen many things come and go. And when projects fail, you can easily say "I told you so" and "here's why."

Here's the problem: being a *know-it-all* may backfire. Eventually, you might be placed in the driver's seat. And when that happens, you won't have enough practice at moving from strategy to action. You may have developed skills to preserve the status quo. When it comes to being on point for being a driver, there's a skill set gap and the clock is ticking. You will never deliver in the hot seat without these skills. Your best alternative is to learn a method like Decision Sprint because it will teach you in months what has taken me about 25 years.

**Takeaways.** Get out of your comfort zone with haste and shift from a know-it-all mentality to a "learn-it-all" mentality. Become a champion for a smarter way to address unknowns through methods like Decision Sprint. Modify your skepticism into the neutral zone by raising them as matters and clarifying questions. Decision Sprint allows you to do that constructively and can become part of your growth as a leader.

## Change Agents

You're a high-energy leader who likes to drive novel ways of working. If it can push the customer experience or business forward, you lean toward making it happen. You may not be the decision maker, but you'll go to bat and have the right conversations to set it in motion.

Change agents who team up with intrapreneurs can be a powerful combination. It's especially the case when the change agent sits with the company's existing operations, as they then speak the current "language" of the company.

When I transitioned from Amazon into the C-suite of McDonald's, our CEO introduced me to James Floyd, a change agent who was able to open doors. The wildly successful digital transformation you've read about earlier in this book was not possible without partnership with James and other longtime employees.

James was the VP of operations for the McDonald's locations operated by the company (instead of those being franchised). Even though we operated just 10 percent of the locations instead of franchising them, the sheer size of McDonald's made this a footprint of thousands of restaurants. The internal lingo for these restaurants is McOpCo.

"At the time, I was the general manager and vice president of McOpCo Restaurants, which are company owned and operated restaurants," James recollects in an interview:

> 66 We used those restaurants for a few reasons. One, to test concepts so that we can talk with the franchisees and have proof of how things work. We experimented with these company-owned restaurants so that if concepts were performing in sale and cash flow, we would transfer any of that knowledge to the operators, just to give them confidence. We also wanted to operate those restaurants so that if an idea didn't work, it may take a little while to come back for a second bite of the apple. It was a testing ground, but also a cash flow generator. That was my role.
>
> When Atif came in, our CEO who hired him said, "This is the first time we've ever done anything like this. Atif is going to be bringing a distinct perspective, and he's going to stretch

the thinking of a lot of our people. And I need you to help him navigate our environment."

People would say, we make hamburgers, right. But you know what? We had to extend ourselves and figure out a way to get to that next level, because just making hamburgers was not going to keep us number one moving forward. So our CEO had the vision. He also knew it would be a challenge because that wasn't in our language and is not in our DNA. We just thought we'd continue to muscle things through, and things were good. And we weren't going to be able to get to that next level just doing what we were doing.

James was a great partner who had learned how to build support: "We had to get with the right people—management, franchisees—on the same page to build that support and start leveraging the momentum. And that was the role."

**Takeaways.** Channel your energy by teaming up with the innovators to help land their ideas. Use the exploration content to achieve this. Open these doors when it comes time to test or put experiments in the real world. Help innovators translate their ideas into the language the rest of the company can understand.

## Action Junkies

Your lack of patience can lead to moving quickly on the wrong ideas, or to misreading. Action junkies can be less curious than business problems require them to be. Before jumping to conclusions, they should ask a few questions to gauge the rate of learning and clarity being created in the project. Redirecting energy into the exploration phase is a great way to channel the action orientation. Channel your energy into feedback on the exploration, alignment, and decision-making quality.

**Takeaways.** Pivot your focus upstream from decision mode to exploration mode. Help the team determine what needs to be understood and whether exploration has been developed robustly. You will make relevant decisions with more influence.

## *Coaches*

You're a force for stability in the organization and eager to reduce conflict by seeing many shades of the issues. One of your highest values can be to reach the standalone innovators as mentor. Mentoring a standalone innovator to be more effective at landing ideas can be a big contribution.

In one of my stints in the C-suite, a peer of mine fit this persona. He was a supportive voice for the innovators I brought into the company from Google, Amazon, Spotify, and startups. He made not have understood all of their expertise, but he was encouraging nonetheless. And since he had been in very senior positions, it made a world of difference to people trying to find their way in a 90-year-old company.

**Takeaways.** Identify the right people to mentor, typically people with bright ideas but less understanding of reading the tea leaves, concerns, and barriers to alignment. Coach them on building in these inputs for the formulation of their ideas and recommendations.

## INNOVATION AND ITS PERSONAS

I offer these eight personas based on innovation work over my 25-plus-year career. I've had the chance to come at innovation from all corners. Innovation in the core, innovation from the top, innovation within a standalone team, innovation in a startup, innovation at innovative companies, and innovation within incumbents who've forgotten the innovations that placed them on the map. I'm confident these personas will cover every persona you'll work with in the business contexts around innovation, growth, transformation, or moving into new territory.

# Land and Expand

What is land and expand when it comes to innovating into the unknown?

It's the idea of starting with a small number of meaningful project explorations. Your organization doesn't need to apply Decision Sprint to every strategic initiative or innovation project to test its value. You don't need to revisit the overall project flow that Decision Sprint feeds. No change is required in your organization's governance process of project, strategy, or innovation efforts. Most project or planning processes tell us what milestones we want to achieve but not how to get there. Decision Sprint plugs in the missing elements perfectly.

For example, we've covered the gaps in exploration and how teams reach alignment or decision milestones on weak footing. Build and run explorations to feed these milestones. Decision Sprint enables a team to reach those milestones in a position of readiness. It brings a method to work that currently takes place with little structure, low transparency, and inefficiency. You can use Decision Sprint to drive processes for the milestones that comprise your company's or team's overall process. The takeaway is simple: there is no dependency on how your company governs or steers innovation projects. Keep that intact and use Decision Sprint to improve the quality of thinking, alignment, and decisions for the key problem statements the projects will face.

Having said all that, you can see why I'm a proponent of team-up adoption to Decision Sprint. And while I expect CEOs and C-suite leaders to sponsor Decision Sprint as an integral part of their management systems, there is no better reflection on a team than a bunch of self-starters. It's much easier for C-suite leaders to amplify and spread the existing work of self-starters than to initiate down into the organization. Trust me, leaders would rather throw their weight behind methods that a team already has up and running. (See Figure 11.1.)

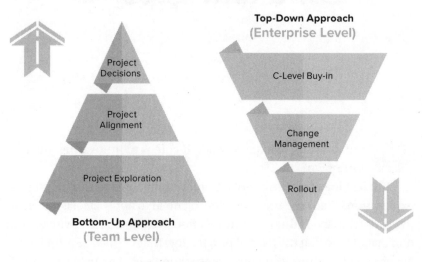

**FIGURE 11.1** Two ways to adopt

So where should Decision Sprint land? What type of initiative? A nice-to-have? Or something critical and more meaningful? It would be self-serving to say the latter, but it's the correct answer. Here's why: there's a tremendous upside and little downside.

An initiative core to strategy cannot afford to suffer from slow and ineffective decision-making. It's challenging enough to sort through the unknowns on the path to creating clarity of thought and direction. You've seen how today's approach falls short. The downside is limited as well. We're channeling time in a different way. A messy flow of team brainstorms, deep dives, and project reviews pivots to a more purposeful sequence. Instead, we source the right input at the right time to solve a puzzle. We want to direct team collaboration to surfacing, solving unknowns, and feeding alignment and decision-making. There is limited downside to infusing purpose when it comes to the upstream work of teams.

With that in mind, a good starting point is to work from the highest-level strategies of your company or organization. Most companies and groups within a company have a set of strategic pillars. The pillars represent the focus for the coming years. They represent what will create growth and keep the organization relevant. Each pillar often contains several initiatives to bring it to life.

These initiatives are where Decision Sprint excels. They are often cross-functional, and working teams are formed to collaborate over months and quarters. While a perfect time for Decision Sprint is the initiation of these initiatives, we also know there's a continuous need for exploration. My team established the digital experiences for McDonald's starting in 2013, and 10 years later there are still boundaries to push. In 2017, I cosponsored Volvo's push into a new business model for cars—the subscription. Five years later, it's a significant percentage of the company's sales, yet it feels like the start.

Another area to scan for fit are promising spaces that are not yet committed as part of the company's direction. These opportunities go by many names—innovation, horizon 2, lighthouse, concept, pilot, or exploration projects. Innovators driving these efforts want to graduate from testing the waters to real commitment. The mother ship of the company wants to filter them for their real potential. Decision Sprint can help the right ones make the leap, instead of becoming missed opportunities.

In some cases, these initiatives don't yet have awareness in the organization at the senior levels. That makes it even more critical for the innovation or concept teams behind these initiatives to tap Decision Sprint. It will help these teams with readiness. When the window opens to pitch the concepts, they will be framed with the right breadth and depth of understanding. What level of sponsorship is required for Decision Sprint? How high should involvement be when it comes to landing? Decision Sprint is primarily a method for teams.

Don't get me wrong. I believe there is a huge role for the most senior levels of a company when it comes to expansion. You will read about how the most senior levels can use it to create rituals that will transform a company's culture. Executives are the key to making years of change in a fraction of the time by adopting spreading strategies. Adoption will grow organically when the value of Decision Sprint becomes visible throughout the organization. Executives can make this go even faster through the strategies we will cover shortly. But none of this goodness will take place if Decision Sprint doesn't make it out of the starting blocks. Here's how to do that.

## STARTING A SPRINT, STEP BY STEP

To get started, teams need the right entry point. First, the team needs to lay out a looming problem statement and the internal milestones they need to manage against for recommendations and decisions.

At the very start of a project, this is precisely where a team finds itself. There are no decisions or even strong recommendations on the table. Maybe some hunches and convictions, but far from readiness to set a clear direction. Looming time frames mean the pressure is on.

That said, a project that is underway always has the next frontier. We've talked about the need for continuous exploration. What is the team trying to figure out next? What's on the list for upstream thinking?

It's perfect to initiate Decision Sprint once a meaningful problem statement has been drafted.

To recap, we've covered two things so far:

- The type of initiative where Decision Sprint should be applied
- The entry point for Decision Sprint into the project

Now it's time to cover the who. Who gets the ball rolling? Three common ways a team can initiate Decision Sprint follow.

### 1. Sponsor Initiated

As the sponsor or cosponsor of a strategic initiative, you have much at stake. At the same time, your plate is probably wide, time is short, and expectations will only grow. It would help if you had the wind behind your back. Tailwinds, not headwinds. Decision Sprint is the tailwind you can gift the team and yourself.

Introduce Decision Sprint to the working group and charge the project lead with taking it on. Use the kick-off in Workflow #1 to explain the benefits and how it works. When the team understands the intention is to simplify getting to alignment with sponsors, they will have a strong incentive.

## 2. Team Initiated

Any leader on a working team can bring the innovation of Decision Sprint to a project. Leaders come in wide varieties, including project lead, product owner, general manager, corporate strategist, and transformation lead to name a few. Use a regular team meeting or project review to introduce Decision Sprint and propose an entry point for it. The next step is the kick-off in Workflow #1.

When should the sponsor(s) be brought into the loop? Make it easy for a sponsor to say "yes, more please." Accomplish that by tapping Decision Sprint behind the scenes and using a concrete output with sponsors. The quickest, most tangible output to share is the exploration canvas (Workflow #5). It's the output of the sourcing input step with some cleanup. Sponsors will value the transparency and the ability to provide input before the development of recommendations go too far ahead.

## 3. Team Initiated (Presponsorship or Pre-project)

As a working team, you may not have a sponsor group at the moment. Perhaps you and some others have self-organized around a bright new idea or a problem that needs to be tackled. The effort is not yet "official" as a project. We've talked about this presponsorship scenario and why it's so critical for teams to be ready. A bright, mature team wants to be prepared for that engagement when the time emerges. A less mature team runs on wishful thinking that an idea will skip the sponsorship stage and magically get the commitment and investment. If you're an innovation squad, this is meant for you, especially.

Don't rely on wishful thinking. Decision Sprint helps you ready the initiative for alignment and decision-making that will take place with more senior stakeholders. The key is it will propel a level of input that gets you out of the comfort zone, which will be critical to achieve shared understanding in the wider organization. Your initiative will not suffer the fate of many that have painful fits and starts based on weak input sourcing and gaps in exploration. Taking a step back, teams have plenty of opportunity through off-sites, hackathons, innovation days, and so on to look into promising concepts even before sponsorship is sought.

## THE THREE NECESSARY COMMITMENTS

As Decision Sprint is being introduced, you might wonder what type of commitment is necessary. As a team leader, what are you asking of your colleagues? As a sponsor, what are you asking of others? To give Decision Sprint a genuine attempt, focus on three commitments.

### 1. Experience at Least One Life Cycle (Typically 90 Days)

A life cycle is defined as the stretch from building exploration, to running it, to using the outputs of exploration for something tangible like an alignment session. The good news is the team could see value quickly in building an exploration (and the confidence this brings in avoiding blind spots and surprises). That may take no more than a week or two. I'll explain further why the 90-day rule still makes sense.

### 2. Staff a Strong Program Leader

Moving Decision Sprint along is more than herding cats with timelines for input and tasks to be completed. It takes a bit of education and coaching into the team related to the workflows. Given the company's specific governance and steering process, how does Decision Sprint fit in detail? In what order are the workflows and toward what milestones? How do they infuse purpose?

### 3. Participation from the Working Team

A core team might consist of five to eight people who are actively involved. That's a good brain trust to develop the main inputs to explore and should provide a diverse perspective on the conclusions to draw. But it has to be an open approach for this collective intelligence to flow—the working team needs to be engaged.

# ORGANIC ADOPTION

If you're reading this book, I imagine you are way more ambitious than getting to first base. You are seeking the full transformative potential of Decision Sprint. When a team and its sponsors can experience a better way to reach an alignment or decision point, they will want more of it. For this to happen, everyone needs some practice together. Practice means enough attempts where the pattern is noticeable—that means, when applied, Decision Sprint noticeability improves the quality and speed of upstream work. It's apparent at various levels, from the working team to the sponsor group.

Again, if you're reading this book, you're probably seeking lasting impact. Lasting practices. More than a successful pilot of Decision Sprint. You're trying to promote adoption. The best way to do this is to make several life-cycle attempts. That could mean running further explorations under a given project simultaneously, or it could be running more than one iteration on a single exploration.

What is the happy case? Organic adoption.

Let's say you're part of a working team or perhaps the sponsor of one. The initiative is more streamlined, the recommendations seem smarter, and the lift to get there is lighter. You will spread the word and start establishing Decision Sprint in your next initiative.

Or perhaps as a C-level executive, you notice the same dynamics around an initiative and ask why this particular one is set apart from the others? What is the approach behind the scenes? The working team will gladly share the engine they've established to power the content and interactions with you. They will be happy to share the methodical workflows that are designed for taking on initiatives with constant unknowns. This would likely come as a pleasant surprise. Not only is an initiative standing firm on its merits, but there is also real innovation in the underlying methodology. The innovators have innovated into the unknown. You'll be sure to ask them to relate this knowledge to the most important priority on your plate that is similar.

Organic interest will emerge in many directions. People will seek out those familiar with Decision Sprint to learn about it for their specific efforts.

## ADOPTION SPREADING STRATEGIES

Once the innovators have innovated into the unknown (aka landed Decision Sprint), the time has come for massive amplification.

The work of the most senior executives takes place as signs of organic adoption are materializing. Sure, they might read this book and seek out a pilot or two. That will be handoff with a check-in maybe a few weeks or months later. But there is so much more to actively promoting Decision Sprint adoption, which is anchored at the most senior level. Now we will walk through four of these amplification opportunities.

### 1. Adopt Standard Language

Trigger the right behaviors by using terminology. For example, when you encounter new problem statements with many unknowns, you might suggest "there is upstream work to do" and use the "upstream work" label. Establish the right frame of mind by asking the team to start with an exploration and share a canvas of what they intend to explore. Set expectations that exploration feeds alignment and that alignment without exploration is a bad compromise. Four terms will make all the difference in the world. Upstream work and its three components: exploration, alignment, and decision-making.

### 2. Work Backward from Milestones

Collaborate with teams to lay out milestones fed by the phases of Decision Sprint. Put Decision Sprint to work by allowing it to connect to milestones where alignment or decision-making is set to occur. The 13 workflows I've elaborated on provide the building blocks you can use to make these connections. Senior executives play a huge role in calibrating the sequence of work because groups plan meticulously for governance or steering meetings with them. Senior executives can create space to implement the key workflows and experience better governance or steering meetings. It's smart and efficient to lay this out from exploration to alignment to decision-making steps.

### 3. Link to Cultural Change

Established companies are often amid cultural transformation, especially as digitization picks up pace. Newer companies are working actively to establish culture as they bring on new people and expand. Time is of the essence in all cases.

We've talked more about using Decision Sprint for cultural change in Chapter 8. The link frames cultural expectations around behaviors that enable employees to deal with unknowns, ambiguity, and uncertainty. We know problem-solving takes place against these challenging factors. And we know the problem-solving of a collective nature is necessary to grow and innovate.

Decision Sprint is a fertile approach for setting cultural ambitions. Here are some behavioral norms it invites an organization to adopt: break down silos, promote collective intelligence, create space for purposeful exploration, avoid a rush to judgment, emphasize clarity of thought, prioritize critical thinking and reasoning skills, invite big thinking, and collaborate to widen shared understanding.

A great case in point is this phrase: Group People Around Challenges. Hakan Samuelsson, Volvo's CEO, crafted it. It was printed on an 8.5 by 11 piece of paper and taped to the entrance door on the fifth floor of Volvo's headquarters. When meeting with Hakan, an employee would scan a badge to pass through this door and absorb these words in those microseconds. Another useful catchphrase I developed as a president in the Fortune 500 is "Calibration over control." It's one way of explaining a management style where we don't tell people what to do, yet help ask the right questions to point in the right direction. I elaborated on both phrases in Chapter 8.

## 4. Invest in Education

The growing demand for innovative methods like Decision Sprint can be served through organic interactions. Organic interactions come in many forms. One team would like to hear about the practices and invites a more experienced one to a team meeting to provide an overview. An executive creates time in a staff meeting for one team member to share it with peers. There are follow-up meetings to go through the details. Soon the company creates a Slack channel, and word of mouth leads to a growing number of users who can ask questions and share insights. These are certainly the natural ways in which "expand" takes place.

Yet we can go further. Decision Sprint can spread quickly and efficiently through small educational investments, which senior executives can sponsor.

Here are some examples:

- Crafting cases studies
- Appointing coaches and giving them 20 percent time for office hours
- Opening a Slack channel for education
- Workshops for interested teams
- Creating certificates and badges for experienced practitioners of Decision Sprint
- Providing time during all-hands meetings for "How we did it"

Some of these may already be in place, and senior executives can sponsor these efforts by creating awareness and providing formal channels. Sponsorship speeds up adoption. It puts into motion the cascading of information. You can imagine that people working for a senior executive will socialize these ideas within their teams. And so and so forth.

The cost for education efforts is time and space for practitioners to share. If you're a senior person in a company and have experienced the value of Decision Sprint, communicate that you're supportive of the time involved in educational efforts. Recognize it as an innovation that is worth creating space for. Assist people involved in supporting education with shifting priorities to take it on.

As the expansion occurs, there will be a real opportunity to look at team-based problem-solving through ambiguity (upstream work) as worthy of investment in specialists for coaching, and formal skill development. Leading companies look to create this infrastructure. In Chapter 13, on mission control, I will explain the key components. In that chapter, you will learn how Decision Sprint becomes the basis not just to drive a project, but to become the center of your company's management system.

# PART FOUR

# A BOUNDLESS PLAYBOOK FOR GROWTH

# Digital Tools

In this chapter, you will learn how digital tools help us in four respects: (1) convenience for everyone involved in Decision Sprint, (2) shifting more work to asynchronous activity and thereby reducing meeting load, (3) helping teams remain super collaborative in a remote work model, and (4) generating powerful new data sources that can enable analytics and AI.

After these benefits, I will walk through approaches for implementing digital tools, which is likely to be the dominant approach adopted by teams and companies.

Let's start with the benefits.

## CONVENIENCE IN A BOX

First up is the convenience of performing Decision Sprint workflows. Each role involved in Decision Sprint can see immediate benefits.

For example, administrators might spend a good amount of time herding cats for inputs—perhaps when sourcing for matters and questions. Or it could be follow-up with those assigned to answer or review answers to questions. With digital tools, convenience for the administrator comes in the form of alerts and notifications. Rather than spreadsheets with dates and milestones, software keeps members of the working team on track. Whether there are three or ten team members, software does the work of reminding. For working team members, this is equally convenient as you can stay on top of deadlines and see all your tasks in a single place. When providing input, it's logged, and there's a form of acknowledgment that may not be recognized in old-school meetings. That's an additional benefit—a way to have a voice that cannot be overlooked like it might in a meeting with louder voices. Let me reiterate that point. With digital tools, contributions can speak louder than personalities.

Administrators also keep team members focused on tasks and not racing ahead. For example, we've discussed the need to collect input before jumping to conclusions. Digital tools help manage this. They allow us to lay out milestones to in an easy-to-digest timeline. Working team members can see the current step and know which comes next. This kind of anchoring is easily accomplished by software. You've read about the 13 workflows in Chapter 7.

Input is great, but it can also be overwhelming. Consider collecting input in a typical meeting when people are chiming in at different points. It's more than taking notes. The discovery and delivery of input can be hard too. With digital tools, we place a structure around input.

Let's say there's a digital tool people can use to suggest matters or questions to include in an exploration. This input is more likely to be clear and well-structured. Why is that? The right tool knows how to prompt for the right input. It's not a blank text thread or unstructured email. With clear prompts for specific input types like matters and questions, digital tools for upstream work help make input more useful.

Team members enter their input into a digital interface rather than being spoken in a meeting, where the precision of the input may be lost.

When it comes time for an administrator to review inputs, having a single interface to view it in list format simplifies things. Administrators likely need to scrub the list of information from working team members for better wording, removing duplicates, and so on.

Let's talk for a moment about security. Digital tools can help by exposing only the necessary data. This reduces security risks by keeping all confidential information accessible and by identifying who has accessed what data. Companies can encrypt their ideas and problem-solving efforts. In the following chapters, you will read how the intellectual capital from Decision Sprint is measurable and valuable. That's why security matters.

Digital tools also hold promise for sponsors and higher-level stakeholders of initiatives. In most companies, visibility and transparency to progress are limited. Let's say someone initiates a project, and a few weeks later executives are slated to review the proposed direction. We've discussed the opportunity to share an exploration a team has built before running it. Sharing an exploration canvas via digital tools can be a simple way to create visibility. It combines the list of matters and underlying questions into a single view. A stakeholder could comment with suggestions or click "looks good." The outcome is trust and confidence in the work, even before any answers are available. And with digital tools, the user interface can be as simple as a web page or mobile app screen instead of a detailed PowerPoint presentation.

Software interfaces can communicate how stakeholders are structuring the exploration, so why create an extra burden with inferior documentation? The workflow of exploration automatically generates documentation along the way when deploying the right digital tools. This is the beauty of digitizing workflows.

Speaking of content, as workflows related to answering questions take place through digital tools, the lift to generate content for meetings is reduced. Digital tools can easily produce a list of FAQs after the team completes an exploration. Administrators can select the most relevant FAQs from an exploration to prepare for the next round of interactions (if some matters are more relevant to a particular stakeholder). The digital tools will offer templates of various kinds to export content into a preferred company format. Want a narrative format instead of an FAQ? How about a content template that is standard for your company? Digital tools can take the substance of an exploration and place them into any manner of content output.

Remember, for example, how Amazon is big on written narratives? Your organization may look to produce white papers, one-pagers, or strategy briefings. The right tool will allow users to set up templates so that they can plug in the underlying content from exploration.

FAQs are my preferred content format. They are succinct and easy to digest. Don't forget when people answer questions, they need supporting materials such as tables, data feeds, or files. Digital tools should allow answers to questions and include these supporting materials through uploads or links.

Taking a step back, you can now appreciate how digital tools add a level of convenience and ease in standing up the workflows of Decision Sprint. And there are many automations possible beyond the workflows of Decision Sprint. Collaboration software, circa 2022, includes downstream systems for project management (e.g., Trello, Asana, and Jira), brainstorming apps (Miro, Figma, and Overflow), and messaging tools (e.g., Slack and Teams). Integration with these tools allows context to move from upstream to downstream and from unstructured to structured activity.

## ASYNCHRONOUS WORK

A second benefit is the idea of asynchronous work. Asynchronous work has become highly relevant in our post-Covid world, as teams work in hybrid or remote models. What is asynchronous work? It's the idea of work that happens independently yet together.

Decision Sprint lends itself to asynchronous work at several stages. Take, for instance, sourcing input. A working team should provide input on matters and questions to include in exploration simultaneously. But they don't need to gather in person to make this happen. Instead, we can give each working team member the same duration (number of days) to make their suggestions.

Doing this independently has benefits we've walked through earlier. And that's why it's perfect for asynchronous work. It's work that can be submitted independently yet synchronized to a common timeline. Digital tools enable this asynchronous work. People can open a browser or app and provide suggestions without needing a meeting. This allows individuals to organize their work to their own timetable. Communication can happen when it better suits the individual, if it is timely. Remember, meetings are the most expensive tool at any company.

Of course, I am not suggesting that we do away entirely with meetings. We can, however, make them more constructive and purposeful. Take, for instance, the workflow of answering questions and reviewing an answer to a question. Digital tools allow people assigned these tasks to work asynchronously. Answers can flow in, and the review can take place at the reviewer's convenience. When that process hits diminishing returns, it's time to meet. We can meet when face-to-face interaction or dialogue is more productive than asynchronicity. Meetings can be more purposeful.

## CREATE BELONGING IN HYBRID WORK

In a world of hybrid or remote work, we need digital workspaces and platforms where teamwork can happen and give us a sense of belonging. Digital tools for upstream work provide this. That's the third benefit. Team members belonging to a project can see all the contributions in one space. It's not guesswork "who is doing what" despite distributed locations. Let's say a team member in Europe answered a question, and it was reviewed by another in New York. The reviewer suggested an improvement and that made the answer better. Or taking another example, let's say most team members are in a particular geography and a few reside outside of it. Those outside the geography of headquarters can have their contributions in the form of suggested matters, suggested questions, answers, and so on clearly available in a stream of contributions under their "profile." A fellow team member may review these and think, "Wow, this person asks really great questions! She is the question guru who helps us see around corners." I wonder how much more objective these perceptions will become versus today's reputations, which sometimes reward loud voices over those with substance.

## REVEAL HIDDEN DATA

A fourth benefit comes from the fact that digitization of anything helps surface previously hidden data. How much upstream data is hidden from us today?

Imagine voting or weighing recommendations. This can become a more analytical approach rather than simply reading the room.

I dedicate an entire chapter to this game-changer for companies (see Chapter 13, "AI as Mission Control"). The raw data for analytics and AI come from digital tools. The more the workflows are taking place through digital means, the more information we collect.

Enabling Decision Sprint through digital tools for as many initiatives as possible is important. That's the key to developing big data sets for comparisons, pattern recognition, and the kind of radar you'll learn more about in the chapter on mission control. The upshot is this: companies will benefit from more precise signals on the actual level of progress on their initiatives through the raw data that comes with adopting digital tools.

## SOLUTIONS

I hope that your organization will lean into these digital tools for Decision Sprint. That may leave you wondering where do I turn for this software?

Let me elaborate on three potential solutions.

First, there are generic software tools that are like a Swiss Army knife. They don't bring knowledge about Decision Sprint, upstream work, or taking strategy to action. They offer generic workflows that a group of people with this know-how can spend months tailoring.

For example, your company can hire a software consulting firm who's read this book to apply generic software tools to Decision Sprint. Your organization could have its own Decision Sprint system. I'm not an advocate of this approach over the ones you'll read about further below. This approach is not the best path to create an advantage for your organization. Advantage lies in the degree to which the workflows of Decision Sprint are adopted, and not whether the digital tools are proprietary to your company.

I worry about the usability of tools developed for proprietary use. It's possible that in-house development would fall behind a best-of-breed provider. An in-house solution could be hard to maintain, and there could be a material capability gap over time.

Don't get me wrong—I have nothing against consultants. In fact, I believe coaches for Decision Sprint would be an excellent investment. Coaches who can train teams in your organization on Decision Sprint (as a set of methods) and help it spread. The software your organization uses to bring Decision Sprint to life is another story.

A better way is to use purpose-built software intended to serve a wide community of users with upstream needs.

Which brings me to the second option. Software that helps manage innovation or develop strategy through templates has probably existed in spades for decades. But can you name one? That's the point. These solutions treat innovation like a routine where you fill in a template and then it's done. But we know that ideas that involve unknowns require collaboration and that collaboration has its pitfalls. The pitfalls are behavioral—meaning the human factors come into play—and need to be anticipated. That's why I feel strongly the future of software comes with a point-of-view. It has a little attitude, like saying, "Oh yeah, you want to make a recommendation, well, where's your exploration? Where's the question list?" You do not pass go.

As of the time of writing this book, there is no such alternative other than Ritual. Ritual is the company I've cofounded to bring Decision Sprint to life via software. Rather than a generic workflow, Ritual has a built-in design to get exploration, alignment, and decision-making right. The method is in the software. They are one. It has a point of view that is entirely consistent with this book's practices.

I believe the future of business software will come from tools that take a point of view. For organizations to keep up with increasing velocity of business, software needs to do more than provide generic capabilities like messaging, chat, forms, workflows, voting, and so on. How boring. These capabilities need to be applied to human factors that exist in business. Tools that bring deep understanding of their domains—including the pitfalls and human behavioral factors—and infuse methodology will help companies and teams move faster and smarter. That's the *future of software* in our post-Covid era.

Let's take a step back. Digital tools do more than just help scale Decision Sprint and add convenience. I hope digital tools will allow companies to pivot how people use time. The pivot is less time on time-consuming low-value tasks and more time on higher-value work. This means more time for strategic work that will help companies grow.

# AI as Mission Control

You are probably right if you think Amazon is the case study for how a fast-moving, strategic company behaves. In this chapter we look further out than today's state of the art and what might come next. What might be the management hallmarks of the next Amazon? How might AI and management come to work in a seamless fashion? I will walk through detailed examples, and even algorithms, for how management will be fueled by AI. We will dive into the deep end, and even geek out, but first a reflection on where we are today.

Looking back on the last 10 to 15 years, Amazon has been unique in finding ways to enter new spaces and continually deliver growth. The results have shown it.

I remember traveling back to the office from a companywide meeting in 2013 and running some mental math. In the fourth quarter of 2013, I worked for a company that added $25 billion of revenue. That figure was more than the revenue of 380 companies in the Fortune 500 at that time. It's extraordinary for a company to add more revenue in a single quarter than the total revenue of many companies in the Fortune 500.

How long could it keep it up? That question was on my mind in 2013.

In the last 10 years, the company grew the top line by 20 to 30 percent despite being huger than huge to begin with. Let's place that into context. To grow by 20 percent in 2016, the company needed to add $21.5 billion of new revenue. For it to increase by 20 percent in 2019, it needed to add $46 billion of new revenue. And to grow by that same percentage in 2021, it needed to add $76 billion of new revenue. These figures are new revenue on top of what was produced earlier. In each case, it exceeded the mark.

The company's performance is no fluke. It's a testament to the system the company has in place. Interestingly, Amazon has established an innovative management culture through the way it defines leadership. You learn a lot through osmosis and observation of how people think and operate as leaders. In my view, the Amazon methodology is not formalized into specific workflows.

## AFTER AMAZON

As we think about what could come after Amazon, I think of a more AI-driven approach to managing. It relies not only on the individual's embrace of management principles, which characterizes how Amazon works. It adds the element of analytics and AI to the day-to-day workflows to help managers determine where things really stand.

In this chapter, we will look further out than best in class as time stamped in the first half of the 2020s. Let's look beyond Amazon. Let's look beyond any agile company you're familiar with. Let's look at the engine of the future. The engine I'm referring to sits above any given project or initiative.

I call it mission control because it's like the control tower at the airport that teams up with the pilots. Another term for it is *metacognition*. That means a higher level of understanding of how the overall system is performing.

At the project level, companies focus on possibilities to grow, enter new territory, and innovate. We already realize that embracing upstream work and Decision Sprint can unlock growth initiatives. Decision Sprint is a systematic way to create an enduring growth engine that can power a company for decades. The upside is much more than lifting up a few strategic projects to produce faster and better results.

Now we will look at creating a management system to unlock the growth possibilities using analytics and AI. AI is already teaming up with humans performing complex activities to work better and smarter. Consider Copilot, a product by GitHub, which can suggest the next line of code as developers type in a development environment. What about other types of knowledge work? Can ChatGPT answer questions better than today's knowledge worker assigned to a key initiative? It will raise the bar on the process of developing the right questions to begin with, and the quality of the answers that follow. But it's more than "bar raising" questions and answers. AI will replace the guesswork of knowing how well teams are progressing ideas into action. It's the mission control we've been missing.

How does mission control fit into upstream work, and how will AI fuel it?

## RADAR AND SIGNALS

Let's talk signals. There's an important initiative that is getting a ton of energy and focus in your company. Time is being spent, but is the right level of progress being made? Signals can help inform whether exploration, alignment, and decision-making are on track, or not.

In this chapter, you'll learn how data scientists work with Decision Sprint to generate signals. And how project teams and stakeholders can tap these signals to address problems before they grow into larger ones. Mission control is about setting up the environment for these signals to be visible.

That's where data to fuel analytics and AI come into the picture. Analytics and AI are not synonymous. Analytics are data constructs that humans set up to inform how things are going. We might set up analytics to compare if an initiative is on track, slow or speedy relative to similar ones. It can be as simple as measuring how many days an exploration has taken relative to other explorations.

On the other hand, with AI, humans don't set up the constructs. AI finds interesting patterns and makes suggestions. Patterns are clues to inform us that something could be on track or not, and provide the lead time to take action before small problems become big problems.

What are analytics when it comes to upstream work like exploring a problem, creating alignment around direction, and coming to decisions?

This is perhaps the most exciting facet of what Decision Sprint enables. For the first time in the history of management, companies will be able to pinpoint why initiatives are stuck without the guesswork.

We first need visibility to determine whether initiatives are stuck. As of this writing, most managers primarily operate in the dark. Initiatives can be stuck at any stage (the workflows I've provided help us determine where). Teams could be stuck identifying matters, diving deep on them, driving alignment, or taking a decision. Too often, we find out after the fact. The stack is already overflowing.

Often when projects are stalled, stuck, or lacking momentum, there's no clear agreement on why. Analytics are the way to solve this. They surface patterns most of us can't see at the project level. There are so many analytics that are possible to construct.

To understand why this will be possible, reflect on digital tools. When workflow is digital, we are constantly logging a ton of data. It's the nature of digitization. We know what exploration the team used to make what decisions. We know about the level of alignment in place before decisions were made. We know how the team and stakeholders felt about the quality of the exploration before and after it was run. We may even know who contributed what to the exploration and the makeup of the contributors in terms of personality attributes and personas (from attributes of personality tests). It's a field day for big-data lovers.

There is nothing short of a mountain of data generated by using digital tools that I've elaborated on in Chapter 12, "Digital Tools." How can this data be leveraged to develop signals? Companies will need to get organized for it.

### Mission Control

As you might imagine, mission control is more of a big-picture activity than project work. It's centralized only as much as is necessary. Mission control work infuses existing parts of the organization with new insights on performing their work. It's not about creating a sizable central function at all. It's about enabling the existing processes and project teams to perform at the next level by providing signals. You can get signals on a specific initiative by comparing them to a larger sample. Organizing comparisons of a specific initiative to samples, and developing actionable data is a dedicated activity.

There's another component to mission control beyond data science. It's coaching. Certainly, the coaches I've talked about in Chapter 11 can sit in mission control to plan which initiatives receive education and onboarding to Decision Sprint. Coaches can help educate on the various aspects of Decision Sprint, from workflow to content. I'm not a huge fan of waiting on centralized resources, which is why such teams should be focused on self-service approaches and learn everything they can without outside hand-holding. At the same time, coaching can consult with a project team through Decision Sprint workflows. This may be appropriate for the most strategic initiatives of a company or in cases where some recalibration is necessary.

The contribution of mission control goes well beyond coaching. Let's take examples of analytics. We will get into AI later on in the chapter.

## SIMPLE ANALYTICS

Here's a simple example to start with. A team has gone through the workflow of sourcing input for an exploration. The matters and questions within the exploration are laid out and visible to team members. Team members are prompted for their confidence level around the exploration, given the way it's been canvassed. This has a few elements. Have we captured a strong breadth of the matters? Have we captured the sufficient depth of each matter? These are the known unknowns.

There are of course, the unknown unknowns. What's the intuition of the team around that? No one has a crystal ball, but collecting input on that frontier is a useful data point to capture. We collect data about the *confidence level* across these areas. Mission control helps compare the *confidence level* to similar projects completed or further along.

A sample of successful initiatives serves as the basis to compare against. What is the median confidence level for projects that turn out to be successful at a comparable stage? This simple analytic can be useful. If the confidence level doesn't compare favorably, it could make sense to take a pause, perhaps do an iteration.

How can a team figure out what is lacking? It can be as simple as surveying the team for why their confidence isn't as high as it may be and what kinds of inputs or perspectives would fill the gap. There's nothing terribly advanced about this scenario. It's a matter of building feedback loops and tapping a sample of data from prior initiatives with similar characteristics. It's about catching the outliers in the earlier workflows of Decision Sprint. This may not sound groundbreaking. However, today, it's really not until the very tail end of Decision Sprint workflows that we often get clear indications. The structure of Decision Sprint and each workflow provides a point in time to collect metrics.

When picking a sample, it helps if we categorize projects into types. Is this project part of core company strategy or a concept that is not yet embraced as core? Some companies use the language of "innovation" versus "core" to differentiate. What is the horizon of the project? For example, companies often use the term *horizon one* to imply an extension to today's business and *horizon two* to imply a new space. Compare initiatives into new horizons against each other. Compare extensions to current product lines against each other.

Here are some analytics that can provide useful signals:

1. **Exploration confidence.** After a team has built an exploration but before running it, we want to get a high, medium, or low measure on the confidence level. The confidence relates to surfacing the right breadth and depth to the exploration, and the level is based on a benchmark for high, medium, and low across a relevant sample.

2. **Recommendation quality.** After a team has used exploration to develop recommendations, we want a measure of how sound and exhaustive these recommendations appear to be. The data for this would come by presenting a list of recommendations to stakeholders, and prompting for feedback. Comparisons can be made to benchmarks for high, medium, and low across a relevant sample.

3. **Alignment level.** After we prompt for the degree of alignment to recommendations, we are very curious as to whether it's enough support. Comparisons can be made to benchmarks for high, medium, and low across a relevant sample.

Across these analytics, the samples play an important role. The benchmarks in the sample need to be similar (as discussed previously), and we need to have some data on their outcomes as well as the sentiment trends at various stages of the workflows. Clearly there is some data capture and setup necessary for this to be possible. And are the specific analytics shared previously the best ones to help get ahead of problems? Better signals will emerge.

AI is going to be a huge enabler of shedding light on the right signals. It will put the analytics on steroids. Let's take a look at how AI will usher in a level of predictive analytics. And how these predictive analytics will come to define management over the rest of the century. Yes. It's my belief that AI will shape how executives spend time as we look over the next 50 years. Rather than replace executives, AI will enable them to zero in on where to spend time to apply their intellectual capital. Today it's a lot of guesswork and based on which way the wind blows. Tomorrow it will be guided by the raw data that Decision Sprint provides, riding on the rails of digital tools.

The power of AI is to alert our attention to issues before it's too late to remedy them. It's about error correction.

## AI AS ERROR CORRECTION

Have you mistyped a word while writing a sentence, only to have the error spotted and corrected by the app you're using? Grammatical errors are fixed as you type. Can we leverage this concept into the world of management? Can we correct for errors before the complexity makes this really painful and challenging to accomplish?

Let's get concrete. A project will suffer if it operates under the assumption that exploration has been adequate only to discover missed inputs later. A project will suffer when alignment is assumed, only to have it fracture as time goes on. A project will suffer if only some stakeholders are ready to make a decision. A project will suffer if a decision is on the table and devolves to an opinion fest, lacking an objective way to sort through it.

How can data from Decision Sprint help with each case? When enough initiatives run through it, we can imagine a good amount of raw data being collected. It's like a big data set. Running a current initiative through Decision Sprint creates a living system where big data with the right AI can surface amazing insights. Over time, with deep learning techniques like feature extraction, AI will help us determine what factors of the upstream work are more important than others. Here's one example related to which personas to involve in a collaboration. Think about a personality test and the attributes collected from it. Now think about the nature of a project and a world where AI can inform the perfect combination of personality attributes to group around it. For example, the best makeup for an exploration could be to include at least two analytical personas and two creative personas early on. That could lead to better results down the line.

The following are some possibilities where AI could help. These are the kind of "keep you up at night" and "make you toss in bed" questions that management faces at every company. Instead of being in limbo about whether there's a problem, AI can alert us with accuracy based on data.

# AI USE CASES

### Have We Run a Strong Exploration?

We will never operate with perfect information about the problem we're exploring. Every initiative faces this condition. And yet some work out well. Putting aside luck and timing, do successful initiatives have some things in common? In an earlier example, I provided a simple analytic to determine if exploration was on track. In that case, a person had to pick a sample set of initiatives, a metric like the team's confidence level and compare it to a benchmark data.

When we introduce AI into the equation, none of this will be required to determine if exploration is proceeding well or not. The machine will do the heavy lifting. See "Hey AI, Are We on Track" on the basic mechanics of AI to learn how.

## HEY AI, ARE WE ON TRACK?

Three things will happen upon completing an exploration. First, our AI will look at comparable initiatives across many facets. We won't need to determine the sample set. AI will determine project similarity. Second, the outcomes of the sample set will be pulled. This means that the level of success that was captured from the life cycle of the sample set will be gathered. This will include pulses of where the project is trending along the way, as well as outcomes once the project is in execution and results are visible. Third, the feedback loop from the stakeholders for the initiative in question will be collected at the exploration stage. This feedback is the level of confidence or satisfaction with completed exploration. Historical data will also be pulled for each initiative in the sample.

With these three steps, AI will determine the pattern of "where we need to be with exploration" for it to be likely to contribute to a successful outcome, and compare that to where things actually stand. Where we need to be is really "What set of features are important for a successful outcome?" These features could be almost anything from pace of the work, to quality level, to confidence levels. The AI is comparing where things stand now against where similar initiatives stood at the same point, and using the outcomes of that sample to give a predictive measure. Are we on track or not? AI will signal.

An additional prompt for feedback can help provide clues on what the problem may be with the exploration. If a stakeholder is not very confident in the exploration, the system collects feedback on why. We can make this easy by providing a few choices like: (1) key matters are missing, (2) key questions for a matter are missing, or (3) answers to questions do not meet a quality level.

When it comes to the quality of answers, some common issues can include not enough supporting evidence or reasoning, incorrect assumptions, or missing considerations. These might also appear as precanned options for feedback when the quality of an answer is not meeting expectations.

As you can see, taking into account feedback loops on the confidence level, AI can look for interesting patterns. It can find relationships between the feedback and potential outcome. AI may surface relationships between features we didn't even know existed. I love the domain of personality attributes (of those staffed on the project team) and project fit. It's an example of where AI can inform some patterns that only the most intuitive people can place their finger on today. AI will go even further to help pinpoint or provide clues on how to get it on track.

Let's take an example. An exploration may have the right matters and questions (breadth and depth) to it. But the most critical questions may have answers lacking to the degree they will steer the project in the wrong direction. It could be that a couple answers are shallow, creating weak links. AI can look at cases where this has occurred previously and raise a concern signal.

What's different about the analytics or AI-driven approach to verifying exploration? Compare it to today's approach, where stakeholders need to need to probe and dig deep to understand where things stand. I've often started meetings with a series of clarifying questions. And it's a heavy lift to get right. I have to understand where the team stands, poke holes in the right areas, and assess on the spot.

Rather than run this manual verification process, a manager can get a good signal using AI. That's valuable when the manager is, for example, the CEO and needs to deal with a large set of priorities and initiatives. They may not have time to run deep-dive inquiries. The signal coming from the AI will help this leader focus.

Of course, there is a feedback loop required to assist the AI. This example is feedback on the quality of answers and their importance. Provided a decent number of people across a working team and their stakeholders (say, 8 to 10), this should be sufficient feedback.

## *Have We Achieved Alignment?*

Humans don't always voice their inner feelings so transparently. A more common scenario is that forums where we gather don't make it easy for enough voices to come through. Time constraints and personalities can get in the way. That's why data-driven approaches to measuring alignment, like we find in Workflow #8, can achieve breakthroughs. They take the ambiguity out of alignment by allowing stakeholders to be specific.

Imagine a scenario where we understand the level of alignment across various conclusions or recommendations. We also have a view on the importance of each of these factors. For example, we have high alignment on the key recommendations, and there are less influential recommendations where we're not as sure. We've walked through this simple data-gathering earlier; now it's time to take it to the next level.

Where do we mark the line of concern when it comes to alignment? How much alignment is enough? How much of it can be missing while still moving ahead, instead of zeroing in to sort through it? Armed with big data, we can know. Big data against a sample of similar initiatives will tie project success with alignment characteristics of the initiative you're working on. AI will inform us if the level of alignment is enough to promote project success. AI will uncover and weigh the hidden features of alignment (who, how much, when).

Compare this to how alignment rears its head today. Someone speaks up in a meeting and questions whether we have alignment based on a specific concern. It could be a loud voice, as opposed to a widespread one. It could be drawing a conclusion based on a limited connection to the underlying exploration. A perception could develop on weak grounds about the level of alignment or lack thereof. This perspective should not carry much weight.

How can AI help? Let's say during the workflows around recommendations there was a good amount of support. They were rated as sound and exhaustive. The data is correlated with successful outcomes. AI gives us the confidence that we should continue, despite a strong dissenting voice.

In too many circumstances, the current approach to driving alignment is like reading tea leaves. It's hard to do and not entirely objective. Of course, there is a feedback loop required to assist the AI. In this example, it's feedback on the level of agreement with the recommendations under consideration and their significance (some are big commitments and others less so). Provided a decent number of people across a working team and their stakeholders (say, 8 to 10), this should be sufficient feedback.

## Are We Ready to Make This Decision?

Reaching a decision point is often not an easy thing to determine. There can be differences of opinion on readiness. How can we reach these points more objectively and confidently? AI can help avoid premature decisions or dragging them out unnecessarily.

We've talked about rushing to a conclusion based on poor or little exploration. This can happen in a risk-averse culture. It can lead to closing the doors on an opportunity or thinking very small about it. On the flip side, being cavalier about decisions and going forward without enough understanding can lead to big problems down the line. Be careful, especially when entering "one-way doors."

When it comes to dragging out decisions, we know this can lead to losing out on market opportunities and a ton of employee frustration.

The role of AI in determining whether we're ready for decisions will also tap big data sets. For a given initiative, we will have feedback on the quality of an exploration and the level of alignment on its recommendations. Now imagine we captured data on decision points across a wider sample of initiatives. Did they occur too soon, too late, or within a reasonable time frame? We can collect this feedback at intervals after the decision points (a month, a quarter, and a year later). The wider sample of initiatives also comes along with data on the quality of explorations and level of alignment.

AI can find patterns to triangulate when we're ready for decisions based on the quality of the exploration and level of alignment. It considers the instances of timely decision points across a sample of initiatives. It finds more mature initiatives that met the right quality bar of upstream work and lets us know if we've met it with a current initiative—in other words, readiness.

Compared to today, this approach is far less subjective and emotionally driven. When are decisions made in your organization?

Sometimes decision points depend on schedules. For example, when an initiative is reviewed monthly or has a place on an agenda in some biweekly forum, the result can be that decisions are delayed until the schedule allows. When a decision is socialized, there can be fear of making it, and objections can kick the can down the road. It's easy to punt when one influential or forceful voice raises an objection, even when the upstream work is solid. On the flip side, we might be impulsive about decisions to keep things moving or avoid becoming bureaucratic. In the AI-driven approach, a system can simply alert us. There are timely decisions to make. It can also work the other way; decisions are being pushed, but the upstream work has not yet met the quality bar to make them.

Of course, there is a feedback loop required to assist the AI. In this example, it requires feedback on the timing of decisions, from a sample of initiatives that are further along. It also requires ratings on the quality of exploration leading up to them as well as the level of alignment for these decisions. Provided a decent number of people across a working team and their stakeholders (say, 8 to 10), this should be sufficient feedback.

### What Should the Decision Be?

In this section, I will walk through a specific algorithm to make decisions. It's the pinnacle capability Decision Sprint will enable. Everything the workflows enable lead up to this most coveted aspect of management—strength of decision-making.

With Decision Sprint, we can see the thread between a proposed decision and the underlying exploration. Stakeholders do not have to ask how you arrived at this recommendation or that proposed decision. The connection will be a direct one. A stakeholder group can read the relevant aspects of the exploration for the context.

When it comes to analytics and AI, we go even further.

Let's talk about a more analytical approach to start. Think about a proposed decision, and let's assume the options are yes or no.

Now think about a set of matters that comprise the exploration related to this decision. After reading the FAQs for each matter, a stakeholder is asked whether they are inclined or not inclined to support the proposed decision. This connects each matter to the decision. There could be five or six matters connected to a decision, so this would imply five or six inputs from each stakeholder.

On top of that, the relative importance of each matter is compared against each other matter. This is called a pair-wise comparison—you ask for each pair of matters to be compared in terms of relative importance. This provides a weight for each matter.

Taken together, this provides a quantifiable way to take a position on a decision. It uses the matters, specifically their influence on being inclined or not inclined on a decision and weights, to generate a quantifiable decision. That could be a strong yes or no, or a value in the middle.

AI comes into the picture with what we'll talk about next. Over time, the company will get a sense for project outcomes like success or failure. And teams will conduct retrospectives. A retrospective is a look back at where things went right or wrong, using hindsight. Hindsight can help feed AI and turn it into foresight.

During retrospectives, teams should evaluate the weights given to different matters at the decision points in the past. What was overweighted? What was underweighted? Next, we turn to how individuals weighted matters and understand how accurate they turned out to be. There are amazing, game-changing possibilities armed with this data. Let's say you're an individual involved in a wide array of projects employing these methods. And let's say you've categorized these projects into operational, innovation, strategic, tactical, and so forth.

In what type of projects is your weighting of factors more accurate? Is your judgment a better fit for types of problems and challenges a company faces versus others? AI can learn about the patterns. What would be done differently with this insight? AI will help us figure out what weights to apply to different people voting on decisions based on their track record.

AI will score each individual's input on weights based on their track record. The more accurate an individual's track record in previous decision-making exercises, the higher their score and influence on decisions of the same nature going forward.

Compare this to current approaches.

First, decisions are hard to explain even after they are made. What factors were considered? Which were deemed more important factors than others? And why? And then who was involved? Were some factors over- or underweighted based on the people in the room? Are the loud voices helpful or hurtful to decision-making?

There has to be a better, more objective way to make decisions. The analytical approach I mentioned will help make it more objective and easier to explain the why behind decisions. AI will refine that approach, allowing companies to build a graph of whose judgment is most relevant depending on the problem's nature. How different is this state of the world compared to how your company works currently? It's the future state that will become common to how a company is managed.

Of course, there is a feedback loop required to assist the AI. In this example, it comes from the retrospective. It's the reflection on how each matter impacted the decision and how they should have been weighted for the right decision to have been taken. Provided a decent number of people across a working team and their stakeholders (say, 8 to 10), this should be sufficient feedback.

## MANAGEMENT FUELED BY AI

As you can imagine, the work of management can shift in new and meaningful ways powered by AI. Going back to the idea of mission control, it's an opportunity for human + AI partnership.

For starters, it provides a new way to look across the range of initiatives in a company and understand what requires attention. A dashboard will be a critical ingredient. Think about one that covers the top initiatives, the stage of their effort across upstream work, and AI signals about whether things are on track.

## Dashboard of the Future

A dashboard with higher-level comparisons will become a norm for AI-driven management. What's interesting is the dashboard will change dynamically if the workflows of Decision Sprint are enabled through digital tools. For each initiative, new data will come into the picture as the workflows unfold. In other words, it's a living system. Management will know much faster about where things really stand. The work of management can shift to become more real time. I'll build on that in Chapter 14, "The Upstream CEO."

The main idea is to reduce guesswork and listening through the grapevine about what requires management attention. Instead, it will be possible to pinpoint more objectively where teams and initiatives may be stuck. When the confidence level or level of alignment around an exploration does not signal a high chance of success, management can focus on where progress has stalled. It can be a thought partner where it is most needed.

Dashboards will be used for more than signals on potential problems. Dashboards will be used to accelerate progress.

Think about the pace and velocity required for an initiative to be successful. An initiative may not be stuck, but can we do better? What type of pace and velocity do we need to see in an initiative for it to fit the pattern of our most successful ones? AI can inform this comparison.

What about improving velocity and pace over time? Are our top initiatives experiencing better velocity and pace (while preserving quality levels) now than in prior quarters and years? They should. Building explorations. Running explorations. Achieving alignment. Reaching decision points with confidence. These workflows should be easier and faster over time. Dashboards inform whether that is happening. It's the idea of continuous improvement.

Management can evaluate and take certain actions in order to improve velocity and pace. This could include validating which explorations are taking place, identifying missing talent or competencies within an exploration, paving the way for these resources to materialize, nudging the right participation, providing forums for decision-making, and promoting the adoption of workflows.

Stepping back to the big picture, you can imagine a shift in management's time. Management will spend more of their time consuming and analyzing data about project workflow through dashboards.

How will these dashboards be generated? That's where data scientists come into play. Many companies employ data scientists to provide insight on customer-facing activities. For example, e-commerce businesses like Amazon, Shopify, and Etsy use data science to test and learn about a range of issues from website layout, to checkout flows, to product merchandising. When upstream work is established and takes place through digital tools, a company can tap data science to develop AI models and big-data environments. They will inform how upstream work is unfolding through the dashboards we've discussed.

The opportunities for data science to create insight for a company go well beyond the project workflow.

## INTELLECTUAL CAPITAL AND DECISION SPRINT

Consider the rate of new knowledge being created in the company about an area. Let's say there is a strategic pillar on a company's road map. For McDonald's it could be new service models like curbside pickup or delivery or plant-based food. For Volvo it could be a subscription business model or sustainability of cars. It will be interesting to see if projects in these areas grow momentum and traction as new knowledge about them grows.

To make it concrete, let's look at the FAQ level. As a reminder, these are the questions and answers underlying exploration. Let's assume new FAQs are developed as part of exploration. On top of that, their quality and importance are evaluated. Not all question-answer pairs have the same value to unlocking an opportunity. Some provide more clarity than others, usually addressing more ambiguity. That's why assigning a relative value for each FAQ (some type of strategic importance score) is something to consider. As more quality "answers" are shipped, we might look to data science to understand if there's a correlation with project outcomes or progress. I would imagine the answer would be yes. Clarity of thought often paves the way for teams to put together better recommendations and drive better decisions. Better decisions improve chances of seeing good outcomes. The eureka moments make it clear what actions should be taken.

You may be wondering what the big deal is about FAQs or answering some pertinent questions in an exploration. These FAQs are intellectual capital. Intellectual capital is any unique knowledge or understanding. It's like being ahead of the curve on how a puzzle works. I use the term *understanding* in the definition because we don't need to know with certainty the answer to a question. If it's a clear line of thinking considering the known unknowns, that is intellectual capital.

Data science can inform whether my hypothesis holds true (by creating AI models that look for these patterns). Is the rate of producing new intellectual capital a signal of success? If a company continues to pile up strong understanding about an area, will that correlate with results?

If so, this is a huge game-changer for companies. It means upstream focus (asking the right questions and developing strong perspective on the answers) is a quantifiable indicator of future success.

This provides great leverage for managers. Management will obsess over the production of new intellectual capital in strategic areas. Great leaders already do this today. It's why upstream CEOs focus on input over output. You'll hear from upstream CEOs in Chapter 14.

In Chapter 1, I shared a bird's-eye view of my experience at McDonald's shifting a meeting from output focus to input focus. I knew that if we've thought deeply about the right issues and developed clear thoughts, then we would develop the right plans. I was seeking to understand if we had the right level of intellectual capital. Where do we need it? Do we have it? What needs to change to get there? These are the higher-level questions that C-suite executives should focus on more than on specific opinions about what course of action to take.

## BLOCKCHAIN, AI, AND UPSTREAM WORK

In these next few sections, you will learn how upstream work, AI, and blockchain can usher in a new way to value companies. You'll learn how upstream work generates a new asset for companies in the form of intellectual capital that can be ascribed a value.

Rather than waiting for current downstream measures to show up or trust subjective forecasts of future performance, we can unlock new data to value companies. This is a huge concept, and I recognize that many details need to be worked out. People smarter than me will develop the right mechanisms and algorithms. Let's take a look at some high level possibilities and use cases.

## INTELLECTUAL CAPITAL AND VALUATION

We've talked about the building blocks of intellectual capital—the FAQ. Let's assume the organization is scoring the importance of each FAQ. Remember, each FAQ is part of some exploration related to an initiative. And let's assume the exploration that an FAQ is associated with is understood to have some expected value. This could be a function of the market opportunity or size of the prize. If the exploration holds a certain value $X$ and this FAQ has a certain importance in the exploration, some quantifiable value can be ascribed at the FAQ level. How much is this puzzle piece worth relative to that market opportunity?

Next, we need to factor in the quality score of the FAQ. If the FAQ has a high-quality score, meaning the confidence level is high around "how right we believe the answer is," then more of the value or worth is being realized.

To recap, we need three building blocks:

- An expected value of the exploration
- The relative importance of each FAQ in the exploration
- A quality score for each FAQ

What could the output of these building blocks look like? It comes in the form of a backlog of upstream initiatives and the expected value creation of these upstream initiatives.

Imagine a management team having visibility to a backlog that shows the future value of initiatives in the pipeline, even before financial models can be created. Or think about the common dynamic in financial modeling where it's difficult to show the work behind the assumptions being made.

Having started my career at Goldman Sachs and having created hundreds of financial models, I can readily admit that most modeling comes down to laying out the framework. The work of populating assumptions into the framework can be no more than educated guesswork. Nonetheless, it's the premodeling phase where management can get a good sense about the extent of value on the table. I think this is a huge spur for innovation because many innovations die before they reach a stage where a model can be developed.

Now you can't simply run these numbers and claim that certain future values will be created. The upstream needs to cross over into the downstream, and new unknowns will surface along the way. Financial analysts would call this a discount rate.

That's where AI comes into the picture. Across a portfolio of prior initiatives, AI will look at the value conversion that occurs from similar stages of similar initiatives. AI will look at the upstream stages of comparable initiatives that are further along and how value materialized further downstream. Of course, this requires feedback loops on the value creation of the portfolio we're comparing against to provide a data set. If you think this is far-fetched, consider that the kind of algorithms and feedback loops I'm referring to are so mainstream you don't even hear about them (search engines, recommendation systems, and Siri suggestions).

To make it concrete, let's say we have a comparable initiative that has migrated from upstream well into the downstream. At the upstream stages, we mark an expected value for the explorations, and we follow the life of these explorations as they proceed downstream (when the decisions or actions from these explorations were taken). We mark the value creation of the explorations at the downstream stages. AI can tap into these data sets to estimate the likelihood of a current upstream initiative converting on its potential value. It would apply a factor to the expected value from the three building blocks I presented earlier. It could be a factor that would discount the expected value, but it could also be a factor that would grow it.

There are several complexities to solve for on the path to using this approach:

- The value of an exploration can change. (It could be smaller or bigger based on externalities. As of writing this book, crypto and Web3 seem like huge new markets, but if the hype fizzles out, that could discount the size of the prize for a related initiative in your organization.) That's why they need to be "marked to market" periodically.

- Assigning relative importance and quality scores can be subjective. We need to develop objective approaches and have independent "bar raisers" in companies.
- Good comparative data needs to be available. Life-cycle data is required to feed AI. We need to develop enough critical mass of data for comparable initiatives across their life cycle. The habit or ritualization of this is a dependency in order to populate a big data set.

Yes, there is a ton to figure out and establish as methods in the organization.

I am a huge believer in valuation fueled by AI over the guesswork of management forecasts. The building blocks and approaches to how it would come together provide the basis for this.

Why is this important? It's a huge unlock for CEOs. It's hard to convince investors to play for the long term. The transparency and visibility provided by AI-fueled valuation is a way to overcome this stalemate and conflict. Many investors don't have patience for amazing new ideas; they can come across as wishful ambitions of CEOs that are very far away from impacting results. Tomorrow, the picture can be entirely different.

## THE ROLE OF BLOCKCHAIN

There's one more ingredient for AI-fueled valuation to work. It's blockchain. If you're not familiar with it, here's a description from IBM: "Blockchain is a shared, immutable ledger that facilitates the process of recording transactions and tracking assets." Many things live on the blockchain, like currency and digital art. Why not intellectual capital?

Blockchain is key to enabling trust from the external community of investors. It's a record at specific instances that can't be tampered with. It provides assurance that the data used to estimate the value of intellectual capital in the company from upstream work is true. This cuts both ways for management teams. It builds trust that a valuation is truthful. When initiatives are going well, that's great. When initiatives are struggling, it can't be fudged with to look better. Management teams have to own up to the reality of initiatives.

## MARKETPLACES ON THE BLOCKCHAIN

If we want to go even further, think about intellectual capital as a real asset. It not only impacts the company's valuation—it can be traded. Long before companies sell off units or divisions, they can trade intellectual capital with each other. That's where blockchain becomes key.

Let's take an example. Your company has developed a novel and new way of thinking about a loyalty program. It's going to reward customers for doing business not only with your company, but with a network of other brands. The team has put tremendous effort into it and figured out a lot. Some real intellectual capital has been developed.

While your company will implement the new program, it sees more value if it can let another company run with the intellectual capital and sell an offering to more businesses in other industries. Your company does not want to become a B2B provider of a loyalty program. Your company wants to stick with B2C. Rather than creating and funding a new unit within your organization to do this, the blockchain allows for an alternative. The alternative is to trade the intellectual capital today (while still having access to use it internally).

How might this work?

The exploration (FAQs) lives on the blockchain. And the right third-party domain experts have access to evaluate it and ascribe some value to that knowledge. Maybe another company in a separate industry is keen to operate a loyalty program business. They are comfortable being a B2B provider. The intellectual capital provides a head start. Maybe they are not great at developing new ideas and innovations but are stronger at scaling them. So they look to a marketplace to get a channel into growth opportunities. Blockchain, with some independent validation of the intellectual capital and its worth, can help companies trade value in this new way.

# BETTER INPUTS FOR
# EMPLOYEE PERFORMANCE

Another huge area for data science to shape how we run companies is employee performance.

Think about the potential to better quantify the contribution of an employee to an initiative. Decision Sprint provides many opportunities for contribution. Asking a good question is contribution. Sourcing a relevant matter is contribution. Answering is contribution, as is improving an answer. Building an exploration with the right breadth and depth is a team-level contribution, as is completing an exploration that makes alignment easier. Coming up with nonobvious yet important recommendations is contribution. We can go on and on.

With feedback loops, it's possible to get a measure on the value of discrete contributions. For example, which answers are most important in drawing conclusions or making recommendations? What was the quality level of answers provided? And what difficulty or complexity was involved in providing those answers?

Why does it matter to quantify contribution at this level?

Imagine tying project outcomes with these contributions. A unique contribution influenced the outcome in a positive way. We want more of that. It should be recognized and rewarded. Today these contributions are hidden. Tomorrow they can be revealed.

The data can feed into performance evaluation and talent planning. You can probably imagine a performance review in the future moving from the general to the specific. Instead of using our best recollection of contribution to a project, we can be specific. A performance review can cite very specific contributions, attribute them, and identify their value.

## *Planning Talent*

We've discussed AI related to "what the decision should be" and learned how companies will be better able to assess the judgment of individuals. Some people have more relevant judgment on certain types of problems than others. From a talent-planning perspective, here are some higher-level questions managers should be looking at fueled by AI:

- Do we have the right kind of judgment or competencies to match the problem-solving ahead of us?
- Have we staffed initiatives with the right mix of these judgments and competencies? A mix of the right contributions may be linked with better project outcomes. For example, we want people who ask great questions as well as those who can provide great answers.
- When we look out quarters and years, what kind of competency mix do we need? What shifts need to be made? Are our hiring and recruitment aligned to those needs?

As you can see, the big opportunity is to match the ongoing and future needs of the organization with the capabilities of talent. AI enables a new way to look at this matching process. It may be clear what types of opportunities and problems a company will be facing. Often, it's less clear what individuals are good at contributing when it comes to day-to-day work, such as asking the right questions, poking holes, shoring up holes, answering questions, synthesizing recommendations, or identifying the concrete actions tied to a recommended direction.

Decision Sprint surfaces this information, whereas it's largely hidden today.

Human capital and intellectual capital are really intertwined. Decision Sprint is the bridge between the two. It gives us the means to surface data on the contribution employees are making to knowledge that helps our companies take action.

## THE LONG AND SHORT OF IT

This chapter has definitely geeked out. If it caught your interest, you might find yourself returning to it several times to allow the concepts to sink in. I hope you do that for one reason. It's not to make this book more widely read. I've written this chapter to plant seeds. It's my hope that more specialized (and smarter) people will build on these concepts. It will take a community of specialized talent to turn these concepts into practice for managers and leaders of organizations. With AI enabled by Decision Sprint, there can be quantifiable data about the progression of ideas and their expected results into the future. AI can tie the dots. AI can even help investors get onboard. As a CEO, this is why you need to embrace upstream work in the new way provided by Decision Sprint. You are building a system for the next era of business. Looking back, today's approach will seem like child's play. AI-fueled management is inevitable, and Decision Sprint will provide the raw materials.

# The Upstream CEO

'I've always imagined the time when a CEO starts a day with the assistance of radar. What kind of radar? It's one that provides signals (or clues) as to where the most attention is needed *now*, as opposed to being constrained by a predefined schedule. The right answer is somewhere in the middle.

A predefined schedule comes from planning ahead on touchpoints for relevant issues and initiatives. At the same time, this box can be limiting. I'm referring to a feeling in the bones you get about something that is calling for your attention when leading a big business or being in the CEO position. You may be several levels removed from the issues or initiatives, and there are so many under your remit. Somehow the intuition has you wondering: Is there something more important calling for my intention *right now*?

In the future, AI will help fuel this radar. It won't be a matter of intuition alone. Great CEOs act on their intuition by redirecting time despite regimented schedules toward what is most important to place attention into now. But this takes a certain personality, confidence, and practice to do well. It's more art than science, according to Volvo's former CEO Hakan Samuelsson:

> A lot of managers think, we need to be very efficient, so let's define the target and measure how people do the job.

Then they ask people to "deliver your numbers." Everybody then adapts their way of measuring to be able to say they have reached their target. You need to go deeper into how things are done.

People say, what you cannot measure is not worth doing. Totally bullsh\*\*, because often the most important things to do, you can't measure. You must discuss what and how to reach understanding and commitment on the right actions. Then the results will come. We focus too much on output such as results and targets.

We should focus more on input, the right "what" and "how" actions. That is something I learned in my first company. We didn't do management by objectives, but management by means, methods, and principles. How do we run production? What methods do we use to improve quality? That defines a way of working that people can relate to much more easily. 🙽

Through decades of effort, Hakan has developed his ability to cut through and get the clues. AI will enable this as more of a science. It will democratize this ability. It will provide radar to act on. It will help more CEOs place attention on what matters most now. It will speed up resolving issues and help avoid costly pitfalls.

This approach doesn't imply that schedules are obsolete or that CEOs disrespect preexisting commitments. It just means there is no hesitation to recalibrate the use of time. Bend schedules when there's good reason.

Let's talk about schedules for a moment and use of time. Having been in the C-suite of three Fortune 500 companies, I have an appreciation for planned touchpoints on key initiatives.

My teams consisted of hundreds or thousands of employees, and there could be a dozen or more initiatives that needed attention at any moment of time. Often, I would work backward from milestones such as decision meetings to build in time to review explorations and create alignment. Schedules help us slot these interactions. I loved slotting these in advance so that we had the space.

Schedules allow us to bring the workflows we've discussed in Chapter 7 into an overall timeline. But I was very clear with my assistants and teams that schedules are a juggling act. And I set expectations for roughly 20 percent flexibility in my schedule over the horizon of the next 24 to 72 hours. What was the use of this 20 percent flexibility? It's the space we allow to become more real-time about our availability. Do the math. Twenty percent daily flexibility implies a good number of hours per week to allocate to real-time needs.

To me this was a norm. It's how I create flexibility to respond to issues or initiatives calling for my attention now. Priorities should be based on real-time status of affairs, not old information on where things stand. In my view, great executives constantly baseline their priorities and see what the stack should look like. I would do it daily, if not several times a day.

A great executive instantly processes new information about issues and initiatives to determine priority. And when that priority runs into conflict with schedules, they don't hesitate to create space. Mediocre executives are by contrast slaves to predetermined schedules and can be hard to reach for days or even weeks, leaving teams in limbo.

Interestingly, I found Hakan to be one of the easiest persons to schedule time with while I was at Volvo. He was an incredibly involved CEO internally and very outward facing. The demands on his time were terribly hard to fathom, yet he felt really accessible. Why is that? It's his instinctive radar about what mattered most now.

In the previous chapter, you've read about how AI will help provide this radar. And provided you have the courage to act on it, you will see the gears in your organization move in better harmony. This is your highest contribution. You must develop radar about where your attention is most required in the moment and apply it to unlock others.

## UPSTREAMING NOW

If you run an organization and day-to-day performance is stable, you're in a great position to shift the use of your time. You can delegate more operations and increase availability for upstream efforts. In fact, you should seek out the most meaningful upstream work. Demonstrate openness to engage with teams that are embarking on the upstream journey. Swap downstream activities such as detailed quarterly business reviews with the problem statements that shape the next wave of results. Work from the strategic direction of the company and the initiatives that are expected to take flight. Find interactions to calibrate as you explore these initiatives; make sure they are aligned, and check in that decisions are being made on high-quality exploration. I spell out these workflows in Chapter 7, including the specific ones where the CEO can interface.

The more stable your organization and the more predictable today's performance, the more you can shift attention upstream. Not every organization or leader is so fortunate. That's why before talking about how CEOs will spend time in 2030 or 2040, I start with today's reality. As a CEO, you may feel far away from freeing up time to focus on upstream.

What typically happens when an operational problem occurs in your organization? For example, a customer-facing system is down. Or parts are missing for production and manufacturing. Or there are lines and queues impacting wait times. We must "drop everything" and make it right. Look to Decision Sprint as a way of addressing those problem-solving efforts.

Some organizations grapple with persistent operational issues, and it becomes a situation of whack-a-mole. Problems are being solved, but the company is not moving ahead. All the attention is downstream. Organizations can get addicted to this mode. Work becomes troubleshooting the latest operational problem. If these problems persist, today's results will be impacted. The company will suffer. So might your career. And there won't be the same opportunities to land tomorrow's grand visions.

A company of firefighters can, at best, maintain the status quo.

CEOs and executives can become hostage to these environments. They may craft lofty ideas and work through them. But fire drills on today's operations will take up a good amount of energy across the organization. There won't be the capacity or energy to tackle the new. The organization will lack the practice of working through innovation or strategy.

You may have witnessed a certain dissonance in companies. The executives are in the clouds, and the day-to-day reality is about fire-fighting. Executives are not wrong to think about the future, but they need to change today's reality.

If your organization is a pure downstream player, meaning it's all about keeping today's operations afloat, it will take a big push to reverse the tide. But it is possible. I call this process upstreaming.

When it comes to today's operations, identify something strategic to upstream. The organization may be expecting to address an operational challenge in the same old way with bandages and duct tape. Quick fixes. But there's an opportunity to rethink, a more strategic way to go about crafting a plan and direction. Yes, it's Decision Sprint.

The problem may need an immediate solution. But don't let the team off the hook so easily. Keep the tiger team fixing the immediate problem assembled so that it can peel back things much further. These can be parallel tracks. For example, set expectations that in parallel to shipping a fix, the team will be running an exploration to address more strategic questions like, "What does good look like?" or "How do we make things 10 times or 20 times better than today?" I took this approach at MGM Resorts when guests across our properties (like Bellagio, Aria, and others) on the Las Vegas strip could not check in to rooms due to a system outage. The immediate pain of manually checking in customers was resolved within hours. The upstreaming effort took weeks, and in the course of it revealed a number of bigger vulnerabilities that could make us a less-resilient business. With sponsorship from the top, the teams could invest the time, energy, and resources to prevent not only a future outage but a bigger problem.

Doing this has three benefits:

- It begins to train the team on upstream work and teaches new muscle.
- It will reduce the likelihood of operational problems from this specific area as the fundamental issues will be understood and addressed. While it won't happen overnight, at some point, the organization will experience stability.
- The stability in this area will create space to address new opportunities proactively.

# TRANSFORMATION AND UPSTREAMING

I've led major functions within global companies where firefighting was the norm at the start. When I first took on those roles, there was not enough capacity to act strategically. I've elaborated on an example of this in my first day on the job as Volvo's Global CIO.

The ambition of moving from firefighting to acting strategically, and doing it within two to five years, is called transformation. Many large companies find themselves within transformation. These can be supply chain, digital, business model, or strategic transformations of some kind. This was the challenge faced by H&R Block CEO Jeff Jones, as captured in our interview.

*Excerpts from an Interview with Jeff Jones,*
*President & CEO, H&R Block, on Communication*
*as a Strategic Tool*

**Atif:** In terms of critical initiatives and innovations that your team has been driving, what is your management style? What lessons can be shared from how you communicate and encourage teams to work together around ambitious goals?

**Jeff:** Well, first, the framework of exploration, alignment, and decision-making is right on to me. We are where we are, and we need to be brutally honest about where we are. We all need to see the problems and opportunities the same way to understand where we need to go.

I've always believed, and I brought this to Block, that work must be done by the organization and not outsourced to a consultant. It's just super important that if you want the management team to learn a strategy, they must own alignment from the starting point and not be handed it by somebody they don't know or trust.

Beyond that, there needs to be lots of simplification and communication and repetition of what we are doing. From the first week, we got very clear from the exploration of how we got here that there were five fundamental challenges the company faced. We then asked: What's the antidote to those challenges? What do we have to be or do different to systematically change those things?

One example is the company had been losing clients but raising prices and maintaining flat revenue. The more we were raising prices, the more we were losing clients. The result of that was a decade of flat revenue.

That required a lot of analysis to understand what we could do differently. Then there was exploration around possibilities. We could change the financial envelope of the company. We could set new expectations with Wall Street. We could invest in different ways. We could lower prices after years of raising prices. What's the broadest exploration possible to address the antidote for the problem?

That work led to real clarity. Alignment kicked in again because our antidote ended up reducing our EBITDA margins from about 30 percent to 25 percent and communicating to Wall Street that we were going to make less money. As a result, we were asking them to invest that with us and improve the quality and value of our core products.

Obviously, lots of alignment was required, as well as communication, and shareholder outreach—because we were making a bold decision to say we are going temporarily backward. But if we don't go backward and reset to invest, we had no chance of getting to the next pillars of our strategy. Today, several years later, we're delivering some of the best performance in the history of the company and in 2022, our stock reached 15 new all-time highs.

**Atif:** In the decision-making process, sometimes we get in the room and not everyone that is impacted is present. Then people wonder: What did they decide? Sometimes that communication just gets to people through the air. What's your view on the importance of communication and cascading decisions?

**Jeff:** When we talk about decisions around enterprise priorities and strategy, communication is everything. How do you simplify it? How do you repeat it? We communicated across many channels. For example, I am making videos and writing LinkedIn posts. We also bring together a larger group than many companies in the prioritization process.

Think about the top 30 people. Teach them how to make enterprise decisions, how to work through trade-offs, and how to recognize that trade-offs are different when the decision is at the level of your team versus your function versus the enterprise. It's not until you are practicing that together that one realizes how hard it is.

As it relates to Block, and this is different at many companies, if we start asking ourselves how we go faster, the key to going faster is creating shorthand with each other. The way you do that is by building trust. The way you build trust is through communication. It all flows back the way we are communicating, which helps us go faster and meshes it all together.

Upstreaming is a powerful tool for transformation. When we take a current focus area and upstream it, a very noticeable message is sent through the organization. It demonstrates that current realities are being prioritized as opposed to living in the clouds. It's a way of problem-solving that teaches the organization how to embrace unknowns and put together innovative solutions. Jeff and his team demonstrated courage to take a step back in order to propel forward.

The MGM example of a system outage is less glamorous, but it demonstrates how operational matters can be upstreamed. In other words, we took a downstream situation and gave it the upstream treatment. When the organization encounters upstream work in other areas—let's say new ideas that are not yet operational—it will have context for how it works. That's a positive side effect.

If you're the CEO of a company living primarily in the downstream, check out these three takeaways:

- Look for operational pains that can be addressed strategically, and upstream the problem-solving effort.
- Find a portfolio of downstream pains, group them into related areas, and package them as a transformation.
- Establish Decision Sprint to upstream the transformations.

You may need to get enough traction in these areas before booting up the bigger ideas that comprise the far-reaching vision of the organization. There may need to be a solid base or shoring up of today's realities before the organization can tackle vision. This should be motivation enough to shore up these realities. Most CEOs will want to get on with mobilizing for their strategic vision.

## WHAT GETS CEO TIME IN 20__.

Your organization has embraced upstream work. The workflows spelled out in Chapter 7 are running like trains on schedule across key initiatives. Decision Sprint is on the path to being a norm. Upstreaming has worked.

Yes, this may take years to achieve. But what then? What does the plate of the upstream CEO look like? When the hard work of upstreaming your organization is achieved, what lies ahead? What powerful new ways to lead your organization have opened up? What new capabilities lie in the hands of the CEO?

We'll talk about three focus areas for upstream CEOs as we look out in the future. I don't know if this is gazing 5 years ahead or 25, but have no doubt AI will usher in a new era for how CEOs spend time. When AI takes hold, it can radically shift the nature of CEO work.

We'll cover three areas:

1. Driving valuation through upstream work + AI
2. Strategic planning based on AI
3. Calibrating upstream initiatives through AI-based radar

All three areas are connected in a flywheel. I will walk through each component.

## DRIVING VALUATION

One of the main responsibilities of the CEO is to grow the valuation of the company.

In the prior chapter, we introduced a powerful new way to accomplish this. Upstream work can lift the value of a company even before we build initiatives into financial forecasts or move downstream into execution. This is a huge concept to get our head around.

You've spent a ton of time thinking about the biggest value creation opportunities for the organization. You've put your finger on what they are and green-lighted the resources and commitments to get them off the ground.

What is the rate of intellectual capital we are producing on the key initiatives, and how are they translating into value? With AI, you don't need to wait for the answer. You don't need to wait for good understanding, recommendations, or plans to pan out. AI will inform how sound they really are. AI is providing a better indication of how upstream efforts will be creating value out in the future.

Take the entire picture together. There are current operations. Your team has a good grasp to forecast it. With that operational forecast you can drive some value. There are new initiatives, in various upstream stages, and AI is helping shed light on what you can expect as contribution. With this entire picture, an organization can assess what valuation it can justify and what its current worth truly is.

What if it's not enough? There are micro and meta moves we can make. Let's start with the micro.

## STRATEGIC PLANNING

Strategic planning is one of those murky phrases. Every company does some degree of it, but does it really matter beyond a few nice PowerPoint slides? With AI, it can become far more data driven and connected to the day-to-day work.

Often a select group of bright minds do the strategic planning, and then hand it off to doers across the company. AI will create connective tissue between the big picture and how things are unfolding on the ground.

At the CEO level, it's about aligning the growth ambitions with strategic pillars of the company, talent, and workforce planning.

Let's make this real. Your organization would like to double in a period (every 3 years, 5 years, 10 years, etc.). That's ambition that implies a certain valuation. To get there, a company develops a set of strategic pillars from where the growth will come. Each pillar may have several underlying initiatives to support it. This is all standard stuff. Most companies have this in a single PowerPoint chart that looks like a pyramid with purpose at the top, pillars in the middle and the underlying initiatives below. I've shown an example of this in Chapter 3 (Figure 3.3).

None of this comes to life or fruition without people or talent. How do we know if we have the people and profiles necessary to pull it off? AI can help us define talent pools and profiles for the underlying initiatives. A good HR leader or CHRO will raise this concern to the extent they are involved with strategic planning. But again, it's often a matter of intuition and hard to land such a message into the organization. AI can make this a more quantifiable approach.

AI evaluates similar initiatives and the staffing levels and profiles to determine how much and what kind of talent we need from the current priorities. Across the strategic pillars of the company, this is a major exercise in workforce planning. It's one that the CEO should be driving to make big moves, if necessary. For example, a company may have more downstream players than it needs and lacking on the upstream part. Or it has the right profile of players, but there isn't enough capacity given the number of initiatives on the table. Workforce planning based on AI is a huge area to unlock.

A second problem with current strategic planning is it's static.

AI can make it dynamic.

We've talked about valuation methods based on the intellectual capital of upstream initiatives. AI provides a current measure of what the initiatives are on track to produce.

If you're the CEO, there can be a few scenarios to respond to:

1. The initiatives/pillars are not adding up, but they should be. You go into corrective action on today's upstream work where things are not on track.
2. The initiatives/pillars are not adding up, and that's for good reason. It could be that the opportunities are not as meaningful as originally thought. You need to source new ideas and iterate on the strategic planning effort. Don't wait for surprises of planning cycles to do this. I can personally attest not every big idea I sponsored was as big as we imagined in the end.

3. The initiatives/pillars are adding up. It's time to accelerate. You have the space to think even bigger than what's on today's plate and horizons.

The reality for a CEO is life can fluctuate between these three scenarios. You spend a few quarters addressing scenarios 1 and 2. Scenario 3 becomes appropriate to tackle down the line.

Of course, strategic planning is very connected to valuation. The growth ambition in terms of valuation will define the strategic plan.

With AI, it's possible to connect a strategic plan to a current measure of valuation. AI can inform if they are equating to each other, or not. It can help a CEO take various actions to alter the plan or improve the execution of the plan so they come into harmony.

## CALIBRATING INITIATIVES

I opened this chapter with emphasis on acting on the now. AI fuels radar. By now you understand how this radar on upstream allows a CEO to understand what matters most now. It's a matter of what drives the future valuation the company is expecting and whether the AI tells us we're on track to produce the contribution or not. What contributions do we need most, and how on track are we? The size of the deltas informs what to place focus on.

In Chapter 13, "AI as Mission Control," I shared how AI can place the finger on where the problem lies within an initiative. Which workflow is facing a quality issue? Is it the building of exploration? The results of exploration? The level of alignment? Decision points?

For example, let's say things are stalled at the alignment step. With AI-based radar, we can convene a meeting with the project team and sponsors to investigate. Let's say during this interaction, an objection comes forward from a sponsor: "I'm not convinced we have considered matter $X$ enough. My concerns about it are the following risks that we haven't looked into deeply enough."

Does that sound fair enough? If so, the attention moves to error correction. We need to open up the exploration again.

What are the unknowns or key questions around these risks, and who is best to provide input? It's an interaction worth doing. Then we can run the alignment workflows again. We should also inquire why these inputs on matters and questions were missed in building the exploration.

The issues we need to calibrate around important initiatives can come in many flavors. It may not be missed inputs or considerations. AI can reveal that velocity is not sufficient. We are not moving fast enough. Convening a meeting to ask why could help put the finger on why. It could be a resourcing matter or prioritization.

With the radar I spoke about at the start of the chapter, we can imagine a CEO being more able to resolve bottlenecks or mistakes in upstream work based on contribution. It's about spending time "where the juice is worth the squeeze" of the CEO.

## BRINGING THE FLYWHEEL TOGETHER

We've just walked through three legs of a stool for CEOs.

It's about strategic planning, calibrating initiatives, and driving the valuation of the company. (See Figure 14.1.)

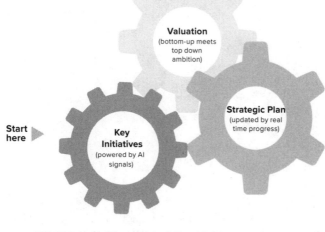

**FIGURE 14.1** Flywheel of the AI driven company

I've elaborated on a future state where AI is informing the strategic plan dynamically with the real progress of underlying initiatives. The growth or valuation ambition of the company can be reviewed against what AI suggests the plan will actually deliver.

Keeping these legs of the stool in harmony and taking the best course of action is going to be within reach for CEOs as we look at systems like Decision Sprint. If you think today's business velocity is high, it's time to buckle up.

# ACKNOWLEDGMENTS

L et me start by thanking my loving family. For my wife of 25 years, Sabuhi Athar, it's impossible to express in words my gratitude for being in the trenches through all the ups and downs of life. We took on a great deal together at young ages, starting a family, moving to Silicon Valley, and navigating my career. Your companionship, support, ideas, and wisdom have made all the difference. My mom, Razia Rafiq, provided the nurturing foundation and academic focus that helped her children transcend our circumstances. I hit the jackpot when it comes to moms. My children have been a constant source of encouragement as have been my siblings. I sincerely thank them all.

Like any good product, this book has gone through iterations thanks to my editors. Donya Dickerson of McGraw Hill has lent expert help from the proposal stage through publication. Herb Schaffer and Kevin Commins provided editorial help as I was in the trenches. Others at McGraw Hill made great contributions: Steve Straus and Pattie Amoroso on the production, Jeff Weeks on the cover, and Scott Sewell with marketing. My agent, Peter Riva, has been a strong advocate for me. I thank my neighbor, Azeem Ibrahim, for connecting us. I also thank Azeem, a proven writer and scholar, for providing ideas and encouragement along my writing journey.

While the ideas in this book are original, they build on the shoulders of others. The books by Carol Dweck, Daniel Kahnemann, and Clay Christiansen that I mention in the Introduction fall into this category. The academic work of these scholars related to neuroscience, innovation, problem-solving, and decision-making has reinforced many of my personal observations about how people behave in companies. While Decision Sprint is a new way forward, the underpinnings are consistent with leading academic work on behavioral science and human psychology.

The CEOs and executives I interviewed in this book are extremely busy people and went great lengths to make the time to share their perspectives. I thank them for reflecting on what works and what doesn't work in business, and distilling it for all of us.

I've had the privilege of working closely with the CEOs of several Fortune 500 companies. I thank them for allowing me the space to "do things differently" and "disrupt from within" in our quest to create growth for the business and to modernize culture.

I could not attempt to operate teams or business differently without amazing and committed lieutenants who shared the North Star. You know who you are. Your partnership allowed us to move quickly and boldly. You carried the ball during the hard yards of making change. Thank you to all the teams I've had the opportunity to quarterback. Executive assistants and business coaches fall within my notion of teams—I thank them for their personal sacrifice, emotional support, and contributions.

Over the last few years, I have stress tested the ideas in this book through Ritual, a software company I created with my cofounder, Mike Vo. Mike's unconditional support and partnership have enabled us to learn how to make my ideas work for real users. The motivation to create Decision Sprint as a system emerged about a year after Mike and I began building software to help teams and companies simplify decision-making.

Two well-known venture capitalists provided input that caused the right light bulbs to turn on. Ben Horowitz, of Andreseen Horowitz, looked at the first demo of our software and suggested it would need to be paired with a big idea or framework in order to really break through. John Lilly, then with Greylock Ventures, pointed out that breakout software companies design for daily usage as opposed to less frequent needs, like the decision points themselves. Their input drove me to ponder the wider notion of upstream work before I had a name for it. I realized an entire system needed elaboration and that I was the right person to develop it.

Software has been a medium to express my ideas and creativity for 25 years, and with this book, I have been able to tap the written word in a symbiotic relationship with passion for software.

The written word can be a powerful mechanism for change. It's why I share leadership and management ideas through my newsletter, Re:wire. What began as an experiment on LinkedIn has grown into a loyal following of over 100,000 subscribers.

The tagline of Re:wire is "meditation and methods" because I believe there is a certain stillness required to perform, manage, and lead at high levels. It's in these moments of stillness where we can see with the most clarity. Thank you to my readers. Your support has given me the encouragement to share novel ideas for the ever-evolving field of leadership.

# INDEX

Page numbers followed by *f* refer to figures.

# ABOUT THE AUTHOR

Atif Rafiq has blazed trails in Silicon Valley and the Fortune 500 for over 25 years. After rising through digital native companies like Amazon, Yahoo!, and AOL, Atif held C-suite roles at McDonald's, Volvo, and MGM Resorts. Rafiq was the first Chief Digital Officer in the history of the Fortune 500, a pioneering role he held at McDonald's and he rose to the president level in the Fortune 300.

Atif was most recently President of Commercial & Growth at MGM Resorts, a Fortune 300 company, where he oversaw a significant portfolio of corporate functions as well as the company's P&L.

Prior to MGM Resorts, he was the Chief Digital Officer and Global CIO for Volvo, where he led efforts to catalyze business model and product innovation. Previously he served as Chief Digital Officer and Corporate SVP of McDonald's (NYSE: MCD), where he led one of the largest digital transformations in the world. In four years, the company went from idea to global rollout of initiatives such as mobile ordering, digital delivery, curbside pickup, table service and ordering, digital menu boards, personalized offers, and kiosk-based self-service ordering.

Previously, Atif had a 17-year career in well-known high-tech companies, including Amazon, Yahoo!, and AOL.

While at Amazon (NYSE: AMZN), Atif was General Manager for Kindle Direct Publishing, one of the fastest growing and most profitable businesses within Amazon.

Prior to Amazon, he worked at Yahoo! as general manager of various divisions, and previously was cofounder and CEO of Covigna, a venture-backed startup. He ran the company at the age of 27.

Prior to starting Covigna, Atif held business development roles at Audible and AOL. While at AOL, he worked alongside the executive team during a time of explosive growth for the internet space. At the age of 23, he negotiated and launched the first major e-commerce partnerships in the history of the internet.

Atif holds a bachelor's degree in mathematics-economics from Wesleyan University and an MBA from the University of Chicago.

While leading business units, teams, and growth for companies, Atif has built a large following as one of today's top management thinkers. Over half a million people follow his ideas about management and leadership on LinkedIn, where he is a Top Voice, and his newsletter Re:wire has over 100,000 subscribers.

He's advised and invested in over 30 startups.

He currently sits on the Boards of Flutter ($25bn public company and owner of Fanduel) and Clearcover (a fintech provider, ranked on the Fast 500). Previously, he's served on the client council for Snapchat (SNAP), and as advisor to Slack (acquired by Salesforce for $20bn).

He is an active speaker at conferences including MIT Artificial Intelligence Summit, Fortune Reinvent, Cannes Lion, SXSW, CES, Google I/O, Twitter Flight, Web Summit, and more. His work has been profiled in the *Wall Street Journal*, *Fortune*, Mashable, *Forbes*, CNET, Tech Crunch, and *Fast Company*.

Atif is passionate about helping companies push boldly into the future. He accomplishes this through Ritual, a software app revolutionizing how teams innovate and problem-solve, and through his work as keynote speaker, Board member, and CEO advisor.

# It's easy to put *Decision Sprint* into practice.

Tap into exploration to move alignment and decision making along faster and smarter. Ritual is an app that makes it easy to build an exploration and solve problems based on the right questions.

Ritual's pioneering approach to exploration covers it all:

- Build explorations based on the key matters and questions
- Organize explorations to collaborate effectively
- Run explorations to develop answers and FAQs
- Share explorations with sponsors and decision makers

Simplify exploration. Get the Ritual app.

Ⓡ **Ritual**
Get Ritual

Transformation

Strategy

Innovation

Then visit **DecisionSprint.com** for additional services and guidance.